Practice Makes... Progress

by Molly Grantham

This book is an original production of Miss Meade Publishing
Charlotte, NC

Cover design by Diana Wade
Text design by Diana Wade
Cover photography by Nicole Taylor

I have tried to recreate events, locales, and conversations from my memories of them. I have only used the first initial of a person's last name when quoting their post from a public Facebook page.

ISBN: 978-1-0881-6421-1

To Wes: For always loving our kids—and me—exactly as we are.

Books by Molly Grantham

"The Off-Camera Life of an On-Camera Mom" series:

Small Victories

The Juggle is Real

Practice Makes... Progress

INTRODUCTION

Metaphorical wake-up calls are unexpected by definition. You're slapped because you don't know they're coming.

Back in early March 2020, my book editor was proofing a final version of *The Juggle Is Real* and said, casually, "Think you should mention this COVID thing? Maybe in an Afterword?"

Huh. Good thought. I quickly wrote a few pages about how a virus had started in China and was rapidly spreading worldwide. I was not flippant. I was unaware. My ignorance had good company—most of us didn't expect April 2020 or May 2020 or the heaviness that would come.

What I did during those long, *long* months was what I'd done since my second child, Hutch, was six days old: I wrote. I wrote monthly Facebook entries on our kids' experiences, the preposterous, and the hit-you-hards as they grow. I wrote about my intense career, rapid headlines, and chaos and coffee in the mornings. I wrote about fights, love, activities, and parenting through texts. Nothing was glazed over or made pretty. What I saw and felt, I wrote.

In the first book, which ended up covering Month One to Month

Thirty, that meant I wrote about wondering if I liked working more than I liked being a mom. In the second book, Month Thirty-One to Month Sixty-Five, it meant documenting my own mom's death and debating whether to let my kids see her sick in a Hospice House. The journey was genuine. You guys replied on Facebook with your own *Small Victories* and how much you understood that *The Juggle Is Real.*

In this book, the raw honesty continues. There is humor. There are lessons. There are surprises. But there is also more.

This book is a time capsule.

Between Month Sixty-Six, where *Practice Makes . . . Progress* begins and Month One Hundred, where it ends, our entire world shifted. COVID gave us no choice but to shift accordingly. We were forced to teach school at home. We watched career responsibilities transform. We embraced Zoom calls as a norm and got disgusted over political divides. At work, I reported long stories about vaccines and tracked the number of available hospital beds. While not at work, I birthed a baby into a pandemic. Creating this book and going back to reread these monthly posts was a window into a forgotten life. I had numbed myself to the big and little obstacles our family faced, and seeing the honesty of what I'd written reminded me of moments distance had erased, and made clear that facts get blurred with the passage of time.

During those long days, though, the fact that many of you read the posts and shared your thoughts helped (and still helps) save my sanity. There is a moving world outside one's own mind, and connection to others, especially when isolated, is a human necessity. I write things down, but it's your comments that create the connection. And yes, I know. It's Facebook. A platform easy to toss aside or mock. To do that is short-sighted. A Facebook page has the potential to be more than just a Facebook page. I believe mine is a community. Hundreds, sometimes thousands, of you comment on each post. It feels right to share a sprinkling of your responses in this book.

Like the two books before this one, what you're about to read is not cut and paste. Much time and love has gone into mining what was on Facebook as a starting point. Editing and reliving those words was an emotional process—both good and bad. In the course of remembering, I added lots of new. In this book, you'll find fresh writing never published. More thoughts. More photos. More reality.

When I started writing about my kids, Parker was three and a half and Hutch was less than a week old. This book ends with her nearly twelve, he eight and a half, and a surprise third baby. Parenthood changes you. I've learned it's not always in ways you expect or welcome. I still love working. I still think I'm a better mom because I have outside experiences. I still believe my fifty-hour-a-week career helps me better value the time I do get with my kids. But a dozen years into this relentless gig of motherhood, I can now say with conviction that being a mom is my number one role. It's more demanding than my job as a journalist and speaker. It's also more rewarding. Anchoring three main evening weekday newscasts is a career. It's an important career and big piece of me, but my children are my future. Without them I might be happy, but not as complete.

My kids and I have grown before public eyes. We all altered parts of ourselves during COVID—or COVID altered us—and I'll just say again, this book feels different. With two kids and two books behind me, you'd think I knew what I was doing, and a third baby and third book wouldn't feel like such a big deal. Not at all. We learn as we go, no matter how much experience is behind us. Each child, and each journey, is different. Some days it's about growth. Some days are just days. Perfection isn't the goal; imperfections are worth noticing. Practice makes . . . progress.

I can't wait to hear what you think.

—Molly

APRIL

MONTH SIXTY-SIX: Silver Linings

There might have been a better way to warn us about the bizarre world in which we now live. People debating this get tangled in no-win bureaucratic battles. I'm not interested in those conversations. As far as I'm concerned, nothing could've prepared us.

Not neon billboards lining highways with a screaming message: *"Buckle up! COVID ahead!"* Not journalists relaying prophetic facts that 100,000 people around the world would die in a month. I don't even think it would have mattered if we all got daily phone alerts telling us we'd have no immunity to the highly contagious germs on the way. I'm confident nothing would've worked, because even if we knew exactly what was coming, nothing could've predicted how this new world *feels.*

Facts and feels are different. Feels hurt more. They kick you in the gut.

We couldn't have predicted how it *feels* to be socially distanced from people. How it *feels* to homeschool in a hallway, to watch mom-and-pop businesses get financially decimated, to drive on empty roads, to witness charities avoid human interaction, to hope scientists race to stop deaths, or how it *feels* to cancel plans, proms, graduations, postpone weddings, and remember entire lives through virtual funerals.

There's a global view, and a micro down-to-our-own-street view. You're dealing in different details than your neighbors, but have a similar understanding of what they face. It makes watching the news more relatable. This isn't a story about a terrible hurricane that hit a town four states away. In that case, you see ninety seconds of video, after which you might empathetically shake your head for those who lost everything, but then turn and go back to making dinner. Your sympathy unintentionally fades as that crisis doesn't impact you directly. You can move on.

Collectively, we can't move on from COVID-19. This virus connects us in its universal horror.

In one month, we've heard dozens upon dozens of forceful, poignant stories. People who can't visit dying loved ones in nursing homes; families on the brink of losing it all; single moms who work in the healthcare industry and can't find childcare, let alone time to teach fractions to their fourth grader.

We've also heard of people suddenly furloughed and spending their newfound time delivering groceries to the elderly; teachers who work from 8:30 a.m. to almost midnight trying to dream up ways to creatively teach online; children pooling piggy-bank nickels to buy bread and deli meat to make sandwiches for Meals on Wheels.

Examples everywhere show how the virus directionally changed our lives. The most major change being time. Time. Time, time, time. We have more time.

Loads of time, actually.

Time to just . . . be.

These past six weeks (five weeks? seven? eight? where are we? who can keep track?) has made many say they realize how much of life they were taking for granted. I get that. I never knew how much I appreciated the ability to meet someone for coffee until it became impossible.

No one can travel anywhere. Quite the predicament for spring break. We're wrapping up a week off work with nowhere to go. This has made me reassess, well, everything. I'm inspecting old relationships and new ones. Careers. Rewards. Motivations—what do I really want? I'm looking at leadership. Motherhood. Responsibilities. My parents, both of whom I miss. My marriage. My children. The past. I'm really into thinking about the fact that there is no crystal ball, but if given the opportunity to hold one, would I want to?

I'm not sure knowing the end helps the journey to get there. Sometimes driving too fast toward a place you know is ahead can make you miss exit ramps that lead to better destinations.

I don't think I'd hold that crystal ball.

Ha. I wrote that above sentence while sitting here six months pregnant with my unexpected third child. Pretty rich irony in me proclaiming, "I don't want to know what's next!" Had I known baby number 3 was on the way, a boy, I'd have lost my mind. Another human wasn't in the plans. My husband, Wes, and I were done having kids. We'd happily gotten rid of most newborn items. My mind had to be massaged into acceptance over this baby we're currently calling, "Tic-Tac."

We all know stuff will happen. But only recently have I wondered if that "stuff"—an unplanned pregnancy or an unknown virus—are the true soil that creates growth.

As awful as COVID is now in April 2020, our eyes are wider. There's more consciousness this past month. I'm more present. I'm starting to see what was always in front of my face, if only I'd taken a harder look.

For example, right now. If I look up from typing, through a

window I see Parker and Hutch playing in the yard. We're not on a deadline to get to soccer practice or dance class or a karate lesson. I have zero phone calls to make. Kid stuff is on hiatus. Extracurriculars are canceled and there's nothing that *must* be done, so, they're outside on a plan-less week off. My schedule is also absent of lunches with friends, emceeing events, and meetings, giving me freedom to absorb what's beyond the glass pane. I've spent a lot of this week sitting and staring—more than I've ever sat and stared. I am doing more than looking. I am seeing.

Here's what I see:

Hutch's quirky sense of self. He's wearing socks to run in the grass. Wetness and mud soak through the material. The dirt must be uncomfortable. And, soft? Squishy? Wouldn't it also be slightly cold? Yet, Hutch seems unbothered. Rather than choose one of two typical options of going barefoot or wearing shoes, he opts for a third path he creates himself. If I were busier today, with less time, I'm not sure I'd notice those things. Shame on me: I might also miss his inside-out striped pajama boxer briefs. Parker chastised him when he came downstairs, "You can't wear pajama shorts for the day. They're only for night!" She'd blurted that before pointing to the backward tag sticking out.

He shrugged in response. That was that. He was wearing them, approval or not.

There's a fingerless Spiderman glove on his right hand. Hutch loves accessories. Some boy-themed, some girl-themed. He breaks societal standards because he doesn't know what societal, gender-dictated standards are. He'll ask to paint his nails or wear a Halloween costume in the middle of April. This morning he walked in our room at 7:00 a.m. wearing his sister's long-haired purple wig.

Hutch is a kid who loves order, but finds ways to break flows. He can be a walking contradiction. If you try to explain why he can't wear only socks outside on wet ground, or get his nails painted, or wear a Halloween costume to school, he'll ask why not. Which makes you rethink your own rules. Why not only socks in the grass? Why not blue sparkle nail polish? Why not a Spiderman glove (or the entire Spiderman suit) to preschool?

Hutch's whimsy shows how many meaningless orders I push on my children. The more I push, the more meaningless the rules seem. I push because it's what I learned: either bare feet or sneakers in wet grass, boys don't get painted nails, and costumes are reserved for special days. Those were my standards, and my parents' standards. But after years of seeing Hutch's big ocean-blue eyes water when I tell him about no socks in wet grass, no painted nails, or—worst sadness of all—no Spiderman to preschool, I've stopped.

It's not like teaching a child to avoid hot stoves or not to shoplift. There is no pain or penalty for being quirky. Restricting his personality doesn't aid anyone. So, call me an enabler. I'll tell you I'm a proud mom who embraces her son's imagination and five-and-a-half-year-old mind at work. It thinks in ways mine doesn't and never likely will.

This first month of COVID shutdown, allowing me to laser-focus on Hutch's view of the world, also reminds me Parker approaches life in the opposite manner. She is a rule follower. She feels guilt if you yell. She is disappointed when she doesn't do things "right." She moves with purpose, and thoughts are written on her face. Sometimes they get spelled out in slogans on her T-shirts. *Mermaid for Life* is across her chest today. The *L* in *Life* is starting to peel at the bottom left letter corner from so many washings. She has a closet full of clothes, but repeatedly wears the same items. Other favorites include: *Girl Boss* and *I'm a Big Sister, What's Your Superpower?*

Her outfits reflect a child who knows what she likes and has something to say. Always. Instantly. Opinions are not sparse in my newly turned nine-year-old.

Contrary to hardly being able to keep up with Hutch's vision, I often agree with how Parker thinks. Her negotiation skills could persuade a hardened jury. She has a sweetness streak a mile wide, but doesn't doubt herself. Ever.

Out this window. Now. What I see. She's trying to convince Hutch to swing higher on the playset alongside her. She's fearless; courage pours out of her pores. Her hasn't-been-washed-in-days hair is knotted around her face in long plaits as she flies back and forth. I already know what will happen. I can see five minutes ahead. She's going to jump off that swing at its highest peak, so high that if I were outside, I might yelp, scared she'll break a bone when landing. She wouldn't—and won't. The process is always the same. She'll soar off the swinging seat, land on her feet or fall on all fours, and pop up quickly, saying, before anyone can ask, “I’m okay!”

So much to soak up with nothing going on.

ꕥ

Tomorrow I go back to work, late night only. I’m the solo-anchor of the 11:00 p.m. news and need to be in person for that late night show, but with pregnancy putting me at high risk for COVID, I can’t be coanchoring early evenings when others could be around. Most employees have transitioned to virtual producing/editing/reporting, but a few people remain in the newsroom. It’s not worth putting Tic-Tac at risk, so I’ll stay away until 8:00 p.m. At that time, the few coworkers there will leave. I’ll come in and sit alone to help research and write the show. I’ll FaceTime the 11:00 p.m. producer, Maggie, who will stack the newscast in her apartment miles away. She’s there with her dog as company. We’ll review and write some of the most important headlines our modern world has ever depended on while not even in the same room. We’ll track COVID numbers, listen to interviews with doctors, and hear soundbites from scientists attempting to predict an unpredictable future.

Homeschool also restarts tomorrow. We are set up in a hallway near our garage. Mermaid Academy—as I’ve named the two desks—will be in full force. I’ll help Parker, now in third grade, review life-science readings and multiplication tables. She and I are both impatient and will get frustrated at least 690 times by noon.

Hutch will stand nearby, possibly in the same inside-out pajama boxer briefs and now mud-stained different-colored socks, wondering why he can't participate. His preschool is shut down. He's waited years for kindergarten to begin and go to school with his Sissy, and now she's in a Chromebook class ten yards away which he can't attend. I'll give him crafts, markers, paper, and tell him that is his work to do, but he knows his tasks are made up and hers are required. It's a cold-hearted tease.

Meantime, our puppy, Rudy, a strong, untrained, adorable mutt who Santa brought last Christmas, will bark at squirrels out the window, and run through the house with a quickness he doesn't know he owns. His presence will create an added layer of stress that Wes and I will try to ignore.

Tomorrow our family returns to our new, unwanted groove. I hope, however, the spring break self-reflection will remain. As much as the past month wasn't what I'd choose, it is providing empty days to view my kids and our world with a more critical eye.

Parker just jumped. I called it. She landed on hands and feet, messy hair blown into her mouth. Through the window her yell was loud but muffled as she stood up like a star athlete: "I'M OKAY!"

Yes you are, P. I hope we all will be.

COMMENTS:

Jan P. I have grown children and looking back, I shouldn't have sweat the small stuff. But when you were raised with rules, that's how we learned to discipline. See you tonight at 11p, but not before (I'd wondered why you weren't on the early evening shows).

Carla F. I am an essential worker and haven't been quarantined to my house, but my mom fell and cracked both sides of her pelvis, and my life has been very different in that way. One doesn't realize how much you miss seeing a person until you can't. The emotions when I was finally able to pick her up and bring her home . . . priceless. No one is on loan. Don't take days for granted.

Alison M. My third, unexpected blessing came seven years ago—my older two were nine and almost seven. We were done. Or so we thought. But alas, we weren't. Our third has been the glue that holds us together.

Hank S. Distance is hard. I've realized there is no substitute for the human touch.

Sherrie O'C. I have been unable to see my grown children during this unreal world. As scary as it sometimes seems, I've enjoyed getting "put-off chores" done.

Sydney L. I'm soaking up all these words, and the feels that go along with them.

Alice C. "Time to just be . . ."

Jack V. It might get worse before it gets better.

Parent Lesson

Today was the first day hundreds of thousands of parents in our area returned to homeschooling after a spring break spent forgetting confusing log-ins and passwords to virtual classrooms.

I'm not a good teacher. Not pretty to admit, but, truth. I particularly hate what's called "new math." It's basically every process you never learned to get a correct answer your third grader will whiningly tell you is wrong because how you got there isn't how she has been taught. She's right. Kinda. You can't teach your child what you knew decades ago because that's no longer how kids are trained. Being wrong, while right, is enough to throw your head against the wall and pray for a substitute. Only, no one is allowed near you and your one-room school can't have visitors. I'm good at finding work-arounds, but there isn't another option except to teach those basic fractions in an unfamiliar way on a computer system that keeps locking you out.

Saw a meme the other day online that was a teacher saying to parents: "Just log onto Zablezoot, scroll down to the Zork! app and have the kids work through the assignments sent through Kracklezam or check the links posted in Drumblekick."

It was supposed to be funny, but that's exactly how it feels. Some Martian language used in another galaxy.

The worst part is doing this in between your own five Zoom calls and video work conferences.

Though I'm not in a studio anchoring early-evening shows, I am still working. Producers have asked me to gather, write, and relay information from home on other digital platforms. This means I'm filtering COVID facts while doing "new math," surrounded by a chorus of Hutch complaints and Parker yells. He'll be trying to get in front of her camera lens in order to "go to school" with her, and she'll be screaming for him to get out of the way so her friends don't see her annoying little brother.

At least it seems temporary. The school district said it'd try virtual education for two weeks, then see where things stand. Wish I could send myself to detention until then.

Just Announced: Schools Closed

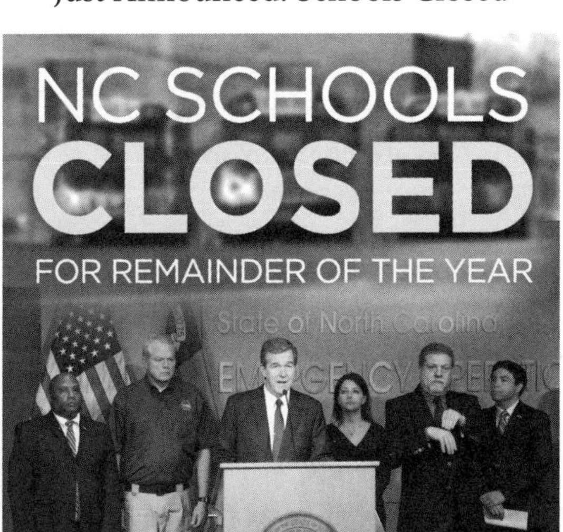

It's official. Indefinitely, most likely until the end of this school year. I post this from the sanctity of the bathroom where I can't be heard screaming.

COMMENTS:

Shannon R. My twins are devastated. Senior year, no final track season. They've made regionals each year, now no chance for that. No final recruiting. No prom either. They're feeling left out of life.

Lauren R. This needs to say: "School buildings closed." Schools are not closed, they just shifted to online teaching.

Nicole D. My kids are getting no instruction. I'm working; they're watching YouTube.

MAY

Keep On Movin'

The third grader rolled into Mermaid Academy this morning. Took me two minutes to realize I had seen it happen, heard the skates, didn't care, and wasn't fazed. We are hitting new baseline standards on a daily basis.

COMMENTS:

Jennifer M. Your hallway is a skating rink; my kitchen table is an art table.

No Choice

Seven months pregnant and biking. All activities remain canceled, so when your five-year-old is outside so much lately, he teaches himself to ride with no training wheels and begs for a bike ride with you, you deliver. (Just hopefully you don't actually *deliver.*) Laugh, laugh, laugh. Laugh all you want. Happy to provide COVID chuckles.

COMMENTS:

Doris S. Yesterday I rode a dirt bike for my son. I am seven months as well. It's crazy. I get it.

Lisa R. As a labor and delivery nurse, you scare and crack me up.

Micah H. I'm more impressed with biking in a dress.

MONTH SIXTY-SEVEN: Ready for Hire

Last full week of Mermaid Academy. Parker is preoccupied. Wes and I are both working. Hutch is left alone to be Hutch with not much to do, like so many days the past nine weeks. He suddenly yells so the whole house can hear:

"I need everyone to be quiet. Do you HEAR ME? I said, QUIET! I have a conference call. I have in earbuds."

His preschooler's voice shatters the silence. His word choices are curious enough to get me up out of my chair. I turn the corner and see his hand near his ear, fiddling with imagination and air. He'd found an old keyboard in our garage trash. It's in front of his blue rubber-cased kid's tablet propped on the wall like a monitor. He looks over at me approaching, annoyed.

"I said I had a call. Just please make sure you're quiet."

Then he looks back at the keyboard. He starts moving his fingers fast over broken buttons, typing absolutely nothing. I try to slyly take this picture. He notices.

"Please be quiet, Mom," he says. "I have another call in eighteen minutes after this one."

I leave.

Like it or not, children are what we make of them.

COMMENTS:

Peggy D. Proof we need to watch what we do and say: little things matter.

Keri J. There's some truth to the old saying, "more is caught than taught."

Glenda L. His imagination is magnificent. Keep sending good vibes.

Angel McC. They sometimes need to be bored so their creativity can bloom.

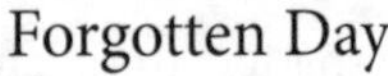

Forgotten Day

Today would be my mom's birthday. I'm writing this at 11:45 p.m., after the day has gone unrecognized. Three years after her death, there's a reason to remember, but no real reason to celebrate.

If she were here, she'd want to be the center of attention. I post this old photo now for that reason. Giving my momma some love.

Bet she didn't even know this picture existed. One of her old friends sent it months ago. You always think you've seen all the pictures when someone is gone. Seeing a new one can take your breath away. Besides that, my mom is beautiful in this photo. I love that it's her and Dad together. Her friend who sent it said it was the mid-seventies. They'd just married. He was Southern and proper. She was a Northern hippie. I'd wear the dress she has on right now.

They got divorced by the time I was four; there aren't many photos I have of them together.

Happy would-be seventy-third, Mom. Your daughter and son texted each other this morning in your honor. We both made sure to tell your grandchildren a story about you. Bet you're on a perch high above, making certain other surrounding spirits know: May 28 is your day.

COMMENTS:

Katrina L. How wonderful to have found a treasure like this—you must have heard your whole life how you look just like both of them. (Might I add, that is a beautiful soft spring dress. Have a seamstress look at the picture and make it.)

Lori W. My mom's birthday is also May 28. I know how fortunate I am to still have her and my dad in my life even if I can't visit them since they are ninety-one and eighty-eight and are trying hard to be safe during this crisis. COVID has taken so much away.

Paula F. I lost my mom four years ago and my heart is still as broken as it was on the day she passed. My mom was my best friend. We talked almost every day. We shared secrets and dreams, and when I go put flowers on the gravesite, I always sit down on the ground and talk about real stuff. When I walk away, I feel her presence. It makes me feel renewed.

Covid Shower

In the middle of this uncertain time, some amazing girlfriends got together and dreamed up a virtual baby celebration for Tic-Tac. One dropped off food (stayed far away on the porch). One had flowers delivered. Together they gathered two dozen people on a Zoom call filled with thoughtful words. There are plenty of things to question in our world right now; the importance of loving friendships is not one.

Six weeks to go.

Hutch, the Graduate

Larger commencements for all kinds of life markers are being skipped. I know preschool graduation isn't comparable to what high schoolers and college graduates are missing, but in Hutchville, today was going to be huge. He was saying goodbye to his mini-school. If we were in normal times, there'd be a nice ceremony, sing-along songs with families, and photos with friends.

Instead, his preschool is hosting a contactless drive-thru. I told Hutch weeks ago we'd be able to return one final time and see his teachers through a car window. He has been counting down to this moment ever since. His smile here? Permanent grin. Been like that since the hour before we went and in the hour since we left. Kindergarten—no matter what it looks like in the fall—get ready. This little guy is rarin' to join the club.

JUNE

End of School

End of Mermaid Academy today. We took a field trip to the brick-and-mortar elementary school to get everything that was left in classrooms the day the students went home, not knowing they wouldn't return. Teachers were uber-organized, smiling behind masks. Some parents were crying. So were some kids. It was bitter-sweet, and a stark reminder of the last twelve weeks. Thank you, once again, educators everywhere who have tried so hard to help clueless parents figure out how to be you.

COMMENTS:

Barb F. I could cry.

Patricia B. My daughter's teacher retired this year. It made me so sad for her because her last weeks were spent away from her class.

Not a Halloween Costume

"I wanna do the mask myself!" Which means minute three now of me silently standing by watching as he tries with adamant determination to find eye holes.

COMMENTS:

Erna E. Some people I've seen wearing masks must have trained with Hutch.

Peter W. Spiderman (glove) to the rescue.

Brandy H. Some people will never understand the struggles of a boy mom . . . especially those of a very independent boy. We want them to be themselves, but phew, it can take up a day.

Surf Camp

Day 1 of vacation: Sun.

Days 2–6: Rain.

Day 7: Finally, sunshine. Well-timed for the start of surf camp. Parker's instructor is a sixteen-year-old sensation who looks like P plus seven years. Another year, another surf camp, and another chance for the future to float in front of my face.

Dad's Day

1999

I have friends who don't know their dads. Some were raised by strong single women, some with deep distance between them and their fathers. Not me. I was one of the lucky ones. Maybe even the luckiest one. My dad loved his kids (I have two half brothers, a term I hate—we're all equal in each other's minds) with such intense sincerity that the four of us knew we were the light of his life. Fourteen years after his death, we still know it. We were his motivation. His legacy. His pride. From him, the four of us learned the art of conversation and making people feel comfortable. We learned joy, jokes, and family. We learned a love of Kure Beach. We learned the importance of manners and handwritten notes and how to skim ice cream straight from the top of the gallon tub so you don't make a spoon dent right in the middle.

As the only girl, he also taught me to go after anything and everything. He instilled confidence by creating a safety net of love. To fail and fall was okay. To not try was unacceptable.

Once a year on this day, our timelines and newsfeeds are filled with beautiful posts and happy photos of daddies loving on their kids. I have those thoughts every day. They are not, I promise, dictated by a calendar. I can close my eyes and hear his laugh and see his open arms. Memories flood that space behind my eyelids. He was not just a father—which sounds more formal—he was a dad. A loyal dad who told his friends stories about his kids, lifting us up even when we couldn't hear him talking. The four of us now own different pieces of him in our personalities.

Though I wish beyond wish Dad was here to be a Pop-Pop and get to know his five grandkids (soon to be six!), I love the overwhelming memories. I don't often write about him. It can seem too hard or too very-very-real. But sitting this morning in his favorite place, watching waves as I type, spending a week a bit removed from reality, it feels right. Makes him feel closer than ever.

Kure During COVID

Kure. You didn't disappoint. You never do. Even in this world where nothing is certain and a first week filled with rain, you came through[1]. You make a mind lighter, skin warmer, a soul more free, and as a particular bonus this year, found a way to have my kids get along and appreciate sibling-hood. Thank you.

1 Let the record reflect: Hutch owns bathing suits. Multiple ones that fit. I don't know why he often changed out of trunks and into pajamas. I don't know why he liked swimming in the ocean in heavy wet cotton. I don't know. I don't know. I didn't ask.

These past ten days were a final time to love on these two before they become three. To watch her surf better and never brush her sea-spun, sandy hair (by night nine, blond dreads were forming), and to study Hutch and his desire to copy her, while living completely and wholly as Hutch.

This year, Kure, you showed me how Parker's more mature face isn't just a look; it's actual age. She's getting older. She owns the title of big sister. No doubt Tic-Tac will have one mom, and one mini-mom. I overheard her telling Hutch she called "dibs" on holding their brother first, once they meet. Hutch, of course, argued back. He hates feeling younger and wasn't about to sit pretty with her manipulative attempts to claim priority. He responded in the way little boys generally respond: by lying.

"Nah-uh," was the exact sound he pushed through his teeth, into her face. "You can't hold him first because I already called it."

His response gave her pause. Did he call dibs already? She wasn't sure. Curiosity spurred her to stomp over and ask me.

No, Parker. He didn't claim first-brother-holding rights. And you can't either. We'll figure it out later. Hutch is just trying to get under your skin.

Which sent her marching back to yell at him.

He erupted with howling laughter. He loves to bother her.

He loves loving on her even more.

That conversation was one memory from these past days; most other thoughts I had weren't as specific. With COVID keeping pools closed, half the restaurants shut down, no aquarium, no

Carolina Beach carnival in the next town, no arcades, no going into Wilmington for a children's museum on a rainy day, and, as an added bummer, the ferry to Southport closed for maintenance, Hutch had to become one with the ocean. Beach was it. Beach was all he got. I'm grateful the lack of distractions made him appreciate gritty sand and hot sun. They've always been the forever favorite for the rest of our family—Parker runs and dives into surf without so much as a big-toe test—but for the first time this year, the beach became Hutch's favorite as well.

We got him a professional boogie board. Too large for his size, but it made him feel like a big boy while Sissy was off in surf camp. He tried and tried to stay on top of the tiny waves near the shoreline. He also continually checked the lifeguard stand for its color flag, that safety system being a process that clicked in his mind. As long as guards showed green or yellow, he'd wade up to his armpits, wrangling his board in front of him, then turn around and ride broken whitewater onto the sand-packed shore.

He'd stand afterward and look to make sure I had watched from my beach chair. After some rides, he puckered his lips and blew a kiss. Be still, my heart.

Beach babies. Both of them. I don't know what next year's June will bring with an eleven-month-old added to the mix. Will Tic-Tac be more like Parker at that infant age, already trying to swim? Or more like Hutch, content to sit in his diaper and eat sand?

No matter how this child inside my basketball-sized stomach forms the future, I will surround him with salt air.

MONTH SIXTY-EIGHT: Heartbroken and Learning

Rudy is no longer a part of our family.

I tell the Good, the Bad, and the Always Real. I don't want to pretend this hasn't happened. I don't want to ignore my parenting fail, or brush over how getting a dog for my daughter as a Christmas present ultimately hurt her and forced tough lessons about love on all of us.

Some of you know the backstory. How much our family cherished Fisher the Wonderdog; how bone cancer in his back leg took him from us last summer when he was thirteen. Fisher was our first child, Parker's best friend, and Hutch's main protector. We all miss Fisher, though Parker might miss him more than the rest of us combined.

Soon after, Parker wanted another dog. We repeatedly told her we weren't ready. She tried to understand, but last year at Christmas, at the ripe age of eight, she wanted one so badly she asked Santa for "a family puppy." On her wish list she specified in parentheses: "(Just make sure it's playful.)" She knew Santa worked miracles, and this was a child's way of trying to make dreams happen.

Wes was against it. I caved. (If you read *The Juggle Is Real*, you know the intricacies.) Bottom line: I got caught up in the emotion of my daughter, of missing Fisher, and gave my insides the green light to start looking.

Weeks before Christmas, Parker and I visited the shelter where we'd gotten Fisher. There, Rudy found Parker. She fell big, bad, hard in love, right back. I pried her away from the lumbering baby giant, saying Santa sometimes surprises, and even if he doesn't bring her Rudy, he now probably knows with certainty how much she wanted a puppy.

My friend, Melissa, worked at the shelter and helped secure Rudy for pick-up on Christmas Eve so he could bound down our house steps as a special delivery the morning of December 25. Santa was a hero. Even now, I don't regret seeing that unbridled joy on my daughter's face. Rudy was licking Parker's smile and together the two of them—dog and girl—looked like Christmas bliss.

I am a big promoter of rescuing rescues. But part of what you accept with shelter dogs is not knowing their details. We knew Rudy was half Lab, half another mix, probably pit bull. We knew he was eleven months old, good with kids, and loved to be loved.

We did not realize his strength.

Every passing week, from Christmas Day until this June, we watched Parker *try* to walk him. Every time she took him outside, I had to drop what I was doing to stand on the porch and monitor. We don't have a fenced-in yard. My role was to make sure Rudy didn't get distracted by a jogger, other dog, leaf, horn, something, anything, because if he did, he'd unintentionally almost rip Parker's arm out of its shoulder socket jerking her in that direction.

My girl was not dissuaded. For six months, she walked him, only to be dragged to the ground repeatedly. (That happened to me, too. I have a permanent Rudy scar on my forearm.) She'd come back with a bloody knee and get her own wet paper towel to clean off her wounds. Hours later she'd hop up again, put on his leash, and take him out. She never complained.

On weeknights, Rudy would hear me walk in after midnight from work. He'd jump up to go out. I was exhausted, in TV makeup, round all over, pregnant in high heels and a dress, walking a freight train of a dog in rain, cold, or on a good night, just plain darkness. Every night I'd plead with him to pee fast before a lone car would drive by and start him barking. It was easy to stay positive by making myself believe Rudy was training me for newborn-hood, late nights, and crying.

Rudy would've never hurt us, or anyone. He'd sleep with Parker, play with the kids, and sit in laps. He had endless energy. He was a strong dog who persisted relentlessly. He was jumpy and exactly what Parker had asked Santa to bring: "Playful."

Parker did this difficult walking routine and I suffered through the late nights through the beginning of the pandemic. Through homeschooling. Through extra-extra-late evenings when I'd be at the station well past midnight to cover protests or breaking news, and not get home until 2:00 a.m. We did this through having a TV studio set up in our home office for three weeks, in a trial run of me anchoring afternoon newscasts from home. He barked too loudly while I was live, so we paid to put Rudy in a doggie daycare to wear him out and let me go live from home. We spent tons of money on dog care, training tools, equipment, and when he wasn't in daycare, we took multiple walks a day.

We did all we knew to do because we appreciated Rudy was a playful puppy . . . but we loved Parker. For her sake, we wanted it to work.

Eventually I asked the doggie daycare owner her opinion. She said Rudy needed to learn boundaries and recommended intense training.

I started researching. Took Parker with me to various places so she could see her tired, seven-months-pregnant mom overturning every stone. We met with an accomplished dog trainer who had advice, but ultimately was too busy to take Rudy into her classes. By May, five months into a world with Rudy in ours, I bit the bullet and signed him into an overnight doggie boot camp. A man named Mark accepted Rudy into his program and kept him there for three weeks.

After week one, Mark texted a cute photo of our beefy dog

looking well-behaved. Every morning afterward, Parker woke up asking to look at my phone to kiss that photo of Rudy through my phone screen.

We were wildly hopeful boot camp would teach him rules.

It did. It worked.

For Rudy.

It did not work for me.

After three glorious weeks at home with no barking or added Rudy stress, our whole family went together to pick up Rudy. Mark wanted to give a human lesson on learning how to speak the language Rudy now knew: we had to use the same directional words, keep him on a strict schedule, and show Rudy to a pet cot where he'd then be able to listen to commands. These were commands we had to say the right way. Mark handed me a contraption with buttons and told me to wear that around my neck. Through continued training with that contraption and by using the exact words and exact timing, Rudy would be a great pet.

As Mark was talking, I knew it was too much. Especially with a baby on the way. With a broken heart, I made a decision. I called Melissa. We made plans.

Then, the unthinkable next step: telling Parker.

It was a Sunday morning. One you might describe as leisurely.

We had brought P into our room, where Rudy had dutifully followed. As we sat on the bed looking at the two of them, they were lying on their stomachs, also on the bed, facing us. Rudy was calm, letting her drape her arm over his back. Their connection was visible which made it worse.

Wes and I were there together, but it was me who spoke. It wasn't fair to give Wes the challenge when he knew it had been a bad idea from the jump. I used direct words. Looked in my daughter's eyes, and told her.

Once the words fell, her tears became waterfalls down her cheeks.

Parker felt the pain, instantly. She sobbed quietly, staring down at the bedspread. She listened, and did not interrupt. She was mature. Open-eared. Believing, as every one of my words rocked her world.

I don't remember my exact language, but I know I gave it to her straight and treated her like an adult by telling her the truth—it wasn't Rudy's fault. It wasn't her fault. It wasn't our family's fault. It wasn't her future brother's fault. Rudy simply needed a fenced-in yard. He needed space to run free, something we couldn't provide. He had a huge amount of excitement and energy, and no matter what we'd do, it wouldn't be enough. I told her not be mad at us or Rudy, and certainly not to resent the baby. I told her how for six months she had shown sophistication in being a dog owner, and how proud we were to watch her be responsible.

I told her we'd found Rudy another home—with the help of Melissa—and he was going to be loved somewhere else. I told her Rudy would never forget her and that we were taking him to the new home the following morning.

"*Tomorrow*?" she sniffled. It was the first time she'd spoken. "*TOMORROW*?"

Tomorrow, I repeated with my own shaking voice. It was decided.

I reminded Parker that she saved him. She found him at the shelter and asked Santa to bring him to her, and because of that, Rudy would never forget her.

She cried until her eyes looked like rivulets of red running through white milk. Her pale skin blotched with pink, she asked to leave the conversation. She wanted her beloved Brown Bear. She returned gripping the stuffed animal, crawled back onto the bed, and returned her arm over Rudy's back.

This picture was taken an hour after Parker lay there with her dog, getting into his face to say things one-on-one. She spent the whole time talking as she scratched behind his ears. In her semi-swollen, squinty eyes of this photo, you can see both pain and love.

As much as I don't remember every detail, I do remember saying this at the end:

"Parker, it can be really hard to love something or someone so much. This is a tough lesson to learn at only nine years old."

Still face-down in a pillow holding Brown Bear, she turned her head toward me sideways and replied with two sentences I'll never forget:

"It's not hard to love, Mommy. It's hard to let go of what you love."

Pause.

Pause.

Pause.

"It's not hard to love, Mommy. It's hard to let go of what you love."

She's right. It isn't hard to love. It is hard to let go.

ꕥ

Rudy is now happy. He has a great new home. Privacy laws prevent me from publicly relaying too much about his new owners, but I am very okay with how it stands. This situation is for the best.

As for Parker, she's incredible. The first week after he was gone was really hard, but her resilience and thoughtfulness has her mentioning Rudy (and Fisher, still) in prayers every night. Two of her girlfriends pooled their own money together to buy her a small stuffed dog that looks like Rudy, who she named "Rudy 2.0." He sleeps beside Brown Bear, a coveted spot. On our recent trip to Kure, she talked fondly about how Rudy had been there once; she liked knowing he'd experienced running on sand and had ocean water on his paws.

I also promised her years from now, when Tic-Tac is older, she will get her own dog. Not a family dog, but a dog just for her.

I'd kicked this can down the road too long, hoping to dream up a solution that didn't involve breaking my daughter's heart, which only made me finally breaking it worse.

Parenting is hard. Do more research before letting Santa bring a live pet. Follow your adult gut—not a child's emotional requests.

And don't judge a family who returns an animal. You never know what they faced before making that choice.

Of course, the biggest lesson learned?

It's easy to love. It's hard to let love go.

ଔଓ

To the mom and daughter reading this right now who are the new proud owners of Rudy: thank you. I'm betting Parker will read these words someday too. I'm sure as much as the hole in her heart will still feel airy, she'll also be grateful knowing he's with people who offered what our family couldn't.

COMMENTS:

Beth C. I did this very thing. Let my child direct us down a path I knew we couldn't handle. I appreciate your transparency.

Richard S. He depended on you and you let him down. You were his life; if you can't keep a pet then never get one. I said what I said, and you can't change my mind.

Kim O. You did what was right for Rudy and your family. Anyone who judges you has no idea how hard you tried or how hard this was. I know it was. I watched your struggle. Much love.

Molly. Thank you, Kim, and to your doggie daycare.

JULY

Last Night of Work (for Now)

Nine months cooked. Five-inch heels. One show left.

Maternity leave starts Monday. Not sure when Tic-Tac will arrive, but doctors say soon. I am ready. After tonight's 11:00 p.m., it's goodbye to the newsroom for a bit.

If past maternity leaves are any indication, I'll be grateful to get back to work in a couple months. Until then, I wanted to send you guys a note tonight to thank you for what is the engaging, warm, and heart-full Facebook family we have built, for caring about headlines respectfully (for the most part), and for so often making me laugh. I appreciate you.

Stay safe. We're living in wildly unique times that make you check what matters. Life is about to change for my family. I can't wait to meet Tic-Tac, and introduce him to all of you.

COMMENTS:

Carrie S. I had my apprehensions going in three weeks ago to delivery our own surprise third baby during this pandemic. But once we hit the maternity floor, it was like the rest of the world didn't exist. It was my most peaceful delivery and we really enjoyed our time alone as three before going home to our oldest daughter (seven) and son (three) just twenty-four hours after delivery.

Margaree H. Can't wait to meet Tic-Tac and see Hutch's expression.

Welcome to the World

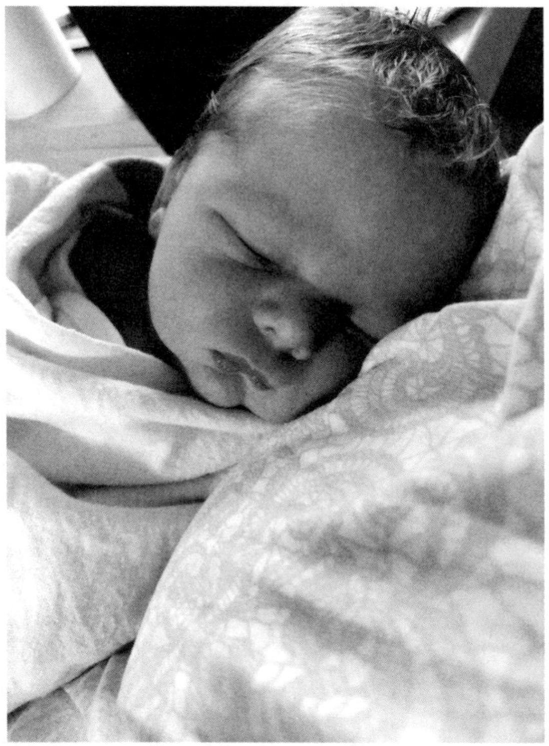

My name is Hobie Michael. I was born last night, July 14, happy, healthy, and with a head full of hair. My mom keeps whispering in my tiny ears how I'm already awesome. I believe her. I'm eight pounds, two ounces, and can't wait to meet my older brother and sister in person. (On FaceTime so far, they seem super excited.) Mom said there's something called a pandemic right now, and they're not allowed to visit the hospital. She also says the good wishes from everyone worked. We're all doing great.

MONTH SIXTY-NINE: The First Week

How can a soul already decide it loves something so much? This entire hospital experience with Hobie feels different than nine and five years ago. More intimate. More connected. Softer. Warmer feelings leave me confused. How can this time feel . . . good?

This was *not* how it was with Parker or Hutch. I remember feeling inferior after having them, wondering when the loving feelings of motherhood would wash over me. Why were those feelings everyone always talked about absent when I held my own child? Why wasn't I, in those early hours, feeling blessed and glowing from within, wanting to stare at the baby now out of me after spending so much time inside? I didn't feel that glow. Hurts to confess, but I didn't then.

I do now.

Makes no sense.

This time, I'm high risk. I'm over forty. This time, COVID added challenges to the ways we were admitted to the hospital and the number of staff who could attend. Plus, this birth got complicated. Hobie's head was lodged in the wrong place the last few weeks. He was breach, up near my rib cage. Ultrasounds showed him standing (or some version of cross-leg-style sitting), on me. I'd be in live newscasts talking about coronavirus, politics, masks, possible homeschooling in the fall, Charlotte's high homicide rate, serious life stories—and would feel Hobie Michael pounce inside my body.

Imagine giving a speech to 100,000 people while acting as a human trampoline. I had those feelings *every night*. The experience was a mixture of awe, horror, and humor. Sometimes I'd loudly exhale relief the moment the red studio light turned off. Chief Meteorologist Eric Thomas would look over.

"Is he doing it again? Moving everywhere?"

"Yes," I'd reply, smiling. "He's doing it again."

"Think anyone could tell?"

"No. I covered it well. At least, I think?"

"One day closer, Molly. You're getting there."

The day before a scheduled C-section, I swam laps in a friend's backyard pool to practice flip turns. My childish attempt to try and turn the baby. I didn't know how else to attempt to get him in the right direction.

Guess we'll never know if reliving competitive high school swim-team races while nine months pregnant is what moved Hobie's head south, but when Wes and I checked into the hospital at 5:00 a.m. on July 14, doctors found him in the perfect position.

Is that why I feel the miracle of this moment more this go-round? Because it was a harder journey to get here? Maybe. But don't say, "You like holding this third baby more because you know what to do." It is not knowing what to do. I've forgotten almost everything about the early hours of a baby's life. Nurses keep asking questions about the first two kids, and I look blankly back at them; amnesia has washed my brain. They are forced to turn to medical records to get answers.

I do remember how to swaddle though, and was confident enough to make my own decisions (READ: no guilt) when disagreeing with two different lactation consultants. I also knew in advance I'd want a specific dinner—no matter how odd—after the baby arrived. This meant a healthy Hobie Michael met the world at 8:45 p.m., and by 9:30 p.m., I was eating sushi in the hospital bed. Cringe, if you need. Extended family did when we sent them photos. But, I'd missed my favorite food for nine months, and Wes knew of a spot that'd deliver if you scheduled in advance.

We overordered, shared with gleeful nurses, and I didn't question one bite.

"Definitely your third baby," the nurses said while eating raw fish rolls and laughing. "You planned dinner around labor."

As Hobie is now merely hours old, I've talked everything you just read into my phone, like a voice text into Notes. I wanted to document. I didn't want to forget this feeling. My stomach is full, my uterus empty, and I am going to sleep for a couple hours. The first real feeding will come soon enough.

☙❧

Ten hours old.

Maybe I was wrong. Even if I don't remember details of past newborn-hoods, maybe some things are like riding a bike: no matter how many years since you last sat on a seat, ingrained knowledge lets you hop on.

Hobie is perfect. I'm staring at him while talking softly into the phone again. Both my eyelids are up; his are barely open. Tall fingers. Tall toes. With morning light shining in long rectangular slits through the closed hospital blinds at 6:45 a.m., I see his wrinkles and a double chin and fat roll circling his neck. How can legs look immeasurably long on a twenty-two-inch human?

☙❧

Eighteen hours old.

Not even a day yet. We're in a hospital bubble. Yet, the world is spinning beyond us and my phone just lit with a breaking news headline sent over the station's news app. It says North Carolina's governor made a decision: while we hoped school in the fall would get to in-person learning at some point, the COVID numbers were too troubling. It'll start next month online, virtually.

The phone alert is to notify all parents they'll be teaching their kids at home.

I look down at Hobie. I breathe. I say nothing.

With one announcement, dreams about enjoying a peaceful maternity leave fly away. No more end-of-August and whole September with Parker and Hutch in school, me soaking up my baby. Gone is the vision I'd had of walking P and H to the bus stop carrying a four-week-old. There will be no bus stop. I show Wes the phone alert. We turn on the TV. We need to know what's facing us when we leave. The press conference is live. Strong voices come into our hospital room. The facts feel heavy. The meaning of the words feels insurmountable: I am holding my eighteen hours old baby, hearing how I need to prepare to teach kindergarten and fourth grade in the hallway next to our garage.

Oh God. Whirling. Twirling. A tornado of thoughts. I start to think of my own career. How will homeschool work when I return full time?

Hobie shifts slightly.

I love my job. I want to work. I will go back.

So, I sit. The news keeps going. The governor is still talking. I'm still breathing, saying nothing.

Wes turns off the TV.

"Think we got the gist," he says.

"Yeah," I reply.

"You don't need to say it," he says. "I know what you're thinking. Let's not talk about what those plans look like yet."

He is a good man. We'll cross that bridge later. Back to the bubble.

ঔ

Thirty hours old.

COVID keeps a parade of people—family, kids, friends—out of the hospital. It's tough to not have Parker and Hutch instantly meet Hobie, but also forces all our focus to be on our baby boy, currently on a hospital's rolling bassinet beside my bed.

Nurses in masks enter when medicine is required. They explain short-term plans about how the baby needs food every three hours and sleep, sleep, sleep. They say the goal in these early days is survival. The backup goal? Education on parenting in a COVID world. My comfort comes in as a distant third.

There are no other distractions. It's just Hobie and calling P and H on FaceTime. Wes's parents came from Kentucky to stay with them, which was wonderful. For better or worse, that's all it is: The baby and video screens. I like the peace.

ଓଃ

Forty hours old.

Our bubble popped.

We're now on a couch back in our own living room. Hutch is grabbing at Hobie's stomach, inspecting his belly button, his arms and nails, and rubbing his own nose into Hobie's remarkable hair. Hutch breathes in his baby brother. He's inhaling him, trying to own him, be him, hold him, love him tightly. I monitor closely, half worried about suffocation.

The hospital sent us home in less than two days. Too many germs, too many fears, too many other people needing beds and medical attention.

We put Hobie down in a crib—Parker and Hutch's old one (one of the few things we hadn't yet sold)—with strict orders to both older kids to let him sleep. Two minutes later, I'm upstairs trying to get my bearings. The video monitor beside me shows movement. I pick it up. The image in my hand shows Hutch, sneaking into the nursery, carefully shutting the door to limit his noise. He's walking stealthily, like a cartoon character. He approaches the crib rails. He climbs up. The video shows him reach toward Hobie. He grabs the bundled blanket to pull the baby closer. I feel like I'm watching surveillance we'd broadcast of a viral video, only it's my house. My two sons. And I'm watching live through a nursey monitor app as Hutch is close to accidentally killing his new baby brother.

This is the first time I've used the app. I see an audio button. No idea what it does, but I press and yell. My voice must have gone through the nursery camera because Hutch swivels his head around, startled, but notably—I think in that critical second—with zero shame. He looks more annoyed about a foiled plan than stricken from being "caught." Thankfully he gets off the crib and walks, smirking, *to the camera.* It's sitting on a nearby table. He looks right into that lens and unapologetically puts his hand over it, blocking my view.

He's smart. I'll give him that. Rather than run from the crime scene, he blocks me from seeing what's happening. But by the time he's done putting the camera back on the table, I am in the room, ripping him out of the nursery. Never have I ever flown downstairs so fast, and I am furious. I start explaining all the dangers of what could've happened, as he stares back at me unfazed.

Parker, meantime, is divinely responsible. She is somehow years older than just days ago when I was still pregnant. How does she already know how to hold a two-day-old? When was she taught to burp after a feeding? She whispers to Hobie, gently rubbing the top of his head. She corrects Hutch for being too rough before I have a chance to do so. With no words, her actions show how she values this role of big sister, again.

ঙ্গ

Ninety-six hours old.

Pediatrician appointment: check.

There is a slight concern about our family having been exposed to COVID. We werein a hospital—being in any medical setting is a risk. Wes also walked to the cafeteria once, though masked. That's apparently bad.

No matter how bubbled, COVID germs surround us. We are told with a newborn it is right to be cautious. However, it's also allergy season. This year is terrible. Our pediatrician said office phones are ringing off the hook because no one can tell if what they have is seasonal or COVID-deadly.

Our family has mild symptoms. Is Parker's stomachache a big deal? Are my watery eyes and body aches the fact I just had a baby or the virus? I had a rapid COVID test when checking into the hospital days ago. It was negative. Has something changed since then?

The pediatrician says it's okay to wonder; everyone is doubting their health. She tests Parker and Hutch, just to give me comfort. We'll hear in a few days.

While we wait, she says our entire family should quarantine.

Back in a bubble, just now at home.

ᴄ𝔖𝔈ᴐ

One hundred thirty-two hours old.

Lockdown is hard. I get it; we certainly don't want to put anyone else in proximity to us in that off chance Parker or Hutch have positive tests. They feel fine, so making them stay inside adds extra hassle. The lockdown also changed our plans. My stepmom was going to drive from Florida to help me these first couple weeks. She now can't. Outside playdates for Parker and Hutch are also out the window. Add to that, Wes has to work. He helps how and when he can, but is typing and talking away in a home office with doors shut.

This means our current reality includes: me, a seven-day-old, a five-year-old, a nine-year-old, the same four walls, and Wes's voice droning through the room using corporate speak on conference calls. Hearing certain phrases makes me want to gouge out my eyes. Things like "circling back" and "revisiting conversations," and how a situation can be a "hard needle to thread." I'm emotional, and want to kill his voice, the jargon, his job.

Remember how I noted that Parker was aging instantly? She starts to mother Hutch, while I mother Hobie. I hear her half yelling at him to "move faster" and "brush your teeth!" and "please put the orange juice back in the refrigerator once you get it out."

She has an edgy tone, clearly picked up by copying me. Not sure I like how I sound through her voice.

Hobie is growing and eating and as of tonight, one week old. Parker has an idea: let's have a photo shoot with the number shirts gifted from an old family friend!

"Because I'm the first, Mom," she said. "And Hutch is number two, and now we have number three. We need a picture to remember how little Hobie is right now."

Hutch proclaims he will gladly wear any number *but* two. "I want to be first or last!" he argues. Parker explains, calmly, this time with logic, the special meaning behind his shirt. How he's the *only* one in the family who can say he's a little brother *and* a big one. This time, her tone is practical. This time, I like how I sound through her voice. He happily changes clothes.

I take a million pictures. They all look pretty much the same: A nine-year-old mermaid who could run the world. A five-year-old mess too cute and crafty for his own good. And an infant with no idea what he's entered.

1 . . . 2 . . . and now . . . 3.

It feels complete.

COMMENTS:

Molly. That feels good to write. Thank you all for giving me the grace to type away. Best therapy all week.

Peggy F. I remember those first days with my babies and wouldn't have traded them for anything. I started reading your articles when you were pregnant with Hutch and I'm so glad you're going to do this with Hobie as well. You learn something new from every child.

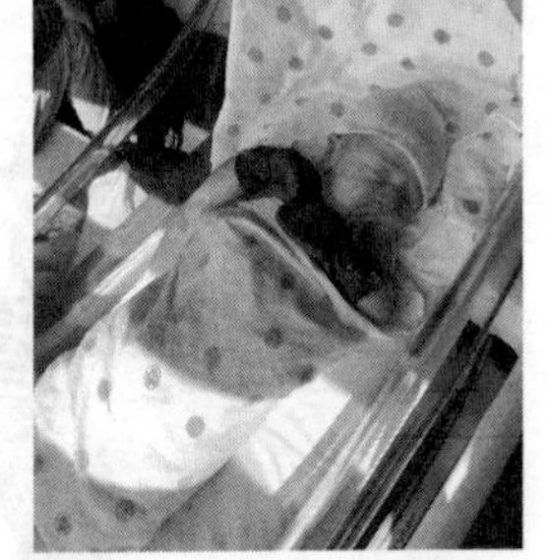

Anne H. I became a Grandma today. So excited to see this one grow.

Erin S. Raw reality. I'm a working mom myself. Thank you for being real and giving everyone insight into the juggle and craziness.

Jill K. This is the only long post that I've felt like reading in full recently. A life-giving message in these challenging, strange times.

Marie W. I feel you with the isolation. I have a seven-month-old. When he was three months (right around the time I was ready to start getting out again) COVID hit. No one comes to visit because they don't feel safe. The walls of the house feel tight. Thank you for your authenticity with motherhood and just life. We will get through.

Lisa S. Truly laughed out loud at Hutch sneaking Grinch-like into the nursery.

It Happened

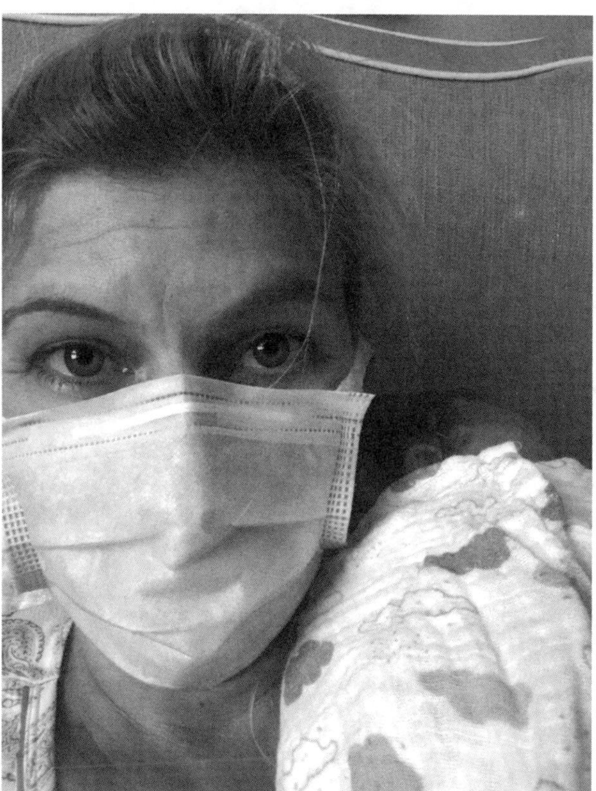

Our whole family has COVID.

That's a direct way to say it; I don't have any bandwidth left to beat around the bush. The past two weeks have been a blur of quarantines, testing, and illness. Just having a newborn right now is surreal. Add to that, at ten days old, Hobie was "the youngest person tested in Mecklenburg County" and "youngest presumptively positive case," according to the county health department. Our lives are beyond surreal. I'm writing now because we are on the road to recovery.

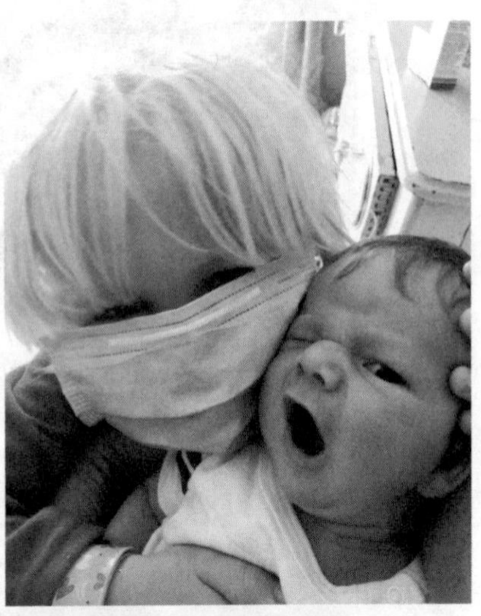

I'll repeat: we are on the road to recovery.

Except that, I'm going nuts. I couldn't script the life we've been living. Parker got it first. Of all the scenarios I played out about coming home with a new baby, none included the whole family in isolation with a potentially deadly virus.

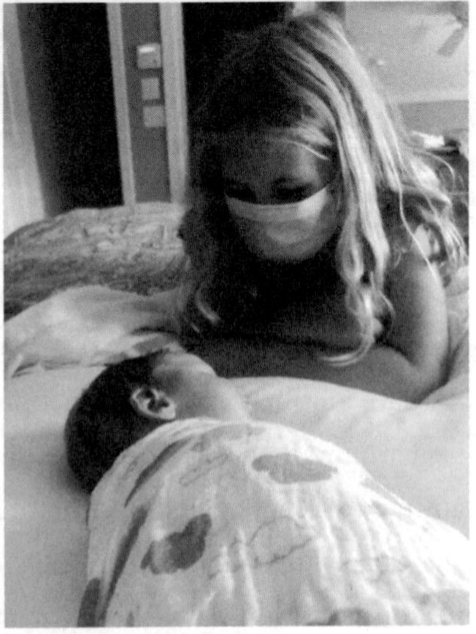

I instinctively want to make a joke about that last sentence. As if it's funny. It's not, but twisted humor has been my way of coping. If you're laughing, you're too distracted to scream.

To be clear, I didn't want to tell you guys until we were out of the woods. I didn't want to cause unnecessary alarm. I also didn't want to post something just to post something. It's why after the last post that ended with the kids in number shirts, I didn't write a word. It seemed insincere and wrong to falsely imply that life was grand when I was sincerely petrified. I didn't want to announce, "We have COVID," without being able to add more.

Now I can say: we are going to be okay.

In our latest video medical appointment three days ago, the doctor said writing details about what our family has gone through might help someone else. We've learned lessons. I understand, in a personal way, more about this virus and its myriad of symptoms. As she said: "This is not a political issue—it's a public health crisis. One your family has been living. Please help educate as best you can."

Education. Got it. I can do that.

So, ready to hear our crazy story?

ଔଷ

Turns out, while Wes and I were in the hospital having a baby, Parker got exposed to COVID. She showed no symptoms for days, so when we returned home with Hobie, and all of us were hugging and kissing the baby, we were all exposed. On Hobie's third day of life—less than eighteen-hours at home with him—Parker started complaining of a sore throat and her ears popping. Allergy-like feelings. I mentioned in that last post that I normally wouldn't think anything about a sore throat. Only, we'd just left a hospital and its multitude of warnings were in my head. I instantly wondered whether it was COVID and got both her and Hutch tested at the pediatrician's office, just to be sure. It was easy.

The pediatrician asked if she'd been around anyone who had it. I said no. At the time I didn't know my mother-in-law, who was watching the older kids during Hobie's birth, had symptoms.

"The cat is out of the bag," the pediatrician also said. "We should be careful, but there's a chance everyone, everywhere, will have it at some point, because anyone can easily be exposed. If you're getting the kids tested for a sore throat, it might actually be COVID. It might not. We hear daily about people who test positive and have no idea where they picked it up. How and where almost doesn't matter. I want you to go back home and quarantine."

We did what we were told. Went back home and told my in-laws. They left thirty minutes later to drive back to Kentucky. I mentioned in the last post, too, how my stepmother's visit was canceled. No family was allowed to assist.

With that, we went into quarantine. Wes got on work calls. We took the number pictures. We had a long first day of isolation, and I wrote that night, posting to the world. Fine. Whatever. At that point it was still non-dramatic.

But that night Parker woke up in a deep sweat. She came to me crying, feeling nauseated, her hair matted back from her forehead, wet and sticky. She slept on our bedroom floor, with soaked pajamas clinging to her from the sweat and one arm wrapped around a bowl.

She never actually threw up, but felt like absolute hell. Wes and I were up more with her that night than with four-day-old Hobie.

I was panicked. Parker and Hutch have had nighttime sickness before, but not during a pandemic. This world in which we now live can make you paranoid and go down dangerous, scary, rabbit holes. Every horrific headline I reported on reappeared in my mind. Watching Parker toss, combined with having a newborn with zero immune system in the same house, and middle-of-night-hazy-unclear-thoughts . . . it was the worst night of my life. I'd feed him, then go wipe Parker's forehead with a cold, wet paper towel, then try to count backward from one hundred in my head to avoid a mental ditch. I was calm and patient all night long on the outside; inside, I was a floppy, fear-filled mess of frightened feelings.

And then . . .

Thank God . . .

Parker's fever broke.

She woke up, early morning, and looked at me.

"Mommy, I feel better."

That's all she said. She knew. She knew simply by looking at my face peering into hers how the night had torn at both of our souls.

By that afternoon, she was back to riding her hoverboard and roller skates in our house, feeling good.

☙❧

Also by that afternoon, Wes had lost all sense of taste and smell. He felt lethargic. He was still in his office, finally telling his bosses—in another time zone—that he wouldn't be on their Zoom video conference later, as he was having to call around to find an available COVID-test appointment. Everything was booked. I, in the meantime, got a call from his mom and dad. They were back in Kentucky, feeling terrible. It had started on the car ride. They'd been tested before leaving Louisville to come to Charlotte and were negative then, but were both now bedridden. My poor mother-in-law lay down in the back seat feeling sick the entire eight-hour car trip home.

Even if Parker's symptoms were similar to a stomach bug, the one symptom that defines COVID is loss of taste and smell. We assumed Wes was positive and felt grateful we'd been in family quarantine. Hutch and Hobie felt fine, and I felt tired, but I'd also just had a baby. Of course my body ached. Of course I was exhausted. I could taste and smell and thought nothing of the other postpartum-like symptoms.

⁂

Days later, Parker's test came back positive. Hutch's was negative, but the pediatrician said to assume it was a false negative or a bad swab, and to consider him "presumptively positive." Wes was still down and awaiting test results. I told her I hadn't had any major symptoms.

Through a professional FaceTime-like virtual appointment, the pediatrician said that Hutch, Parker, and Wes should stay in one part of the house, and Hobie and I should quarantine in another room away from them for the next few weeks. Keep Hutch away from Hobie? In the same house? I thought she was kidding.

She wasn't. And if we had to see each other, she said just make sure we all wore masks within our own home. There wasn't data on newborns and COVID yet. Anecdotally, they weren't seeing many cases, and the only ones they had were very serious, so we needed to protect Hobie as much as possible.

The logistics of staying separate from two kids wasn't realistic. Wes was working remotely with unmatched dedication while fighting COVID in a home office, and I was trying to feed a baby in one room while also getting meals and parenting P and H through walls. We stayed apart a day, but eventually it turned to everyone wearing masks in the house at all times.

Meanwhile, my body aches were getting worse. I had a pounding headache that wouldn't go away. It didn't seem odd. The responsibilities being managed—while making sure to feed a baby every three hours—would hurt anyone's head. I told myself there was nothing to worry about.

◆

Our county health department started calling. We were on its radar.

"You're breaking our precedents," multiple nurses said with an attempt at lightheartedness. "We don't have many families with a newborn in the records. We just want to make sure you're taking care of yourselves."

I was honest: we were doing the best we could.

The health department nurses were kind. They gave me cell phone numbers to text for information. They kept calling, various nurses, and I kept nodding at the phone as if they could see me, as if that would make the calls go faster. I wanted to stop answering questions; the same questions about symptoms and timing and "on a level of one to ten, how tired are you?" that I'd just answered for someone else who had called. Hobie was crying little baby cries, and Hutch and Parker were fighting. Family members wanted updates. Dishes needed to be washed. What were we doing for dinner? Laundry was spilling into the hallways. Everyone else needed me, and I wanted to stop picking up the phone.

Another twenty-four hours later, Wes's test came back positive, and Hutch had a fever. Low-grade: 100.7. I called the pediatrician.

"Keep assuming he has it," she said. "There's no doubt he does. His symptoms are just a week late. Molly—you need to get tested."

"But I don't have a fever," I told her.

"Needing to have a fever is a misconception with coronavirus," she said. "You're at high risk with a newborn and three of your family members are now positive. Go get tested."

Easier said than done. I called hotlines and clinics. Appointments weren't available for days. Right at the tipping point of frustration, the health department called. Again. Just to check in. Now instead of being impatient, I *needed* the lady on the other end. I asked where I could go.

She told me about a drive-up line at a newly constructed clinic. "You don't need an appointment," she said. You didn't even need a primary care provider. It was open Monday through Friday from 8 a.m. until noon. "Get there early," she added. "There is usually a long line."

The next morning I was the twenty-eighth car in line at 7:30 a.m. The reporter in me counted. It was the first time I'd been alone in weeks. I was grateful for the car silence. The line could've taken hours for all I cared. I lay back on the headrest to take five-minute catnaps in between moving the car forward. When it was my turn to pull into a space, a nurse practitioner approached. I was almost disappointed that the quiet was going to end.

Her name was Courtney. She was soft-spoken and had a lovely bedside (car side?) manner. I started coughing while telling her the situation. I really was, I realized while barreling through facts, *exhausted.*

"So, your whole family has it?" she asked.

"Everyone but the baby," I replied.

"Call your husband and have him drive the baby here," she said. "I'm giving you a rapid test, then taking you inside this clinic to get a chest X-ray. You don't sound good. I want your newborn tested as well."

I called Wes. He packed the kids in his car and drove to the health clinic. When he arrived, I knew it was critical, because they didn't make his car wait in line. They waved his vehicle to a parking spot beside me.

Meantime, my results came back. Positive. I had COVID.

The X-ray also showed that I had pneumonia.

Courtney called in a strong antibiotic to the pharmacy.

"You are doing what every woman I have seen is doing," she scolded. "Taking care of your kids and family and ignoring yourself. Get the medicine. Go home. Go to sleep."

With my wrist appropriately slapped, and our quarantine calendar count starting over with a new ten days, I went home and did what Courtney said.

Wes's bosses did not get him on conference calls that day.

ઉ઼

Hobie's rapid test came back negative, but—like Hutch days before—we were told to assume he was positive. The thought crossed my mind that if the newsroom had seen "ten days old" on a press release about daily COVID testing statistics, we'd probably try to track that family down and see if they wanted to share their story. Yet, it wasn't some nameless, mysterious family. It was me. My kids. My baby.

Because he was unable to talk, or express anything to me at his age, and because COVID symptoms can kick in anytime, I was told that when Hobie slept, I had to watch him breathe. That was my task, every time he closed his eyes. *I had to watch every breath he took while asleep.* Courtney said to stand over him, masked, of course, and make sure I studied the direction of his ribcage. If it looked like it was going up and down, that would be good. Keep looking. Keep hoping it went up and down.

If his ribcage looked like it was going left to right. I was told to pack him up and rush to the emergency room.

I write this more than ten days after being given this horrific responsibility and to gratefully say that Hobie has had every breath in an up-and-down direction. I've watched him like a hawk. Over-studied. Inspected small movements on an eight-pound human's rib cage. He also handled the cold-turkey switch to formula really well, being that there was no choice. Putting an antibiotic in my body was going to make my breast milk too strong, and he had to accept a new diet.

Unfortunately, that antibiotic was too strong for my body as well.

I woke up in hives two days after starting the medicine. Watching Hobie's breaths, I felt aggressively itchy. I had an urgent need to scratch and knew before even looking down and seeing red welts over my arms and legs and torso that it had to be an allergic reaction. I got up, went to the mirror, turned on a light, and gasped. My face was a swollen game of connect the dots. I am allergic to all penicillins and have had reactions to medicines before, but never like this.

I set up a video call with Courtney while scratching the massive raised red spots so much, a few started to bleed. She took one look through the screen and switched my meds. "I guess you're allergic to more than just penicillins," she said as the unquestionable explainer.

The second meds made me throw up. But I stuck with them. Am still on them now. No choice. COVID and pneumonia, or puking? I chose the latter. You don't mess with pneumonia.

Photos of Hobie's first weeks of life will make quite a scrapbook. Everyone holding him is wearing a mask, and his mother looks like an uncomfortable inhuman tomato-head.

ఌ

Here's what, so far, might help you:

- You don't need to have a fever—there are many symptoms.
    Parker: Allergy-like symptoms and a fever
    Wes: No taste/no smell, lethargy
    Hutch: Chills, a cough, and runny nose
    Me: Body aches, shortness of breath, headache
    Hobie: So far—unscathed
- Kids are not immune.
- Anyone can be exposed.
- Some side effects are worse than the virus. For me, pneumonia.
- Get checked. Don't wait. Don't assume it's something else.
- This is not the flu.
- One big difference is the incubation period: Parker had it for days before showing symptoms.
- We had no warning anyone had been exposed prior.
- We made a chart of who Parker had been around, and when.
- Then, who *they* were around, and when.
- You'll be horrified with a line graph that starts with your child.
- One case can affect many. Parker alone could've infected dozens.
- All those on our line graph have been tested, and are negative.
- Long-term effects? Time will tell.

ᴄᴓᴈ

For now, I'm glad the fire is extinguished and the smoke around our family is clearing. I am usually eerily calm in crisis situations and am proud for surviving this one, but can't deny how rocked I was watching Parker sweat through the night and my vigilant round-the-clock watch over Hobie.

Relief is an underrated sensation. It covers me right now as I watch P and H argue and Hobie sleep with contentment—we're still watching him breathe, but it has been two weeks with no left-to-right ribcage action. That feels really good. I'm grateful Wes feels better, and yes, I am getting my energy back. Not 100 percent, but I say again, we'll be okay. We survived, and my baby never had to go on oxygen with an uncertain outcome.

As we've crawled back into the light, I've been consumed thinking about the families who aren't okay. The ones who make up the growing statistics day after day. There are many people filled with pain and loss. Currently, North Carolina has had 2,000 people die from COVID; Mecklenburg County, where Charlotte is located, has had over 20,000 positive cases, and over 200 deaths. (Those numbers are end of July 2020; less than five months since coronavirus hit the United States.)

My heart breaks for those families. It did before; it breaks even more now having a small taste of the isolation and loneliness that comes with this virus.

This is not a made-up, fictitious illness meant to be politicized.

You can have an opinion on how it should be handled, but don't fool yourself into thinking it's not real. It's real. I watched my ten-day-old get a nasal swab from a nurse practitioner covered head to toe in a protective suit, while his nine-year-old sister tried to calm him without being allowed to touch him. This, while I was in another car reviewing X-rays with a doctor, looking at nodules on my lungs.

It's real.

Be careful. Share the lessons. Symptoms range from almost anything mild to anything notable. Just, please, be smart. Only spread factual information.

COMMENTS:

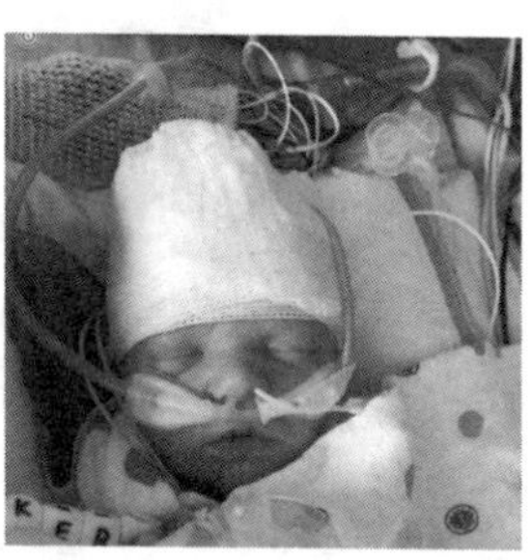

Cindy S. My first grandson came home from the hospital and then had to go back as he was positive for COVID, and so was our family. He's also in a family of five. Our thoughts are with you as well. Here is a picture of my grandson in NICU.

Katie H. How is your mother-in-law?

Molly. Both she and my father-in-law tested positive. Neither was hospitalized, thankfully, but both strong cases.

Della F. If your words reach just one person who didn't believe this was real and change their mind, that's a good thing. I shared your post. Looks like many are.

Michelle S. Thank you for sharing specifics. At times I start to question myself; am I making too much of this? Am I keeping my child from people for no reason? I realize this is real, but it has gone on so long. Many are complacent. Some days it leaves me letting doubt creep. This has reassured me we are doing the right thing.

Astrid P. My kids are scheduled to go back to face-to-face instruction, and I'm overwhelmed with dread. Parenting is hard. Parenting in COVID is hard x 1,000.

Melissa R-G. Beautifully frightening. Thank you for saying you're okay at the start, because I would've been on pins and needles while reading.

Didn't Expect That

The Charlotte Observer

RNC details start to emerge, but venue is still uncertain

WBTV anchor says entire family contracted virus days after she gave birth

I just did what I do. Write. Report. Story-tell. Hours after hitting "publish" on Facebook, I hadn't even gone back to look. Had no idea it was traveling. Didn't realize anything was out of the ordinary until a friend at *The Charlotte Observer* texted: "So . . . wanna talk about it? The fact that you're viral?"

You probably think I sound like an idiot, but I didn't see our family's story about living with COVID as interesting. Guess it's because my mind was clouded. I was living the insanity hour by hour for weeks, and when you live something—survive something—you don't see how the reality in front of you might come off to others. You're just getting through and making sure your loved ones around you are getting through. I was watching Hobie breathe throughout the night. Assuring Parker was really healed. Monitoring Hutch's low-grade fever. Parenting through walls. Taking my own medicine and ignoring my own nausea. Trying to get Hobie to eat new formula while dealing with the repercussions of instantly stopping breastfeeding. (Ladies: the most uncomfortable pain. Ever use cabbage leaves on your body that way? Google if you're not sure what I'm implying.)

Because I lived "the story," I didn't see "the story."

Now that we're thankfully on the other side, I get the appeal: the Facebook post over a week ago was seen or interacted with by more than six million people in its first forty-eight hours. More than 7.5 million after a week. I was live on CNN and CBS News. Reports filled the *Today Show*, Hollywood celebrities and politicians (both political sides) were sharing and commenting, it made the cover story on the *People* magazine website, and I'm still getting requests from *Good Morning America*. Dozens of blogs republished my photos (with no credit or attribution, mind you), and it was one of the most clicked-on stories with UK's *Daily Mail* in London. This morning I was asked through a transcribed voicemail texted to my phone if I wanted to accept a call from an inmate in a South Carolina prison who wanted to send his prayers to our family. I have no idea how he or the prison system had my number. News is funny; sometimes odd connections are out there.

I didn't see any of that coming.

My detailed words about our illness were meant solely as education. I am grateful the message was spread about lessons learned, symptoms, the public health issue, and that kids aren't immune. If describing those things helped even one person, that's a good thing.

Officially, now, we're through the worst. The doctor cleared our family. The kids are back to feeling 100 percent. Wes is no longer dragging. I am still tired and the only one with residual effects, but they're improving and I'd be tired anyway with Hobie. Part of "mothering a newborn" is exhaustion, regardless of whether you just beat COVID and are on the winning side of pneumonia. Sleep is going to be elusive.

Since we're cleared, I think a little Vitamin Sea is in the future . . .

COMMENTS:

Kelly C. I agree that people aren't taking it seriously. I've been sick for two weeks. *This is real.*

Kure Cures

He loves the sound of waves.

AUGUST

MONTH SEVENTY-FOUR: Weeks Old

Dear Hobie,

Today you are four weeks old. Little and loved. Happy one-month birthday.

The world that welcomed you is a circus. Our family has its own ring under the big top, yet you have so far slept through much of the intense show. In the midst of the confusion, your calm nature is a gift.

Your life has been bonkers, Hobie. After our whole family got COVID, there was a hurricane on the coast of North Carolina, an earthquake impacting Charlotte, your sister got stung by a massive jellyfish that wrapped a tentacle around her leg and hand, your brother got a blood-gushing gash millimeters away from his eyeball while playing in the house, and, to top it off, we start elementary homeschool from our hallway on Monday. You will be in my arms as we teach kindergarten and fourth grade.

I sat in on some virtual open house school Zoom calls the other day. You were in a bassinet behind the laptop so I could keep my eyes on you and the teachers. I felt outside of my own body, as if I was watching some other woman. After the open house, I looked down. I'd taken notes on construction paper. Only, I don't remember writing anything. The paper feels like a tangible example of an unbelievable life .

Please, Hobie, be patient with me when Mermaid Academy begins. The school district says students should be in their remote learning environments six hours a day (real school would be seven). The desk next to our garage will be open from 9:15 a.m. until after 3:00 p.m. You and I will be stuck together through the entire experience.

How will remote school work for hard-working single parents who have no one home to teach? How will it work for kids in unsafe environments or without easy access to internet? It seems insurmountable for families like ours with two adults who both have careers, yet we are privileged to even have desks and internet.

You, however, are too young to worry your smooth forehead about these concerns. You're only one month. Your small eyelids are beginning to raise more, like a curtain being pulled to let in sunlight. You're starting to focus on things around you: people. Ceiling fans. Me. Sometimes the pools under those lids seem crystal blue—like Hutch's—but other times they're a murky lake of green-brown. You lie on the middle of a bed for an hour and stare at whatever grabs your attention, usually whatever is straight above.

People keep asking how we got through this past month's sickness, quarantine, and all-nighters. I tell them it was because of your tolerant nature. It's beyond comprehension how adaptable you are at such a young age. Some people say, "So-and-so is such a good baby." I will go to my grave saying, "Hobie is the *best* baby."

Maybe your patience is a sign of your personality ahead. Either way, I want to make note of it now.

A few other thoughts: newborn clothes were too big on you weeks ago, but the snap buttons are now taut around your bottom. Some nights you solidly sleep for five hours in a row, other nights I'm grateful for seventy-five minutes. You only cry enough to let me know you need something, never longer, never inconsolable.

Though we don't yet know your true likes or dislikes, I want to put Kure in your soul. You've been on its sand multiple times, with double or triple shade over your pure skin. Your head always falls toward the ocean as you nap. The mermaid in me thinks your ears are trying to get closer to the sound of waves.

Your four-week pediatrician appointment is next week. We're

cleared from COVID, but I am anxious to hear what they say about your congestion. You've had it since soon after birth. Not uncommon for a newborn, but I wonder. Especially with our past few weeks.

Overall, Hobie, you adapt. You eat. You roll with punches in a miraculous manner, and you almost half smiled the other day. (Parker and I both saw the attempt and squealed like two teenagers at a concert.) All these details of your life seem vividly etched in my mind, but I've learned if I don't write them down, I'll forget them later.

We love you much, my sweet boy.

Happy one-twelfth birthday. Here's to your next eleven months.

Love,

Momma

COMMENTS:

Murphy G. Hutch and Hobie are both going to break your bank in hair-care products when they hit teen years.

Julio M. It is wonderful. The world gave you what you needed in that area.

Lindsay M. Hope that Hobie's congestion is nothing to worry about.

Don't Worry, Beach Happy

His congestion is gone. The world is alright.

COMMENTS:

Taylor N. Oh, the chins!

Here We Go

Night before fourth grade begins. Excitedly setting up Mermaid Academy. I'm in awe of her. She makes me believe we can do this.

COMMENTS:

Lissa C. Mermaid Academy and its kindergarten annex will be wonderful. You've got this. You have to. We moms are following you to see if success is possible.

Kelly C. My daughter's alarm went off at 6:00 a.m.—school already started where we are. She brushed teeth and hair, put on clothes, and proclaimed, "I'm ready." You're right, their excitement is contagious. We *can* do this, we *must* do this.

Casey M. My four children are set up and ready for Virtual Academy tomorrow. I have a sixth grader, a fourth grader, a kindergartner, and a preschooler.

Justin K. This kindergarten teacher is ready.

Sharon D. Look at the bright side. No one really had to get dressed .

Molly I'm making them get up and get dressed. No stumbling down in pajamas, no TV during the day. We'll focus for six to seven hours as if it was real class. The teachers working hard deserve that. I at least have to try to get them to take this seriously.

Look Closely

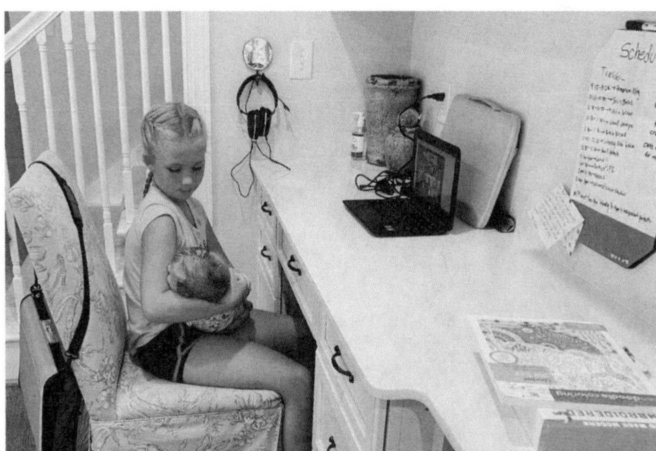

There are challenges to having fourth grade in the hallway, but here's one big bonus: brain breaks can include holding your baby brother.

COMMENTS

Steve M. Parker is experiencing a greater curriculum in human growth and development. You can't put a price tag on this kind of education.

Tina H. Our district policies keep changing. My kids are now even asking what is going on in school. Emotionally, I'm drained.

SEPTEMBER

New Column

This picture is from the day we brought Hobie home from the hospital. It is a marker of time and what *Charlotte Parent Magazine* is using for a new monthly column I'll be writing. The first one went live today. It's called, "Ask A Mom." The editors contacted me to ask if I'd answer questions sent in from all over. You ask, I answer.

At first, I wasn't sure. I shouldn't be giving parenting advice. I often question myself. But that's what the editors liked: I don't pretend to be an expert, and being a reporter, if I don't know the answer, I can research to find out. Love trying something new.

MONTH SEVENTY-ONE: Cracks are Starting to Show

Lil', Mid, Big.

These smiling faces are a bit of a sham.

An upbeat attitude is key in our bizarre world, and, no doubt about it, I'm a glass-half-full girl. But anxiety-packed curveballs continually being thrown are adding chinks in the armor. We will get through these uncomfortable times—I know that. Yet, I feel compelled to acknowledge that sweet photos like this one disguise our daily truths. Photos like this don't show desks in a hallway or pandemic fears. They don't show how I wake up at 3:00 a.m. with a cluttered mind about jumping back into harsh, extreme headlines when my maternity leave is over in a few days.

Photos like this don't show how COVID has made planning anything supremely difficult. For everyone. Holidays. Weekends. We don't know what we can do three weeks from now, let alone Thanksgiving or in December. Anyone have a clue about Halloween? My kids keep asking about trick-or-treating. I give them no hints because there are no details to give.

Photos like this don't show my normally driven fourth grader starting to give up. Her beautiful smile here doesn't show the moments of anger. How there are days her bubbly spirit is replaced with dread for school. She has a growing inclination to fly off the handle, even with me. Maybe especially with me. Moms get the best and the worst.

Photos like this don't show Hutch growing addicted to videos. All types. Live Zooms or bad cartoon YouTube channels. He used to be over-the-moon excited about getting on a big yellow bus and going to sit at his own desk in a kindergarten classroom. Constant screen stimulation has him barely able to sit still at all.

Photos don't show how sports and dance and karate and after-school clubs are either erased or extremely modified. I remember Parker running onto a soccer field with outstretched arms yelling "*Hiiiiii!!*" to teammates, slapping hands, ready to play. The other day it was all I could do to drag her to a soccer skills clinic—she wanted to stay at home and play Minecraft.

Photos like this don't show the meltdowns I've heard friends say they manage their kids through. One day their child will be on top of things; the next day includes a dramatic tantrum over an online project. There are smart kids not doing the work, conscientious kids who can't focus, and moms who have quit their jobs because someone needs to be at home to teach.

What breaks my heart even more than watching my kids starting to drag, fight, and have bad attitudes, is the divide between the haves and have-nots. There are the Ps and Hs of the world right now, and then there are those with no adult at home. No assistance. No computer to do online school or food for lunch. How are households with single parents who work two jobs managing? Or households with a grandparent as the main caregiver who isn't technology-savvy? What about homes where there are two adults, but both work essential jobs and can't be at home? Or the reported 16 percent of households in our school district that don't have internet?

If you talk with school principals and educators, they'll tell you school is the safest place for children whose home lives are unstable and violent. School is the best haven, and teachers the best influences, in households where there is no adult a young child can depend on for guidance and love. What are those kids doing? Where are they?

We got through the end of last year's grade. Then, summer. We're nearing seven weeks of teaching at home this fall. In the beginning, lots of kids had energy for homeschool. I'd even argue there was an excitement, too, from parents, ready to make it work. But, as with all things, time takes a toll. It'd be silly to think anything less.

❧

Those seven long weeks ago, the night before virtual school began, Parker was setting up her desk for fourth grade in the hallway next to our garage. I posted a photo. She loved how we were calling it Mermaid Academy. Her excitement was visible in the way she organized folders by color. As she set up, I sifted through emails. Parker's teacher and Hutch's kindergarten teacher had sent comprehensive notes about apps to download and QR codes to scan for online homeschool programs.

What I didn't cop to then publicly in that short post, was how my mind wanted to fold in on itself. I was trying not to show fear. The emails and codes and happy exclamation points were too much. Parker had no idea about my overwhelmed mental state, or that her natural nine-year-old positivity was the single thread left in the figurative rope we were holding.

"I can't wait to see my friends again," she said while moving things around, as if Zoom was a normal way to see them. "I've missed them this summer. Well, I guess since before summer. When did coronavirus start, Mom?"

"March."

"Yes, March. I've missed them since March." She reached up to take a notebook out of a cabinet above the desk and move it to a closer drawer.

I was silent. Jostling Hobie up and down. My phone buzzed in my palm. Another email. This one needed me to use Sign-up Genius to pick a slot for a parent-teacher conference. And . . . wait. More. My thumb kept scrolling. There was a "Teach us about your child!"

survey to answer. Simple questions. Kinda cute. Didn't matter. Felt like one more thing.

"I mean, Mom." She turned around. "Can you believe this is where we're going to have school? Right here at this desk? I can put things wherever I want! Maybe I'll be able to have more snacks during the school day . . ."

Her stream of consciousness was full of delight. "Mom!" she laughed. "We're going to have fun if you are my teacher!"

I only wanted to cry. Sharing that picture that night before school, showing her excitement, was my attempt to pick me up.

☙

We are now two months invested. I am more well-adjusted. She is less thrilled. There's been a switching of roles. Some days Parker is unaffected, logging on like her old self, full of vigor. On other days it's as if she has been replaced with a daughter I don't know.

The same thing is going on with Hutch. He recently had a meltdown that included kicking, hitting, and screaming, "I DON'T WANT TO GO TO KINDERGARTEN ANYMORE!" This happened after he was called on through Zoom and didn't know the answer. He later told me he felt embarrassed in front of the other kids.

You know, those other kids. His classmates. Kids he has never met in person, yet we say are his friends. He's smart enough to know that feels odd. He's also smart enough to know they can barely see him. The height of the camera on his Chromebook only shows his forehead. He has his name, Hutch, at the bottom of his Zoom square. All the class sees is an inch of floppy white-blond hair, and five letters: H-U-T-C-H under that small image.

The day after his meltdown, Hutch raised his hand (virtually) multiple times. New day. New thoughts. He'd recalibrated, as much as a five-year-old can.

The roller coaster in their emotions leads me to know that our kids need support. Even when they're being brats. They went to school one day in March and didn't go back the next. No warning. They left everything in classrooms, didn't hug their teachers goodbye, and suddenly stopped seeing friends. No more sports or after-school clubs. Then, summer plans and camps were canceled. My kids also had a new baby arrive, got COVID, and quarantined. In Parker's case, she also watched her beloved dog go away. Those changes would impact anyone, let alone a five-year-old and nine-year-old. Even though kids are adaptable, I can't—we can't—expect elementary-aged children to have adult coping skills.

When you stop to think about the past six months, the fact cracks are starting to show isn't a surprise. Stress and tantrums should be expected.

Molly. Breathe. Remember with *hope* that these times are *temporary.* Take comfort in these two words. They're powerful tools. This time doesn't need to be about grades or success. Certain seasons of life are simply survival. Sometimes, that's enough.

At some point, it will feel right again. Until then, I say, notice the cracks. Don't cover them. They are the real effects of these unreal times, and to pretend stress isn't happening only makes everyone else struggling feel worse. Hug your kids. Show grace. Work through screaming frustrations. We are resilient.

We will get through.

COMMENTS:

Mary N. The cracks for all of us are visible and expanding. Our souls are exhausted. Your writing is cathartic for us to identify with.

Tammy T. No day is the same. I tell myself to be a willow tree.

Kelli F. As a teacher, I'm on the other end trying to make school as normal as possible. I miss my kids. I want to hug them and let them know how important their learning is to me. I have gone through emotional days as I Zoom with their parents and grandparents, trying to help them figure it out.

Christy B. I needed to hear this today. My sweet boy has days where he is a child I've never seen. Meltdowns, crying, talking back, hollering at me.

Susan H. I am a preschool teacher. I hear these frustrations every day. My family and I made a COVID time capsule which we plan to open in ten years. I am printing your post to add to it.

OCTOBER

Current Situation

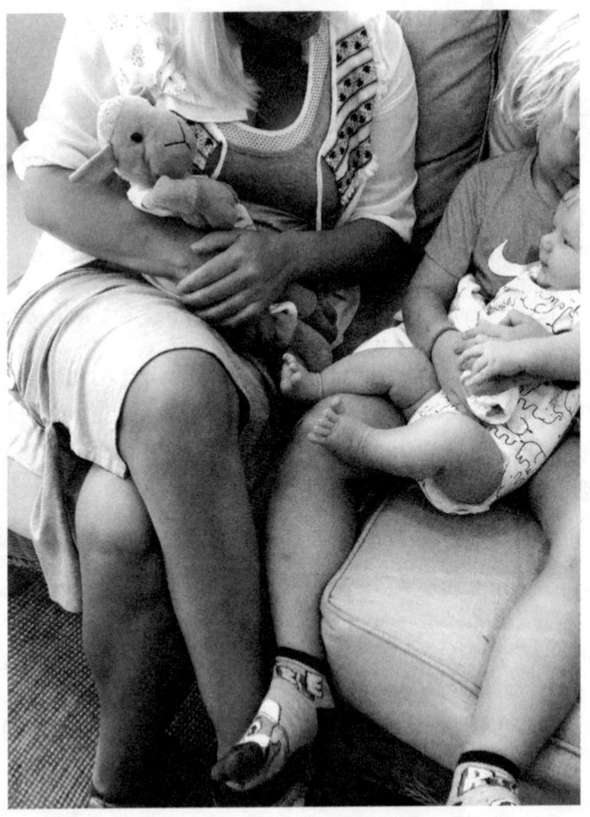

Hutch: "Mommy! Before you get ready for work, let's hold both of our babies!"

Then he handed me Lambie.

The Stand-In

First week back (almost) done. Starting Monday, I asked Parker to help Wes handle Hutch and Hobie while I'm at work. Please get them ready for bed, P, I suggested. Read them books. Get out their pajamas. Remind Hutch to brush his teeth. It's a lot for any one adult—mom or dad—and I'm back to being gone every night. This will help show off your maturity, I said.

Tonight, she sent this photo from Wes's phone.

My bathrobe. My coffee cup. Her humor.

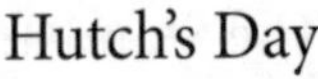

Hutch's Day

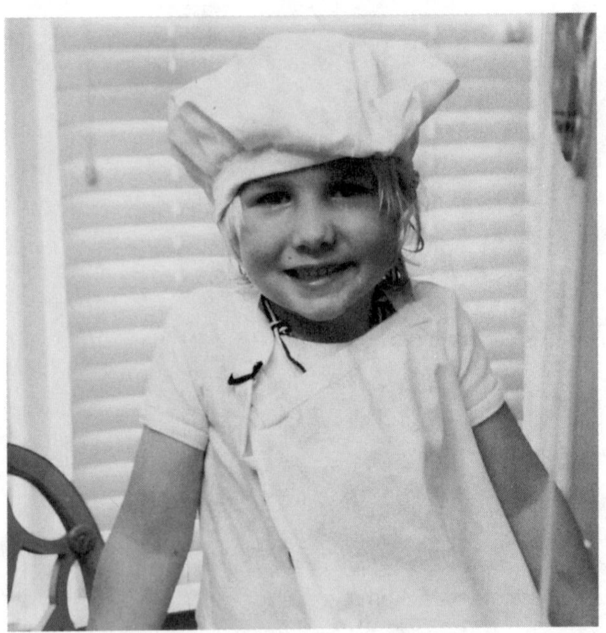

Happy sixth birthday to the quirkiest and most charming little nugget around. Full of joy and pranks with a mind that makes us laugh and think. Love you, Hutchie.

COMMENTS:

Michelle P. Happiest birthday to Hutch. We share the same birthday, forty-four years apart.

Donald H. What idea is he cooking up now?

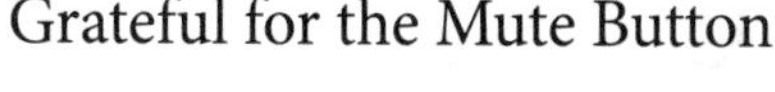

Grateful for the Mute Button

Behind the Zoom.

I was honored to moderate a Metastatic Breast Cancer virtual conference today for women who live with MBC. The camera didn't show me bouncing Hobie to sleep with my foot in a flip-flop or monitoring fourth grade and kindergarten on the couch. A panel discussion moderator seemingly surrounded by all the lovely, calm time in the world.

The magic of multitasking mommas.

MONTH SEVENTY-TWO: Fifth Weeknight

Third week back at work, and we've begun a new routine for Fridays. The fifth weeknight is now defined by meeting for dinner out. Often, pizza. Friday means that there's no school tomorrow. No work tomorrow. Friday nights are later bedtimes and happiness and joy and fewer tantrums. It's sibling hugs and a dinner break that feels free. Even though we know cracks show and tempers flare, Fridays feel easier. Fridays aren't the middle of a cycle—Fridays are the end goal. Fridays are love.

News spins in my mind all day and evening long. That's my career. I don't get an off button. I interview, log, monitor, relay, and inform, no matter how dark or difficult. Maybe *that's* why I have learned to like writing the personal here on Facebook. *It feels good.* Granular off-camera real life is a different kind of truth to acknowledge.

Back in the newsroom now. Still living in that Friday night high of kids and a fast break. I'm smiling big as I type. That feels right to report.

COMMENTS:

Lori C. In this politically-charged, COVID-ridden year, I miss seeing pictures of people's kids and what they were having for dinner. Keep showing us happy.

Luci N. As a full-time working professional, there is something about getting home tired, but an entire weekend stretched ahead.

Bonita H. Fridays are what your kids will remember most when they are older.

Mack S. We've got kids at similar ages. Fridays are our favorite day of the week.

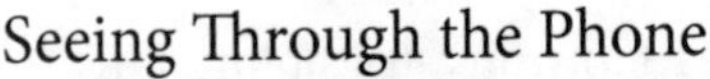

Seeing Through the Phone

Hutch just called. It's past his bedtime. Said he had something to show me and couldn't wait until tomorrow . . .

COMMENTS:

Audrey J. Someone has lost a tooth.

Johnson H. That's an important reason to stay up past bedtime.

Van D. Hope the tooth fairy has money.

The Failed Fairy

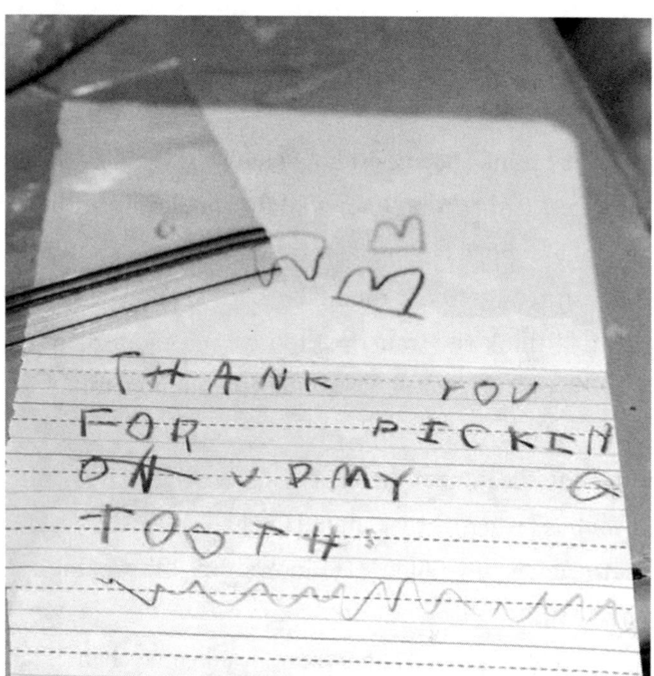

Oh my oh my oh my. Days ago, Hutch had proudly FaceTimed his toothlessness. Hours later, I forgot my tooth fairy duties. Even worse, I hadn't thought about it since. Hutch *never said a word* when he woke up and found his tooth untouched *two* mornings in a row.

Until tonight.

We were on dinner break in the middle of the bustle, I was feeding Hobie, Parker was waxing on about her Halloween costume, Wes was eating, and we were all around a table when Hutch spoke up.

The words whistled through the hole between his teeth..

"I wrote the tooth fairy a letter," he said calmly.

My entire body froze.

"You did?"

"Yes. I . . . I think she doesn't know me."

I could feel Parker, who knows all things, staring at the side of my face. She stopped talking, making it even more awkward.

"She hasn't come to my room," he said, looking at his plate of spaghetti. "I think she wants me to give her more than just my tooth." His voice was sweet. Disappointed, but hopeful. "So, today I wrote her a letter."

I wanted to slide under the table.

"Uh-huh . . . where is that letter, Hutch?"

"I put it under my pillow." He looked up. "It's waiting for her, with my tooth."

Parker kicked me from her seat beside my chair. I almost dropped Hobie.

"Well, that's great, Hutchie. I bet she'll be so happy reading what you wrote. I bet she'll come tonight!"

He smiled. I fake smiled back, drowning in guilt.

I returned to work after dinner and told Maggie—who was now cleared to work back in the newsroom—what I'd done. Actually, what I'd *not* done. As an ultimate in-charge-of-details producer, she promised to help me not forget again.

As Maggie walked out the door after our 11 p.m. show, she delivered. Turned and yelled: "MOLLY. TOOTH FAIRY!"

Turns out, I didn't need Maggie's reminder. When I got home, another girl was looking out for me too. At the top of the steps, a note written on toilet paper in the path of a nightlight, highlighted by a soft beam unable to be missed. Parker's handwriting.

She left me a reply to give to Hutch, thanking him for writing "her" a letter.

Parker was acting as the tooth fairy, assuring her brother wasn't left hanging. Again.

I left Hutch's room after sliding Parker's note and the $1 bill I could find (this fairy is generally not cash-carrying) under his pillow. I came down the hall, turned on the light, and opened his note.

His little Hutch letters and fairy thank-you spurred me to scroll back on my phone to look again at his joy in Monday's screengrab. He held his tooth then with big expectations. Reseeing the photo makes me think about his quietness in the two days since, how he'd been waiting patiently to be remembered.

Parenting is the most wild, hard, hysterical, and grounding job in the world.

COMMENTS:

Leigh R. Everyone can take a lesson from Hutch's patience and Parker's love.

Griffin W. I've done that. It's how our daughter used deductive reasoning to figure out.

Lin V. Years ago I was providing childcare for a family with a single mom. She did the same thing, forgetting the tooth fairy two nights in a row. I found out because I discovered the tooth when I was making up the kids' beds and asked about it. While the kids were playing outside that afternoon, I wrote a letter from the tooth fairy explaining that she'd had an accident and damaged her wing and was in the hospital a couple of days. The mom was beside herself with gratefulness for the rescue. Village, always.

Robin H. We've all been there.

NOVEMBER

Halloween

Hey, Mom and Dad,

I've got a complaint. Isn't it November 2? Should you be dressing me up as a pumpkin today? I know the weekend was busy and you never got a photo of me dressed in this orange circle, but still. It doesn't seem right.

I also heard you, Mom, say that years from now, no one will know the photo of my first Halloween wasn't actually on Halloween. I'm not sure. I feel like a fraud. A costumed, November 2 fraud.

When I looked at you, Mom, as you took the picture and I blew a bubble to question your decision-making, you smiled back and said, "Shhhhhh . . . Hobie. You look adorable."

Parker heard you. She looked at me with pitiful eyes. I think big Sissy knows something I don't. Could this be just the beginning? My first tiny dip into the pool of "just do what mom says?"

As inappropriate as this fuzzy thing feels, I'll play along. Okay? Just don't tell anyone. You pretending this morning is still in October can be our little secret.

Signed,

Hobie

COMMENTS:

Leigh G. The pumpkin photo is *very* important! Locke is fourteen years old and still one of my fav photos to cherish forever. Hobie will be thankful you snapped it.

Misty H. Just like no one will ever know that some of my daughter's "monthly" milestone photos were taken sometimes for two months at a time, just in different outfits.

Carrie G. Last year we did Christmas pictures on December 27. It happens.

Hutch Goes to Kindergarten

This was a morning for Hutch years in the making. He stepped onto the school bus steps, then into the bus itself. First time. He couldn't wait, he said, to meet his class. He even brushed his hair.

That long-ago vision of walking to the bus stop in August with a newborn and watching Hutch and Parker ride off? We know that didn't happen. But here on November 5, there is some version of something. The school board passed a policy: kids must wear masks and carry pieces of paper confirming a current health screening, but they are permitted to ride the bus and enter a school building twice a week. It's a start. One might say it's a small victory. We'll take it.

Take comfort in what you can. Mermaid Academy shifts to part time this morning, and Parker and Hutch go to an actual school. He called it the "second biggest day of my life, after when I became a big brother."

PS: Wanna take bets on if he brushes his hair tomorrow?

Goal-Oriented

Sports are back. It's an accurate chapter title.

Fort School

Too many kids got sick, so Hutch is back to virtual school this week. The principal at Mermaid Academy is struggling and its students are building forts.

COMMENTS:

Tara B. On a day where my project manager brain would love nothing more than a silent workspace to stay focused, seeing this unstructured structure helps. The patience pirates are on full attack while my third grader shares my space for what seems like day 5,462.

Cindy Y. Committed and talented teachers. Flexible and resilient students.

Mental Cauldron

News never stops. Today it's: (A) Incredible support after an officer is killed in the line of duty; (B) separately planning a funeral for a sheriff's deputy tomorrow; (C) the Pfizer vaccine rolling out for the first time at a local major healthcare system; (D) Moderna's vaccine getting FDA approval; (E) a long-awaited pardon for a wrongly convicted North Carolina man; (F) five hospital workers test positive for COVID; (G) a school system suddenly going fully remote because "so many students are sick;" (H) a massive drug bust involving UNC-Chapel Hill, Duke, and App State fraternities

. . . and . . . oh, wait . . . (I) the small, small, we-don't-yet-really-know chance of snow on Christmas. Please cue 82,000 emails.

I typed the above out, top-of-mind. (A) through (I) are in my head because that's my job. I should know (A) through (I).

Tonight, however, another thought is mixed in as well.

In the middle of watching a police procession and asking questions about vaccines, a rogue thought set up shop. Not about work. About family. Kids. School.

Teachers have never worked harder than this year; half virtual, half in person, worried about their own health, kids they can't track down, and being counselors, social workers, and therapists on top of their educating duties. It's hard for them to win in this world. Yet, they don't give up. This thought about teachers was knocking on the inside of my skull despite those swimming headlines, because of a task given to Parker's fourth-grade class.

Her teacher wanted to throw a holiday party, which is hard because only half of the class is in-person at one time. Rather than give up on the idea, though, she told parents to forgo Thursday afternoon virtual class and instead, let students make a gingerbread house on their tables at home.

That's this picture. Parker staying on Zoom, getting off classwork, and at her teacher's request, diving into treats and icing as an independent project at home. When complete, she was told to get back on camera to show off the masterpiece to her friends. She was having fun in pandemic school, and that has been rare. Our sitter, Meredith, knows that, and gumdrops and graham cracker texts from her kept popping into my phone while I was at work.

Meanwhile, I'm miles away from her happiness, focused on (A) through (I), wanting to cry for a police department losing one of its own and curious about which will be the next group to get permission to be vaccinated, while also smiling at my phone seeing her elation.

Also in my mental cauldron? Parker's nighttime soccer practice.

I told Meredith the right time, but gave her the wrong place. Oops. Guess I dropped that ball. I'm getting good at not beating myself up over knowing some balls fall, which makes me think of an email I got today from a woman named Christine. She said I could post this picture of her homeschool, Cupcake Academy, then apologized for the mess. Christine: *the mess is the point.* Feel comfortable dropping the ball of clean floors. You're teaching your child on a couch you named after a treat. Give yourself points and walk by the piles you don't want to see.

Hi Molly! My daughter starts temporary remote learning today. She asked what was the name of her school. I told her about your Mermaid Academy, so we now have Cupcake Academy haha have a great day!

Please look at this image of Mermaid Academy.

Hutch giving up, Hobie alone in the middle of the floor, and Parker, with her back to me ignoring direction. I call that mess, stable.

COMMENTS:

Mitch S. I am a teacher. We are exhausted. Parents can go a long way to make us feel our efforts are noticed.

Amy O'K. Dear All Moms: That "mess" looks like a busy, happy, loving household with children. I see warmth and memories and it's lovely. This year of all years, if your kids go to bed fed, and aware they're loved, that's a win.

Mike W. I was talking to a friend the other day—the word of the year is *shifty*—like a good football running back. As a teacher, I must shift quickly because things change quickly. My friend said the same. It's hard for those of us who like lists, order, and to check off the boxes, but it can be done.

Teresa W. I'm a retired teacher who sometimes subs and can tell you: teachers have never worked so hard and performed so well.

MONTH SEVENTY-THREE: What's in a Name?

I field tons of questions about Hobie's name. Pronounced: Hoe-bee. Not hobby. Think "Kobe"—as in Bryant—but with an *H*. And no, he's not named after David Hasselhoff's son on Baywatch. (Though I did love that cheesy TV show in high school.)

Hobie is named, loosely, after my dad.

If you knew Joseph Michael Grantham, Jr., you might feel good even just reading his name. He was that kind of easy. A man who created positive reactions and was a best-friend guy. After his funeral, multiple grown men said through tears at a backyard oyster roast celebration of life—a party he would've wanted—"Joe Grantham taught me how to be a better dad."

I thought my dad was the best dad every week of my life. He was my hero when I was five years old, when I was twelve, when I turned twenty-one, and when he died, after I'd just turned twenty-nine.

As I've written before, colon cancer stole him. Though I hate cancer with a vigorous passion so deep I can't find enough words to describe, I can also type that first sentence of this paragraph and feel warm dreaming of him, rather than being angry over his absence. I'll never not miss him. But fourteen years later, when I hear his daddy voice, hearty laugh, and long-winded stories in my head, they make me happy. Not sad. The missing will never change, but he's with me and my brothers every day. All of us own pieces of our father.

An awesome piece my brother Jay owns is in his name. Jay's full name is Joseph Michael Grantham, III. The deep meaning passed down with JMG is purposeful—Jay also shared his name with his first son, Joseph Michael Grantham, IV. My brother and nephew carry the initials with pride.

When I was pregnant with Hutch years ago, "Joseph Michael Grantham" was already rightly taken. Wes and I made up the name Hutch—perfect—and moved on.

Late last year when (surprise!) I was pregnant again, name talks followed. If it was a girl, it'd start with *P* to match Parker. If a boy, an *H* to match Hutch. For no other reason than I like alliteration. My *P* girl name idea came to us instantly. But we were empty of ideas if Tic-Tac was a boy.

When last March we cut into cupcakes and Hutch saw blue icing, Wes and I started thinking seriously about names. We were stumped. There couldn't be a better boy *H* name, we said, than Hutch. Nothing jumped out. No website or baby book contributed a name that felt right.

Then, we stopped worrying about names because . . . it was March. Life began to tilt. COVID spread. The world shut down. Homeschool started. I published my second book, anchored the news at home, then didn't because of the chaos, and was getting more pregnant by the week. Life was a series of logistics scratched out on Post-it notes. We waited for more shoes to drop. Names for a future baby weren't remotely top-of-mind.

By June, one month out, I had a rare quiet night. I was thinking about my dad and what might be his view of our hectic household from high above. He'd always found humor in whatever we faced. He was comfortable at an oyster roast on the beach, inside a corporate board room, or changing a tire on the side of the road. He wore khakis with no socks and dressed like a classic Southern gentleman, which matched his formal sounding name. Good thing then, I thought, he had an approachable nickname. "Joby." That's what his childhood best friends called him: Joby. Not "Joseph" or "Joseph Michael." Just "Joby," like a guy next door. How fitting, I thought, as I sat rubbing my belly. My fun-loving dad raised with a fun-loving nickname.

It hit. Joby . . . with an *H*.

Spell it differently, but make it sound the same: Hobie.

Hobie Michael.

Not Joseph Michael, like my brother and nephew. Not Joby

Michael, because Joby was a name unto my dad and there was only one him. But, Hobie Michael. A new name for a new baby. A name inspired by a hero of a man whose DNA runs deep.

Wes instantly agreed. It was set.

Parker, Hutch . . . and Hobie.

Late into maternity leave one weekend, I took Hobie to Kure Beach with two girlfriends who understood the Kure obsession and family memories I find in its three-mile coastline. My dad was a lifeguard there in the 1960s, took us as kids, and after his death, some of his ashes went into Kure's waves. One Father's Day, Wes and my sisters-in-law had a shiny blue fish-shaped plaque engraved with "Joseph Michael Grantham, Jr." placed in Kure's small boardwalk as a gift to his family. That small memorial is where I go sit to honor him. No headstone for my dad: rather, a five-inch fish laid in wood.

One windy day this past September at Kure, carrying my ten-week-old named Hobie, I took him to see Joby's plaque.

I hadn't shared this picture until now, because it feels personally remarkable, and I needed to find the right words to explain *why* it feels remarkable. It probably appears like a mom on a simple walk with her baby, taking pause to smile. But to me, it's my baby boy meeting my dad's spirit.

If something feels right to you, let it be right.

ঔ

Two days after Hobie's birth, a woman named Sonya Parrish sent the nicest email. I never replied. I didn't know how to address her note. She had asked about the origin of the name, and said "Hobie Michael" is the name of her youngest son. Sonya sent along a picture of her Hobie, who's now twenty-five, she said, and a sheriff's deputy. Sonya, I've kept your email all these months. I didn't know how to best explain the origin of my Hobie Michael. Here, though, is an answer.

COMMENTS:

Sandy C. The Old English meaning for the word Hobie is, "bright" or "shining intellect." What a beautiful name to carry the legacy.

Reese H. I will now pronounce Hobie's name correctly in my mind, when reading your posts.

DECEMBER

Adoration

Two mornings ago, he was so overcome with six-year-old excitement about unwrapping presents he ran and jumped straight into his favorite person's arms. She caught him. Let him squeal and squeeze and smoosh her face. Thank God I grabbed my phone.

I'm off this coming week and going to enjoy. Hope you can find a moment or two to take in little things. They're important to notice.

Merry Christmas to all, and to all a New Year.

MONTH SEVENTY-FOUR: Rewind Your Mind

We were hopeful. Wasn't just the first day in a new year, it was the beginning of a new decade. In front of us lay a vast 2020 horizon. We had goals. Lofty resolutions. *Pandemic*, *quarantine*, and *social distancing* were words yet to be said in our sentences, so we felt free to plan futures. Remember hard how this exact day felt one year ago. What is it you wanted?

We didn't know then our year wouldn't deliver wants, only teach needs.

It's easy to slash 2020 to shreds. If for no other reason than to reciprocate how it treated us.

Imagine a prophet coming down 365 days ago to tell us about a virus in a Chinese village that started in a bat, then spread to humans, then spread around the world shutting down borders, grounding businesses, and sending your kids to be schooled at home. I'd have laughed. What a tale.

None of us had a conversation with any future-teller 365 days ago, but thinking what could've been said is almost entertaining.

Prophet: "*Listen. Listen! You have to hear me. I'll start by saying you'll lose loved ones to old age, cancer, and unexpected accidents—things you expect. You'll also lose 347,000 Americans in this upcoming year to a virus. You'll wear masks. No, not Halloween masks. Surgical masks. You'll be asked to spend Thanksgiving and Christmas away from family to protect you and them. The Republican National Convention in Charlotte and the Democratic National Convention in Tampa will be virtual shells of themselves. Charities will stop having fundraising events. Calendars will clear. Time will lose definition. Tuesdays will feel like Thursdays will feel like Saturdays, because no day will get defined. It'll all be the same. Birthday parties, Sunday sermons, funerals, and weddings will become virtual. Vacations will essentially stop. You'll only see coworkers through Zoom meetings.*"

Zoom meetings? Cue my eye roll. I'd have smirked with the confidence that this prophet had no clue.

"*You don't believe me?*" I can, in this fantasy discussion, imagine the sarcasm. "*You, Molly, of all people should believe. You will be forced to work from home in the spring because pregnant women will be considered high risk. You'll anchor the news while a neighbor loudly mows the lawn. You'll teach school in that hallway next to your garage. March and April will feel like five years. In July, you'll have a baby. No visitors allowed. Days later your whole family will get this virus; you'll get it the worst. The strong pneumonia medicine doctors prescribe will cause a bad allergic reaction in your body and an instant cold turkey halt to breastfeeding. While covered in hives, you'll be told to stand over the crib and watch your baby boy breathe. He'll be ten days old. Doctors will give strict instructions to watch the direction of his rib cage.*"

My smirk at Ghost of the Future might then have turned to a skeptical head tilt. (I just gave that face at the computer as I typed.)

"*This is the truth, Molly,*" this prophet will say, with no-nonsense. "*That is what's to come in 2020. Isolation. Fear. Nodules on your lungs, no-contact parenting, avoiding your husband because he, too, has COVID, and watching your baby breathe in a 2:08 a.m. haze. Your head will be heavy. Everyone's heads will be heavy. Ten minutes will feel like twenty-four hours. Some entire days will feel like a month. Nothing will be sensical. The mural in your mind will bleed through lines; facts will be feelings and feelings will become facts.*

"*Then, weeks later, it'll be okay. You will gut-laugh again without coughing. You'll write about it. Some people will thank you for sharing lessons; others will accuse you of promoting a fake virus. You'll repeatedly see, often with no malice intended, how people believe what they want to believe.*

"Twenty-twenty will teach you," this prophet will say, *"that more than ever before, truth was a matter of perspective."*

ꕥ

I just wrote all that with Hobie on my lap, the most obvious bonus and biggest personal marker of the past year. Holding him makes me think hard about 2020. The losses and wins. Most parents teaching homeschool and juggling jobs, family, fears, and life were stretched more than Gumby. But those long days added up to less crowded weeks. The clock didn't matter much.

When P and H were babies, we were go-go-go-go-go. The goal was to get their naps and feedings folded into overscheduled adult days. Constant movement; not a lot of hanging out.

Circumstances changed with Hobie.

Tonight, it's New Year's Eve. We have nowhere to go. I can type one-handed on my phone while jostling a baby instead of getting dressed up. There are no plans for anyone. No evening celebrations, no events on New Year's Day. There is nothing to do this weekend. It's kids and couch and football on TV. Maybe Netflix or HBO. Parker wants to watch *Wonder Woman*. Hutch wants to play UNO. We ordered pizza. The delivery driver will leave it on the porch with zero interaction.

As Hobie sits drooling (let the record reflect at five and a half months, his first tooth is coming), I feel more connected to him than I did the other two at this age. Twenty-twenty gets credit for that bonding.

Twenty-twenty taught us how plans could break, and structure could bend. It taught contradictions: as complicated as the world felt, days were actually quite simple. Stay where you are, value your walls, and love how you can. It reminded us in a down-deep-in-our-core way of how good health is not to be taken for granted. Groundhog Days since March forced us to reexamine our roots rather than race to grow. Instead of days filled with acquaintances, we appreciated good friends who checked on us. We knew in our own minds who we wanted to check on.

The pang of missing loved ones—those we couldn't physically hug because of forced distance and those we lost—helped redefine what mattered: relationships. Information. Love. Light. Empathy. Hope. And of course, survival.

Whenever someone said, "I can't wait for the year to be over,"—did they assume now would arrive, the calendar page would turn, and the culture of 2020 would be gone? Pretty thought. Not the case. The feel of the last year is sticking. Midnight just struck and we're still here, wearing masks and preparing to homeschool next week. We're not back to what we knew as normal.

What if . . . *what if we never get back to normal*?

What if it all needs to be reframed?

What if, instead of "back to normal," it's "the new next?"

A "new next" implies the good in 2020 isn't what happened, but what's learned from its ashes. Let's use 2020's fires to create wider-minded resolutions for 2021. We couldn't have fathomed the year even if that prophet had appeared with a blueprint, but now . . . now we get it. We lived it. We know. We can use "the new next" as code for taking more control. Let's pick and choose, like an a la carte menu. We choose to keep handwashing efforts, but also choose to put kids back in school. Large businesses can opt to hold on to work-from-home systems that benefit employees, but small businesses can choose to open their doors again. We can pick cherishing time, but also choose to add a few obligations back into days.

Remember the needs, let go of some wants.

By doing less, find more.

No, Prophet, I wouldn't have predicted the destructive flames. But maybe you wouldn't have predicted how the story could be flipped and we could gain from what burned.

Amazing how sitting with a quiet baby next to a joke of a candle can set a mind on fire.

Welcome, New Year.

COMMENTS:

Beth S. Saving this. Highlighting the "new next" section.

JANUARY

Pop quiz

I don't post daily difficulties of homeschool—we're still only in-person two days a week—because it is what it is, and we all have them. But on this overly intense morning, I bring you handstands and ukulele-playing. Mermaid Academy is in shambles. Because roughly a million headlines are currently happening at work, I had a Zoom meeting as school began and couldn't monitor class. The result was Hutch on an instrument, and Parker started practicing gymnastics. In the photo, do you see:

(A) My call.
(B) A six-year-old playing live music in a virtual gym class.
(C) A fourth grader who gave up math to turn upside down.
(D) All of the above, at the same time.

Laugh through the journey. No other option.

COMMENTS:

Ey S. As a teacher who has taught virtually all year, I love the extra-curricular activities going on. I've laughed until I cried and learned to embrace all moments along the way.

Andrea D. Quick tip . . . Legos are a great way to teach fractions.

Nicole R. I feel like you are looking into my home. I'm just trying to manage everyone else's stuff.

Corby P. I am a virtual teacher and your posts help connect me to real issues in real homes. I never truly know what goes on behind the screen, but your musings keep reminding me to allow grace with my kiddos and their families.

MONTH SEVENTY-FIVE: View from Behind

What it's like to be Hobie's parent:

"His hair!"

"Oh my gosh, that baby has so much hair!"

"I've never seen that much hair on a six-month-old!"

Once people ask about his name, the follow-up is his curls

covering the front, sides, and top of his head.

They do not, however, curl over the back. *Nothing* is in the back. Hobie has a bald horseshoe.

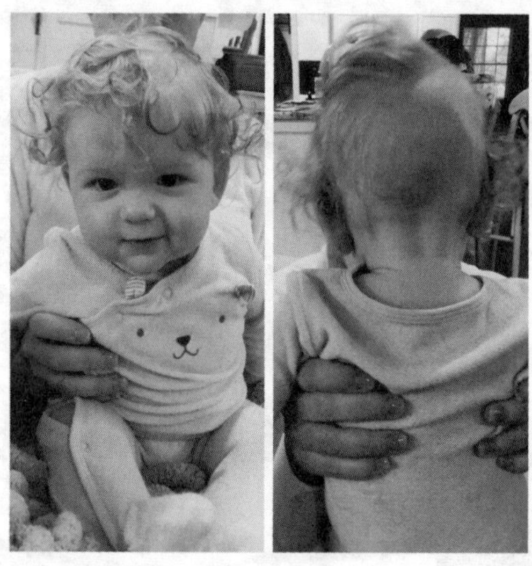

Until now, I've never shown the lack of a party behind. But, the wide semicircle of fuzz has grown too fantastically funny to keep hidden any longer. Our whole family laughs when he turns around.

Every morning, either Wes or I walk in to get him from his overnight sleep and see him on his tummy. He flips himself during the night. We watch him push himself up on his arms to turn his head toward the noise of the nursery door opening. He then gifts us with the absolutely cutest smile you've ever seen. He laughs when he sees us, and we laugh at seeing his half-bald, half-clown-curly profile, and two-tooth grin. It is the best.

If, Hobie, you someday want to kill me for sharing your hair growth with the world, it's the price you pay for having a mom who notices all things. (Also, go talk to your brother and sister. They might have decent advice in this area.)

For those wondering, "Does his odd hair mean something? Is it a sign of illness?" Ahem. I don't think so. Why not? Because I did what everyone does when they have a question in life: Google. After typing in "baby hair growth long in front and sides and nothing in the back" I found this on whattoexpect.com:

> **"Not all newborns are born bald—some arrive on the scene with a shock of thick hair. While a few babies come out with perfectly coiffed locks, the rest look like they're having a bad hair day, with a spiky mohawk, tufted patches, or the scraggly comb-over of a little Homer Simpson. Experts believe it probably has something to do with maternal hormones and the genetic lottery. . . Eventually your baby's hair will grow in and look less like a punk rocker and more like the coiffed baby of your dreams. Exactly when that happens can be anyone's guess—it's different for every child."**

If we realize months from now that Hobie's bald horseshoe is a sign of something more serious, we'll roll. In the meantime, I'm great with a jolly, easy six-month-old whose style sets a good mood.

Love ya, Hobie. From both the front and the back.

Secret Super Bowl Story Revealed

Today is Super Bowl LV. Five years after Super Bowl 50. With time removed, Kristen Hampton, Sarah-Blake Morgan, and I feel this story is safe to retell. There has to be some statute of limitations keeping the halftime police from arresting us, and WBTV can't care too much being that Kristen and SBM no longer work there. So, here we go. Rewind your minds back to Super Bowl 50 . . .

The Carolina Panthers were playing against the Denver Broncos, broadcast on CBS. Seven of our newsroom employees were sent to San Francisco. We were the home team and the home station. By this point, everyone in the Carolinas felt like they knew every player, as the roster was filled with personality both on and off the field. It was the most exciting work trip you could imagine. I have vivid memories and tangible pictures of how the seven of us worked through constantly chaotic conditions and across a three-hour time zone difference to get everything on air, on digital, and on social platforms. San Francisco was electrifying. Taxi lines. Breakfast spots. Jam-packed hotels. Everything was about the Carolinas and Denver. You'd spot Newton and Davis and Kuechly and Stewart and Olsen and Kalil and Benjamin jerseys all over the city. Shaq Thompson, Kurt Coleman, Tre Boston, Ted Ginn, Mike Tolbert, and Ron and Stephanie Rivera were names said in conversations around us. I ran in to Drew Brees in an elevator. Everyone was joyfully talking football and anticipating the star-studded lineup for halftime: Beyonce, Bruno Mars, and Chris Martin from Coldplay.

Game day. Second quarter. Panthers weren't playing well. We were, in fact, terrible. Everyone's full attention shifted to halftime. There was a whole new security line for the halftime show, because lucky fans who had been prechosen were allowed to go on the field. No media allowed unless approved weeks ago. It was made clear to us that no one gets in without a halftime badge and weeks of pre-background checks. Sarah-Blake, in her endless craftiness, was talking to people and working phones. To this day I have no idea how she really did it, but she turned to me and Kristen and said, "I can get three passes. They're legitimate. Follow me."

She can get what? Not sure what you'd do in that situation, but Kristen and I didn't think twice: we followed.

Soon the three of us were in line with Pepsi sponsors. We shuffled underneath the stadium and stood next to Beyonce's backup dancers. It happened so fast. We had been outside, then in line, then herded down steps, then under the seats, then suddenly standing next to

praying women in black leather and heels. The show was supposed to start in five minutes. The three of us didn't know whether to take pictures, act cool, or just stare.

There was movement. The sea of sponsors were pushed onto the field grass. A thump of music began. The Super Bowl-packed stadium went nuts stomping as Bruno appeared and then—Beyonce. A queen, even more so up close. Fireworks shot off yards away from where the three of us stood. We were past cheering—we were screaming. Just like all ages at this vantage point. It felt like two minutes of sexy dancing, though a watch said it was closer to twenty. Our heads swiveled in all directions. We're then told, "Get off the field! It's over. Go! Go!" and were herded back the direction we came. Chris Martin was walking one person ahead, and we felt illegally close to him.

We were trespassing in the most coveted area in America and couldn't tell a soul. We got back upstairs to the large media tent set up beside the stadium that housed reporters from across the world and said nothing about our front-row view to a magnetic, fiery twenty-three-minutes. We silently sat down in front of our TV news equipment, and got back to scripting and editing a show to air in the Carolinas, from California, after the game.

Five years later, I think it's safe to confess our secret trip to the most public show in the world. It was a moment in time, with pictures so good they couldn't be shown back then. No way we got those from the cordoned-off media area. I'm sharing now. Here. The game itself was heartbreaking, but the whole experience, a once-in-a-lifetime memory.

MONTH SEVENTY-SIX: Distance

Slice in time: last week she got off the bus and ran home two blocks to grab him. Hutch was right behind her, but her legs are longer, and she won the race to swoop up Hobie. He saw her coming and giggled with a seven-month-old belly laugh. She picked him up, he bubbled over with noise, open-mouthed, drool falling onto her hair, baby-gurgling so hard it made her smile with raw carefree confidence seen best in a nine-year-old happy girl.

ଔ

It's currently 3:00 a.m. and I'm staring at a dark ceiling with my moving mind carrying intrusive thoughts keeping me from sleep. I just rolled over, unplugged my phone from the charger, and scrolled through the camera. Am now typing myself these words, as the blue screen throws haze into the black of our bedroom. This picture from last week stopped me. Baby joy. Big-girl joy. Nine years apart. Nine years. Notable distance.

Can ages between siblings determine a life relationship?

There is no exact formula, I guess. A certain age difference doesn't dictate whether kids will get along later in life. Each child is their own person. Some relationships will be good or bad as personalities develop, no matter the years in between. But in general, it does seem the closer together kids are in age, the more apt they are to fight, and the farther apart, the greater potential they have to be good friends.

I had a baby nine years after one child, and six years after another. Twenty-five years from now, will they reach out to each other, share meals, and connect? Will they want to be in each other's lives, the way I was raised to want with my three younger brothers, the youngest ones being ten and twelve years behind me? Will it be that way with P and Hobie? Will she protect him? Will he grow to confide in her?

Hope so. But what if my kids don't have that closeness? By that time, what I want won't matter. They'll be who they are, living how they live, in touch with their siblings—or not.

3:23 a.m. Even in the dead of night where reason and logic can be elusive, I'm smart enough to know that while one can hope, one cannot plan.

Hello, 3:42 a.m. Sleeplessness is real. I've now worked myself into over-analyzation by moving to study the relationship between Parker and Hutch. At three and a half years apart, they are textbook siblings. As the younger one, he adores her every older move. Her name was one of his first words, he thinks of her even before himself, and steals *all* her ideas. If she orders chicken fingers, he'll order chicken fingers. If she switches to grilled cheese, he switches to grilled cheese. If she wants to do homeschool in a couch-cushion fort, he leaves Mermaid Academy's hallway to set up his own the same way. It drives her mad. She can't stand him shadowing her.

The oldest of my younger brothers, Jay, annoyed me the same way growing up. Tables later turned. I missed his adoration as we got older. *Someday*, I figure, *Parker will do the same.* Plus, COVID has bonded them together in a way that wouldn't have happened in normal times. They're in homeschool together, dance in the playroom together, and jointly play Among Us and Roblox (if you know, you know). Their maturity falls on separate levels, but I don't think it's an insurmountable distance.

But darkness makes a mind tumble and now, 3:54 a.m.—why am I thinking about age differences right now? Why?—it makes me go back to thinking of the larger gap between baby and the older two.

Quick math. When Hobie starts kindergarten, Parker will start high school. A mini-mother. Then she'll be off to college and will not even be around for long stretches. Hutch will be in fifth grade at the elementary school Hobie will enter. As eleven-year-old King of Hallways, will Hutch take Hobie's hand? Will he want to introduce a five-year-old into his world?

Hutch is so currently and consistently obsessed with his big-brother status, I can't imagine any different scenario, but you never know. That's why I type during off hours, putting my thoughts down. I don't want to later forget the feeling of this photo between P and Hobie, or of Hutch owning the role of big brother without knowing how the future looks.

I should sleep. 4:03 a.m. Stop the mind. Get out of this blue light. Close my eyes and know that the 7:00 a.m. baby cries are coming, a six-year-old will need to be repeatedly told to brush his teeth, and a nine-year-old will argue with me over brushing her hair. None of these early-morning thoughts will matter then; may not even be remembered. By morning light, it'll just be life.

This Thursday after the bus, maybe Parker will get distracted and Hutch will win the race to grab Hobie first. Either way, the thread that ties them in a triangle will be invisibly obvious. A triangle always has perspective of its other two corners, forever connected.

That's a calming thought. One that helps a mom's eyes close.

COMMENTS:

Ross T. So glad to see someone else doing the night wonderings.

Carmel G. I am thirteen years older than my youngest brother. I thought I was his mother. To this day he and I share a special bond like no other. He and I are closer to each other than we are to our other siblings. Even though we both have strong marriages, we worry about each other and in times of sorrow, seek each other. P, H, and H (can I call them your initial nicknames?) will be fine.

Jade H. My sisters are ten and eight and a half years older than me. They always let me hang out with them—maybe playing Barbies in their room while they chatted about teenage things with their friends. We're best friends now and in our own way, were best friends then.

Tiffany E. There are nine years between my younger sister and me. She got on my every nerve growing up, but we're so close today. What's crazy is she says she doesn't really remember me living at home.

Amanda S. I love this so much! We tried for years to have a second baby, and I didn't think it was going to happen. Then at forty, I found out I was pregnant. Last month my oldest son turned fifteen, and my little guy turns two in April. I spend many nights thinking about these exact same things.

Shea A. Age gaps are the best. I have a sister eleven years younger than me and I have kids ten years apart. I don't stress the little stuff too much; I know the tough phases pass, and so do the good ones. They all learn so much from one another.

MARCH

Baby Steps Ahead

Tonight is the school district's board meeting where sources say a vote will send kids back to more in-person learning next week. We're told elementary kids will go Monday, Tuesday, Thursday, and Friday. We're also told traditional high schools and middle schools will split into two groups instead of three, each group going twice a week, and K-8 schools will follow the elementary school schedule.

I can see this shred of light peeking from the tunnel. If you're a virtual-school parent, teacher, or staff member who has become a human rubber band, bending and snapping to schedule changes in every direction, maybe after tonight you will have a more consistent plan. Maybe next week Hutch will get only one lunch in school, instead of twenty snacks a day from our pantry the days he's at home, and one dedicated teacher, instead of a mom who's over it.

MONTH SEVENTY-SEVEN: A Retrospective

This picture is from March, one year ago. The world had begun shutting down, and I was the only one at night in the newsroom. (You can see the back of my head, center of photo.) A few other people were sprinkled around the building—a meteorologist in the weather center, a production director, and someone working the assignment desk still permitted inside—but for a job in journalism defined by noise, multitasking, and the ability to adapt well to crisis, I'd never before seen a newsroom so still and quiet.

A couple of weeks prior to this photo was March 11, 2020, when the World Health Organization declared COVID-19 a global pandemic. On that day, there were only eight confirmed cases of the virus in North Carolina. Over 1,200 in the United States. I reported the breaking news that all schools within the University of North Carolina system would end in-person classes due to the spread of the virus.

It was also the day travel plans would change. President Donald Trump announced a thirty-day restriction from Europe to America while COVID gained ground in other countries.

That was also the day actor Tom Hanks and his wife Rita Wilson revealed they had tested positive while filming a movie in Australia. They put known faces on a virus many didn't understand.

Also on March 11, millions watched as just minutes before an NBA tip-off between the Oklahoma City Thunder and Utah Jazz, fans filling the arena heard the game was cancelled. Thousands of stunned, annoyed people streamed out of their seats, into the aisles, and outside. It was later learned that Jazz player Rudy Gobert had tested positive.

The NBA suspended its season. The first professional sport to do so.

Most pro sports followed, as did college ones. The annual sixty-four-team bracket challenge of March Madness never happened.

Announcements felt like punches, knocking people out. I'll never forget writing bullet point lists at night a mile long—they'd take me two hours to compile because so much came into the newsroom every hour. I'd post nightly, trying to share daily information. It was hard to keep up with how fast the world was spinning, all while large numbers of people continued to die. Schools went remote. Small businesses closed doors. Restaurants laid off employees. We were told to hunker down and worry about anyone who coughed, but also congratulate healthcare workers who couldn't stay home.

All that was one very long year ago.

All of us have different experiences over the past year, but we are connected by the commonality that whatever kind of life we knew was upended. The word of the year last year was *pivot*, or so declared the Association of National Advertisers. That means everyone turned in new directions.

I'd like to think the word this year is the opposite of *pivot*. I'd like to think the word this year is *hope*. It's March 2021. We have the gift of retrospection. We know what we came through, and can look ahead with wider eyes.

It feels good to type that. To feel that. To feel like we are looking ahead with positivity. We have to be careful, though—every night on the news this last week we reported warnings from both local and national officials studying data, worried about another uptick. But we also had multiple reports about more and more people getting vaccinated.

About the vaccine: it is every adult's own decision whether or not to get the shot. Some people are hesitant and have reasons why. This post isn't to convince you. I'm writing about hope because of the undeniable fact that with more people getting vaccinated, the world is emerging again. States are easing restrictions. Students are returning to school. Businesses are looking to hire. Airlines have more customers. Companies are discussing safely bringing people back into offices. Even nursing homes and skilled living centers are allowing residents to see loved ones for the first time in a year. (Those long-awaited embraces are the best videos you'll see on any newscast.)

There's more. Birthday parties and large weddings are being planned. Charity groups are looking ahead to having in-person events. Stores are busy, malls filled, vacations are getting set, summer camps are back on for kids, and March Madness is happening, albeit in empty arenas. Our brackets are, once again, getting busted.

I'm okay with my picks losing. We're winning because the games are being played.

Things are looking up. We have overcome. Wait—wrong. Let me be safer with the word choice: we are overcoming.

Our sense of accomplishment is strong tonight as I stare at this stark, bleak picture, a year into this journey we didn't want. Yet, we're still here.

Onward and upward. To whatever might be ahead.

COMMENTS:

Teresa L. I read your bullet points every night. Kept the news on every day, terrified to see numbers growing. Hard to believe it's only been one year. Seems like many have passed. I am thankful my elderly parents survived and my family is healthy now.

Becky C. I do feel a little bit better about my life since I finished my two COVID vaccine shots in February. I am still extremely careful, but not terrified anymore. I do wish all of my family would get the shots, but it has all been so politicized.

Bob N. Hope springs eternal, and I am feeling it. I was overjoyed when I received my vaccines. I wasn't expecting to feel like that but . . . hope.

Kathy S. One long year of terrible, horrible, no-good, very bad days, over and over again. You forgot to mention the toilet paper shortage.

APRIL

Turning Ten

Ten years ago this morning, Parker Meade was born. How did this tutu-wearing preschooler get to double digits?

P, you are taller, your hair is longer, your face more mature, your vocabulary more robust. But your determination is the same.

Whether three years old or now ten, you have a competitive edge and the smarts to go after what's in your sight. Combine that with how you still value kindness, and you are the jackpot.

Your reaction to this morning's surprise macaroon cake at a French bakery for a birthday breakfast was the excitement our whole family needed.

Left side: Six years ago. / Right side: This year.

Everyone tells you, "It goes fast." I wish they were wrong.

We love you, P. Never stop splashing.

MONTH SEVENTY-EIGHT: Convenience's Evil Twin

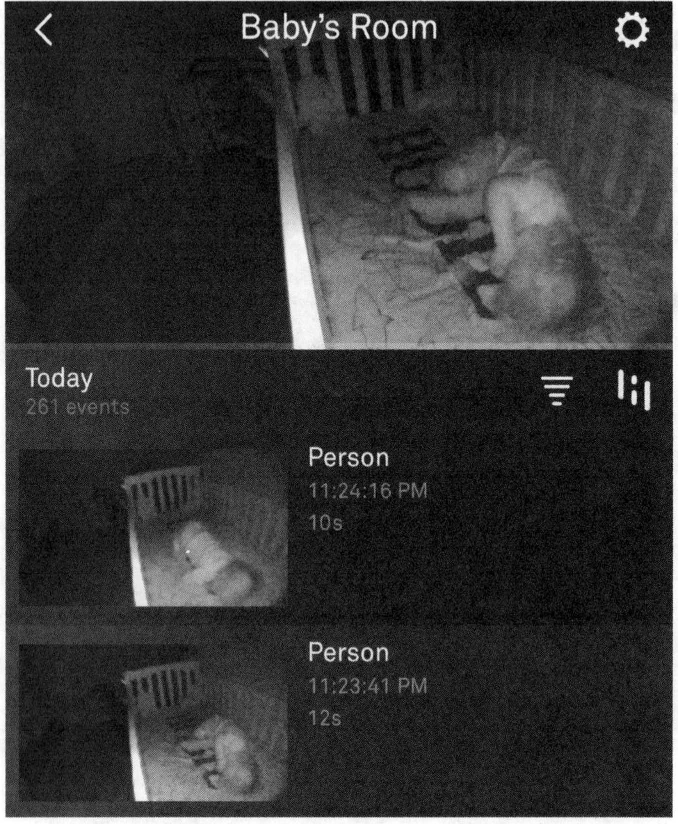

This is a screengrab from my phone that sits on the news desk beside me every night, while I'm anchoring the shows live. Let me explain why I share it now.

ଓଃ

Last night. 10:59 p.m. This is what I said, exactly, about our top story:

"A double funeral today for two deputies being felt across North Carolina tonight.

The images are powerful: a bear hug from two grieving fathers.

A K-9 officer lying beside his partner's casket.

The presentation of an American flag to a widow."

(pause)

"Good evening and welcome to your 11-o'clock news.

I'm Molly Grantham.

Let's get right to it . . ."

Those words fell from my mouth and into your home through a large square camera and its bright red light. I'd written them an hour earlier, put them into scripts, which got transferred into prompter, and as I said them aloud, the descriptions washed over. I could feel my face painting a solemn picture to match their meaning. You, maybe, were watching from the comfort of your bed, getting your day's headlines before sleep. I knew that, felt that, and was living in the weight of the words of honoring two men who had died while leading lives in public service.

Just as I was ready to launch into more, my phone screen on top of the studio news desk near my hands got bright. I didn't look down, because I already knew the notification would show what you see here. Hobie had moved.

While standing inside the TV studio, my phone was alerting me to his actions miles away.

Hobie's nursery monitor is linked to an app—as most monitors are nowadays—that shows if my almost-ten-month-old coughs, cries, or if someone opens his door. It doesn't matter what I'm doing in that moment or that his nursery isn't nearby. It only matters if the camera senses stirring. So, if I'm talking to 100,000 people about two men ambushed and killed, but Hobie drops his binky or rolls in his sleep, those things will both be in front of me.

The mightily powerful and quite trivial, blurred.

Thirty years ago, I would have returned to work after dinner with no clue as to what was then happening at home. I wouldn't be FaceTiming about lost teeth, or texting Wes to remind Parker about the next day's soccer schedule, or seeing my baby through my smart phone app while talking to you live.

We live in a society where whatever you need is on your phone. Information is rampant, sitting in your palm. Having life at your fingertips has dissolved boundaries. Most of us need phones nearby so we don't miss a minute.

It makes information very convenient.

It's easy to forget about convenience's evil twin: dependence.

Compartmentalization takes effort. You can do it, but it must be consciously done. With our work lives no longer just at work, and our home lives not just at home, or this past year with school days not even at school, we must acknowledge how these worlds can intertwine. What bridges them is our access *to everything*—finances, deliveries, meals, entertainment, emails, even a live look at your grandchild's baseball game if you can't make it to the field—through our phones. Brains hear (and see) all these life silos at once.

This struck me deeply, instantly, when notified last night about Hobie rolling over as I described a double funeral on air.

For those of you thinking: "It doesn't have to be in front of you! Just take the nursery monitor off your phone so it doesn't distract!" I add this: no. If I removed the nursery monitor app at night, I'd have to put it back on my phone in the morning when Hobie and I are together, or when he's napping before I head to work. Then I'd have to take it off again. Then add it back. Then remove. That process is way more hassle than occasionally ignoring a flashing screen.

Besides, the nursery monitor is only one example to make a broader point: our pace of life is swirling, and boundaries, I do believe, will only continue to get more blurred.

Keep your eyes open for the mundane mixing with the dramatic. Someday these twisted slices of life might be hard to remember.

PS: See you at 11 p.m. Maybe I'll see Hobie then too.

COMMENTS:

David W. Yesterday was an emotional day for Watauga County and everyone who felt the loss of these two officers. The importance of community and using the right words to relay something that cut so deep to many of us can't be undervalued. As a bonus to relaying last night's news that impacted many of us, thanks to technology, you were also able to see Hobie safe and sound. I'd call that a win.

Marie R. So many emotions going through my head and heart at any given time. We all feel the strain, often lots of strains at the same time.

MAY

Done

Mermaid Academy is pleased to announce it is closing.

Today is the first week to go all five days. No more remote. No more iPad lessons in the hallway next to the garage. Hobie and I are closing up shop. God bless the teachers.

COMMENTS:

Corinne W. You do know there are only three weeks left until summer break, right? Rest up! I'm laughing with you, not at you.

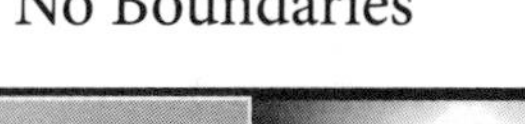

No Boundaries

High level executive leadership meeting.

On a work call today, the duo running the meeting finally addressed my mumbled pacifier words and the game of airplane I was playing. I hadn't thought twice about pacing and carrying a baby on my shoulder during our discussion. We're fourteen-months-numb to what we show. Shots are being called and real decisions being made with a binky in my mouth and a baby flying near my chin.

COMMENTS:

Kate S. Yes! Sometimes your kid is given a magazine about ground beef so you can get through a work call.

MONTH SEVENTY-NINE: Fourteen Love Letters

"Mooooommmmmmmmm," he moaned dramatically from the back seat. He had that tone people have when they're trying to sound overwhelmed and rocked by busy-ness, but are actually proud of their task at hand. "Mommmmmm. It's just sooooo much. I have sooooo much writing to do."

Why was Hutch fake-complaining? What writing? No one had to write anything the night before the most warped year of kindergarten wrapped for good.

"That's okay, Hutch," I replied, as a clueless, distracted parent who wasn't interested in investigating. "I'm sure you'll get it all done."

I quickly glanced in the rearview mirror and saw him smile.

Whatever "writing" he was bemoaning, he looked happy. That was good. It left my mind as I turned into the driveway, thirty-two minutes into my dinner break from work. Wes was traveling, and

I'd picked him and Parker up from swim team practice, and gotten home to meet the sitter staying with Hobie. I knew I still had time to unpack their swim bags, heat up food, hug all three, then hop back in the car and return for the nighttime editorial meeting. I was playing Tetris with life, trying to fit things into each other like the video game. Hutch's unknown writing wasn't a priority.

Fast-forward a few minutes. Ready to leave again.

"Come say, 'Bye,'" I yelled throughout the house. "Mommy's leaving." Parker came running. The sitter was already with me and Hobie. Hutch was missing.

"Hutch!" I yelled again. "Come on. I'm going."

Still nothing.

"He's in Mermaid Academy," Parker said casually before spinning away. "He's using markers."

Huh? Mermaid Academy was closed. We'd gratefully, ceremonially, shut down the desks. I didn't dread that space in my house anymore. I headed that direction.

"Hutch?"

"Mom! How do I spell 'Patterson?'" I could hear him, but not yet see him.

"Patterson? Like the girl in your class?"

"Yes."

I was getting closer. "*P-A-T-T-E-R-S-O-N.*"

"Okay." His voice was louder as I was fast approaching. "How do I spell 'Hollis?' What comes after the *H* and the *O*?"

Hollis is another student in his class.

"After the *O* there is an *L-L-I-S*."

"Thank you." I walked into view to see him hunched over with a fat purple Crayola marker in his hands, head down close to neon yellow and pink construction paper. "How do I spell 'Alivia?' I know she begins with *A*. She always tells people it sounds like 'Olivia' but it's with the letter *A*. What comes after *A*?"

He was writing cards to his classmates.

Every. Single. Child.

There is a sensation you feel when put in front of a surprise so emotionally pleasant, it gets described as heart-exploding. That's what happened when I saw my wet, shaggy-haired Hutch leaned over art supplies at his desk, intensely writing in block kindergarten letters names of kids I don't know, but who he considers his social network. Even though he has only known them through masks and six feet of distance over the past few weeks, not an entire year.

"Whatcha doing, Hutch?" I already knew but wanted to hear him explain.

"I'm writing my friends. Tomorrow is the last day of school."

He hadn't looked up at me. "Can I see the ones you've done already?" I asked.

"They're over there." His arm that was not being used to fist-grip the marker jutted from his side to loosely reference a space to his left in an over-there-where-I-tossed-them-for-now manner. In true Hutch fashion, all the completed cards were in a messy pile, spilling onto the floor. No organization, no system, no neatness. Just kindness and colors. I walked toward the construction paper swirl.

Each one had the same exact message with a different name at the top:

“__*(Name)*__. *I love you. Form, Hutch.*”

I hate that my first thought was his misspelling of *from*. Blame that gut reaction on the fact I edit scripts all night. Milliseconds later, though, my heart kicked out logic and I zeroed in on his message.

“Hutch, this is so nice,” I said. “You’re telling all your friends you love them?”

“Yes.”

“That’s really . . . special. Why are you telling them that?”

“Because I do. And I won’t see them again until first grade.”

I sat down on the floor, knowing that if I didn’t sit myself down, I might fall over. Sat right there in my fancy work dress and quietly watched him finish every card, pulling every student’s name out of his head, making sure he didn’t miss one.

When he was done, he went through a verbal checklist out loud and let me find the child’s name in the pile to assure him that no one was missed.

I was late returning to work. Didn’t care. Upon my arrival, I told Maggie this story. She fully understood, and said it reminded her of being in second grade and picking out who got what paper Valentine cards that you tore off perforated sheets, and then shared in the classroom party.

ଔଓ

This morning, before the last day of Parker and Hutch taking the bus until August, Hutch got up extra early to get his things together. I asked if I could take a picture of him with his cards. He happily obliged and smiled proudly, wearing his favorite blue striped socks, purple shorts, orange shirt, and holding his neon papers written with love.

Sometimes you need to stop for a minute, (sit?), and let life wash over you. On the last day of school before summer break, I bring you this story of a sensitive-souled six-year-old who has an unscripted personality and continues to stun his mother with how the world can be viewed.

Please, Hutch, don't ever change.

Let's look to kids. They know what they're doing. We adults could pick up a lesson or two.

COMMENTS:

Sam S. Hutch will never know the impact he had on his classmate today, and me. This is why I have Facebook.

JUNE

Your Basic Britts Breakfast

Sign our family knows what month we've hit, even with no nearby calendar. Dozen and a half, gone.

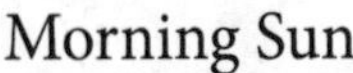

Morning Sun

Early time with the cutest nugget ever.

COMMENTS:

Darlene B. The curls!

Cynthizuna C. Those currrrrrrrrrls.

Little Miss Curious

We've hit the stage where she likes to wear my T-shirts. This one is her favorite.

COMMENTS:

Richard L. A mini-Molly, version 2.0.

Joy H. I loved those books as a child. Didn't realize their rich lessons until I read them to my own son.

MONTH EIGHTY: A Brilliant Beach Business

Photo credit: "Alex Hayes Sports Photography"

A young surfer with a large zoom lens stands on the shore with his camera and monopod. The hard-packed sand helps stabilize the equipment. His bleached-out long hair (not unlike Hutch's) is half tucked behind his ear. His eyes are covered with wrap-around mirrored glasses, his nose painted with white zinc. He swivels his position every so often. One mirrored eye will bend to the viewfinder while his forehead gently rests on the back of the black camera. I watch his index finger repeatedly click. He clearly knows what to look for.

I—meantime—am standing next to him with the same view, but am visually lost. I see thirty dots on the water. Two of those dots are my kids, but there's no telling which ones. They're out far. The glare is blinding. I'm distracted by Hobie crawling around my legs. To be honest, I don't even remember what color rash guards Parker and Hutch put on before paddling out with their instructors. Pink? Blue? Gray? Green? Even if the sun went behind a cloud and floating dot details emerged, the shade of shirt probably wouldn't help identify them.

The photographer is friendly, but also used to parents striking up conversations. He's professionally noncommittal when you ask, "Can you see my kid?" Says he watches all the surf campers. Adds that he'll send these pictures he's snapping to the camp owner, who will send a link when camp ends. I walk away. Poor guy must be bothered by moms like me often.

As promised, I received that link the week after surf camp wrapped. It held hundreds of images that gave great clarity to every one of those thirty dots.

This one is my favorite of Parker. It's saved on my phone and I look at it at least three times a day. It's her mental focus. Her intent coolness, arms extended in dancer-form perfection. Funny to think that tutu training from years ago now shows up on a surfboard. She's angling her board nose down, not out, to keep on the best part of the small wave.

In another photo he took, she's waving to someone. Literally surfing past them, waving. The point isn't who—I have no idea—

it's that he captured her natural reaction to be friendly.

The photographer got Hutch too. My original beach bum boy riding a whitecap, balancing well. In my favorite one, his bright-blue shark trunks are so clear, you see the black outline of every shark on the material. His wet white hair is neon and invisible at the same time. His face is both gleeful and petrified. He's surfing by himself, unsure about the whole thing, but determined to be like Sissy.

I see all those things because the laid-back photographer and his lens saw those things for me.

Memories last forever. The two-week vacation earlier this month provided new vivid moments for our family. Nothing can take that fun away. But now that vacation is over, I love how these photos show the expression and action I couldn't see in real life. They explain personality with no words. They recall beautiful beach days and a world where daily calendars don't stuff a mind, and life seems magically juggle-free.

COMMENTS:

Dana F. Fairly certain if your news job doesn't work out you can find a role in promoting small, laid-back beach businesses.

Angela Q. I'm the photographer in our family. It is great you were able to live in the moment while someone else handled saving the memories for you. I have caught myself missing that sometimes.

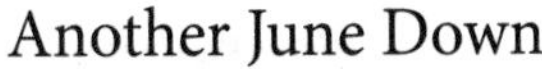

Another June Down

Many memories made over two weeks at my favorite place with my favorite people. Walking. Surfing. Eating. Stunning 6:00 a.m. sunrises with coffee. Eleven-month-old Hobie finally finding his voice (and the ability to throw pasta) in the middle of a restaurant. Parker and Hutch had fewer fights, Hobie semi-lived in a sand bucket and it only rained twice.

Ten, six, and almost one are great ages to observe and absorb. Salt water definitely runs in the veins of all three. Now it's back to work. I'm ready.

Feels Good

Hi.

COMMENTS:

Margaret M. And all felt right again.

Mike B. For us, this is your home.

Shevaun T. I see you kept some beach on . . . starfish necklace?

Brilliance

She's laughing because I just went through the Dunkin' drive-thru, ordered, paid for one large hot coffee with cream, and drove away. Headed up the high hill. Pulled into work. Parked. Got out. Took five steps. Realized I never actually gave anyone time to hand me the coffee. Turned around. Got back in car. Drove down the hill, up to the window, saw her waiting, coffee extended, smiling.

"We've all had days like that," she said, before I could utter an apology. Kept me from having to speak. More grateful for that, I think, than the coffee itself.

JULY

Sissy Away

Only took a week of her off at camp for him to appreciate being the oldest at home.

COMMENTS:

Tom L. Looks like he holds the role well.

Camp Growth

The package has been picked up and secured. It grew about three years in two weeks at camp.

COMMENTS:

McSwain D. When my kids left for college I kept saying, "It's just like summer camp and I'll see them in a few short weeks."

Accidental Invention

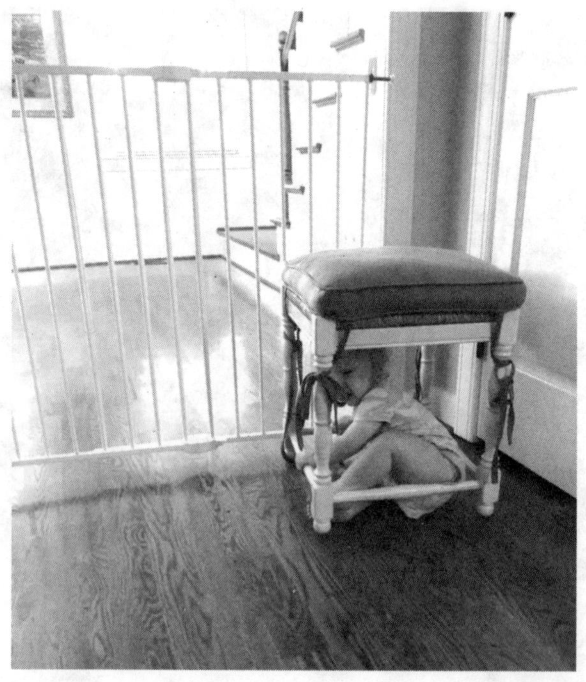

Crawled in there himself. I got more done in the twenty minutes it took him to figure out how to crawl back out than I did in the past thirty-six hours. He didn't cry, instead he took time to resourcefully attempt escape. I feel no guilt.

COMMENTS:

Wanda R. Engineer in the making.

Dan S. Whatever works. He seems happy.

Hobie's First Birthday

Staring at his wrinkled, gorgeous baby face a year ago, I couldn't have predicted anything to come but here we are. Content, healthy, and grateful. Emphasis on the healthy part. You complete our family, Binky Boy. Happy birthday.

One.

I can't believe it.

MONTH EIGHTY-ONE: A Note of Adoration

Dear contraption on my kitchen counter,

You popped onto the market sometime between child two and three. I don't know when you were invented or by whom. Your name makes no sense: "Baby Brezza." Say it six times really fast and a tongue gets twisted. You are bulky. You take up space. You are also what parents of babies never knew they needed until you suddenly arrived.

When people would visit and ask about the odd coffee pot sitting next to the stove, never to be put away, I'd smile dreamily and reply with a corrective description: "Oh, that? Not coffee. It's like a Keurig for baby formula."

An exhausted parent puts an empty bottle on your little plastic bottom shelf, punches in how many ounces of baby formula needed, then pushes start. It's as if a coffee drinker would put down a mug and decide how they want their brew: strong, medium, or light.

Within five seconds, the perfect amount of powder magically mixes with the perfect amount of water and spews the ideal combination of liquid at room temperature into the waiting bottle. Done. You twist on the top and hand it to the baby. Takes two minutes total.

Over the past year, I've made bottles while sleepwalking, one-handed, and often asked Hutch to make them for me. (He likes buttons. This was his favorite "chore.") Never once did I have to boil water, unfreeze breast milk, or test the temperature on the inside of my wrist. I'd hear Hobie cry, walk by the machine, and press "start." Beautiful is the machine that lets a mother get away with zero advance planning.

As accustomed as we've become, BB—my nickname for you—as much as you have been depended upon in our daily life, it is time to pass you on. Hobie turned one last week. Pediatrician's orders are to clear out bottles and move to whole milk in sippy cups. Therefore, I've boxed you up to bequeath to a beloved future momma, one of the four women who got you as a joint gift for me when I found out I was pregnant again. This new mom has pushed aside a large toaster oven to make room for you on her counter. You're about to make her life easier, and are a gift worth regifting. Thank you for the year of convenience.

Please let your creator know if they invent a hands-free way to change diapers, I'd invest.

Sincerely,

An obsessed and grateful fan

COMMENTS:

Julie F. I'm a neonatal nurse. I was talking to one of my baby's moms and she was telling me about this contraption. I was totally floored. It's very cool.

Becky A. Best new baby invention in two decades.

Fernanda P. Oh yes, this is the best! We had twins. My milk never came, and without us even knowing about it we got a box delivered a few weeks later and it was the Baby Brezza. Some dear friends had sent it to us in the hopes it would be helpful. Godsent. Best gift ever.

Pamela P. My daughter is expecting her first child in September. This doodad looks like a present made by angels for new moms.

Jennifer E. I'm so glad to see the positive comments. Was afraid you'd be admonished for not breastfeeding.

AUGUST

What's to Come

Letting go of the steering wheel on this one.

This Thursday at 11:00 p.m., we will air a report of ten-year-old Parker interviewing ten-year-old Rhiya Williams, oldest daughter of former NFL player DeAngelo Williams. D and I have been friends for years, bonded by the breast cancer cause. Our personal histories drive our dedication. This year, DeAngelo's wife, Risalyn, had a great idea: instead of me interviewing D, as we generally do, why doesn't Parker play the role of me and Rhiya play the role of her dad? They both lost their grandmothers to this disease.

It is an unnerving experience to know that such a potentially impactful conversation is playing out with TV cameras rolling. It's also brilliant, coming from a perspective we've never heard before.

This is happening because every year the DeAngelo Williams Foundation raises money to pay for fifty-three mammograms for fifty-three women in the community. DeAngelo's mom died at age fifty-three; it's a significant number in his life.

During the interview, DeAngelo, Risalyn, and I intentionally stayed out of the room. We didn't want them saying what they thought their parents would want to hear. The WBTV crew (all guys) were the only ones able to listen. I later produced it along with the crew; it is edited and ready for us all to watch live this Thursday at 11:00 p.m.

COMMENTS:

Molly. Who runs the world?

Donna P. I could not love this more. What a great idea.

Jessica W. Honestly, I'm surprised this idea hasn't been thought of before. When a parent goes through cancer, their child does as well. Same goes for a grandparent. Can't wait to watch.

Jane O'D. I'm a stage 3, five-year Survivor and know how very important this is. Thank you.

Leslie L. Caring hearts from both girls. Proud of Parker. Feel like I know her. What an accomplishment from the DeAngelo Williams Foundation to supply fifty-three free mammograms for women. Thank you, D.

Julie O. Great testimony from a son to the love of his mother.

First Day of School

Happy first day to the 143,411 students going back today, and to the parents waiting eighteen months for this morning. We did it:

COMMENTS:

Sarah C. We did it:

Robin M. We did it:

Jennifer M. We did it:

MONTH EIGHTY-TWO: Take-Off is Harder than Flying

The relief at having children back in school knows no end. The only reason I can even sit here with an open laptop and the mental space to think those words is because the bus came on time. P and H waved from the window as it drove off. This is day five of school being in session this fall, and it feels like a new weight is lifted every morning. We walk to the bus stop and are happy. Reread that please. We are happy. All of us. I hug them both, remind them to pull up their masks hanging near their chins, and they climb on board. I took this picture this morning.

I'm now back at home. Hobie is napping. Wes is in another room, living the continued work-from-home pace of monotonous conference calls. Corporate jargon bores me, but after eighteen months of it as background noise, it can easily be ignored.

I can feel the circus slowing. Sure there is the usual back-to-school excitement, but this time it's different. Five days in and I can feel the pressure on my insides releasing, like little bubbles rising to the top, making the bottom of my soul lighter. I am not sloshing through the morning. Five days in, I wake up, ready to routine.

It feels utterly excellent to say: school is back in session.*

The big fat asterisk is important. The asterisk means, "for now."

We don't know how long this will last. Mask policies took a step backward recently. Kids could board the bus the next many months, maybe the whole blissful year, or, it could end tomorrow.

No one knows. We can't depend on anything.

Every night the last few weeks on air, I'm reporting about different districts returning in calendar waves. At the same time, I'm reporting COVID outbreaks in schools. It's happening more often in counties with no mask mandates, but every day brings new classroom headlines, new quarantines, and new groups of kids, teachers, and parents quickly transitioning to temporary virtual learning and backup plans.

On last night's newscast alone: one district announced it was going virtual because too many staff members tested positive and they had a sudden employee shortage. Another school reported 50 percent of its people—students and staff combined—were in quarantine. And yet another district voted to extend its mask mandate, set to expire today, because 18 percent of students were out from COVID.

Here I sit, calmly, with coffee, breathing because the bus pulled away, lucky enough to find myself typing "school is back in session" with relief, but understanding that my own commitment to having Parker and Hutch in class doesn't matter. If the buses aren't running, teachers aren't there, and a conscientious principal temporarily shuts school doors, well, that's it. End of story.

If that happens, I'll want to scream like a wild animal, broken and enraged all at once.

But, if an outbreak hits, and elementary school children are put at risk, what are you supposed to do? There aren't long lists of in-person options. Though most people who get COVID survive, is it worth playing Russian roulette with this virus? I've done that. Our family survived a bout with COVID. I don't want a repeat of those fear-gripped nights, nor would I ever wish them on another family.

Statistics say you'll most likely recover. But at what cost? At what long-term effect? Horrific examples are put out there every day. The one I currently can't stop thinking about is a video from last week of a twelve-year-old in the ICU in Columbia, South Carolina. No previous health conditions, but she'd gotten COVID and pneumonia. She was a sixth grader on a ventilator. Her mom stood in front of cameras looking haggard and said, "I want other parents to know: it happens."

That mom's pain felt tangible and everyone watching could see it in her eyes through the interview on the news. I wanted to jump through the screen and hug her.

So, kids can get COVID . . .

. . . I read stories and remember our own experience . . .

. . . and yet . . .

. . . I still want my kids in school.

Opinions are so rigid. Everything feels either-or. I don't agree with these extremes. I think you can be highly concerned about COVID in kids, and still want your kids in school. They don't have to be opposite thoughts.

Parents of young kids have been put through the ringer. With that said, we might be chipped and leaking, but I don't think we're broken. We've kept going. We woke up every day and pulled it together as best we knew how. There was no other choice than to move through a volatile world, hoping our kids picked up a lesson or two about how to function when we had no control. We inched toward the start of school, bought masks as a school supply, and held our breath until the first day.

In my case, I then watched Parker and Hutch board that bus last week with an irrational fear it was going to slam on the brakes after two blocks, shoo them off, and send them home.

It didn't, of course. The bus kept going. This morning for the fifth time in a row.

That's why that even though a mandatory-virtual-school-shoe could drop any minute, I'm letting myself exhale small breaths. Every day, releasing a little more pressure. If Mermaid Academy and homeschool have to start again, as much as I'd hate it, I've been there before. We survived once. We could again if need be.

Take-off is harder than flying. We're now up and coasting in air, more familiar with this flight. If turbulence hits, we'll buckle up and hold tight through jolts. Until then, I'm focusing on the fact we're moving ahead.

ଓଃ

I could've written this month about Hobie's unwanted-wanted haircut. A haircut entry wouldn't elicit comments laced with political vitriol, which this might. Just so you know, I hear hate hurled from both sides. Nasty, nasty stuff. I've been called every name in the book over the past eighteen months. (There is peculiar comfort in being told you're a "liberal mouthpiece with no brain" and a "raging dense Republican" from two different people, complaining about the same exact news report you relayed, but hearing opposite things. When extremes yell at you equally, you feel like you've done something right.)

But I do think I'll write later about Hobie's curls being gone. I hear him waking from his nap now (he gave me so much time!) and his unwanted-wanted haircut is a story also worth documenting. The 360 degrees of life. In future lookbacks, I want to remember schools, COVID . . . and baby firsts.

Together, it all adds up to real.

Four cups of coffee, gone. It feels s good.

COMMENTS:

Malinda C. It's not what you say to people, it's what they hear. It's hard to take a beating for passing along information. I'm not a reporter, but I do work in a school and have to pass along new policies and systems and changing information. I'm exhausted.

Bridges K. I, too, am holding my breath because those steps toward normalcy feel like they were snatched away. I detest the vitriol that is spewed equally from all sides instead of the support we should be showing. Your cups of coffee feel good? Reading this realness feels good to me.

Allyson F. If you're hated from both sides, you're doing something right. You summed up how I'm feeling: glad they're in school and waiting for the other shoe to drop.

Vinesett P. Down-to-earth, raw, fearful, and full of feelings. Handled with grace and honesty.

SEPTEMBER

First Day of Preschool

Dressed to impress in his older brother's hand-me-downs. There is something notable about dropping off your last lil' nugget when you know it'll be the last lil' nugget you'll have. The teachers were kind. He was happy. But after having him with me every morning on top of COVID-isolation and not meeting others . . . I don't know. It's just different. My stomach did unexpected flip-flops as I put him in a new woman's arms and walked away.

Only way to do it.

He cried. I walked away.

His Name is Now a Verb

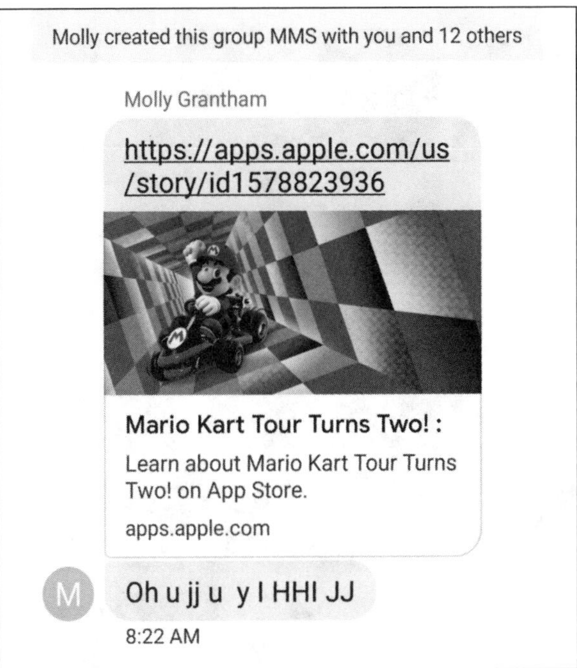

Just when you think your day is going well, you get a message from one of your friends in the FBI. "Did someone hack your phone this weekend?"

Hmm. No. But upon review of my sent text messages, I then saw how twelve random numbers in my contact list—a dozen people completely unconnected—were sent a Mario Kart-looking spam video game with lots of consonants that meant nothing. Took me a minute, but I suddenly knew the culprit without further investigation.

I replied: "Not spam. Child. Think my six-year-old got my phone."

"Ah," she wrote back. "You were Hutched."

MONTH EIGHTY-THREE: Hobie's Hair

(1) Before — (2) After — (3) Current.

He doesn't look like the middle photo anymore. It has been a whole month.

In Month Eighty-Two, I said I should've written about Hobie's unwanted-wanted haircut. That would've been easier than writing about masks, school, and how parents of kids under twelve currently live in a different galaxy. A haircut entry wouldn't have elicited cruel comments and hurled hate. But, as I also said since starting these monthly entries, in future look-backs, I want to remember full-circle reality. The toxic obstacles and the funny good.

Hobie's first haircut falls into the second category.

Let's start by saying that I didn't see how long his curls had grown. That picture on the far left? Don't remember him that way. Don't think he ever looked like that. Although obviously, he did. (Also, would you look at his pudgy, cute-cute-cute baby tummy roll over the board shorts.)

I didn't see the growth because I'd already decided at Hobie's birth that I wasn't going to cut his wild sprouts. I stared at him those first forty-eight hours and rubbed my hand on his beautiful shiny hair and swore to myself that since he had been given that gift, I would let it grow forever.

Was this a silly thought? Of course. Was there any reasoning behind it? None. Was I determined to stick to it because the hormones rampaging a new mother's body had me thinking in emotional directions? You'd better believe it.

Very soon, those smooth sprouts turned into tight curls. I loved them.

Though the self-imposed rule to "let it grow" blinded me from seeing just how long and unruly it had become, it also, sweetly, heightened awareness to other moments. I'll never forget him reaching up to his head and pulling the corkscrews out straight. That baby-fine blond hair would tickle the skin along his jawline, and he'd giggle uproariously. He didn't know how he looked. Babies have no concept of self when staring at their own reflection. But he did know, he liked how his hair felt.

As he grew, my belief in the made-up pact with myself to never cut hair grew, too. Wes didn't like it, but you don't question an undeterred mom who has an idea about her miracle final child.

So, all was good.

Until Grandma Jean came for a visit.

Grandma Jean—Gigi for short—is my stepmom. She walked in, ran for the kiddos, loved and loved and loved on them, then turned around to love on Wes and me, and in the course of the next many hours talked about everything under the sun . . . *except* Hobie's hair.

Gigi saying nothing is an absolute indication she has many thoughts about what's not being said. She's raised Southern. (Does that explain it?) Unfortunately for Gigi, her facial expressions talk. She was also born in the North. (Does that explain it?) Gigi is a total class act, who has strong opinions.

As Gigi sat there, bouncing Hobie on her lap, his hair flopping around, I was talking. Hobie was contorting himself to turn toward my voice. He could hear Momma, but couldn't see Momma because he couldn't see past his hair. His chubby little hand was trying to gymnastics around Gigi's arms to push the curls in his eyes aside, and, even I could admit, the curls in this moment looked less baby-fine-cute and more matted-knots-fried.

Rather than make her say it, I pretended she'd already asked.

"I don't want to cut it, Gigi," I said. "I can move the hair aside to see his eyes."

"What if it's not about you?" she replied. "What if it's about him?"

Hmm. The conversation ended. I didn't answer. I did, however, start thinking.

ᴏᴙᴏ

Two days later, with Gigi still in town, my stubbornness had started to melt.

"Maybe you could give Hobie a trim?" I asked. "Not a cut. Just a trim. Like you used to do with the boys growing up in the kitchen." Gigi always trimmed my brothers' hair as kids. They'd sit in a high bar chair with a towel around their necks. She'd have one pair of scissors, a comb, a spray bottle, and for herself, a glass of wine. The boys looked great afterward.

"Yes," she said calmly. "I'd love to help."

We put Hobie in a highchair with snacks in front of him. (Hobie can be distracted by food in any environment, just like Hutch.) Hobie didn't care about the spray bottle or comb or scissors heading toward his scalp. Gigi was focused. Hutch looked on, fascinated.

"You're going to cut it, Gigi?" Hutch said. "Mommy will let you?"

I answered: "Just a small bit."

Gigi said nothing.

Five minutes and about 100 photos on my camera roll later, some small, wet curls piled on the ground. I gathered them into a Ziploc bag, and labeled it with Sharpie: "Hobie's first haircut."

"Okay," I said. "We're done."

"He looks great," Gigi said. "But let me spray this area again. Maybe a liiiiiiiiiitle more here on the side."

She had it under control. I also couldn't watch anymore. There was something about seeing his hair fall that took me back to that meaningless pact I made with myself in the hospital. I knew it was something I'd established during a highly emotional time, but it still felt weird to watch the promise to myself get sliced through, and I didn't like seeing his hair fall. I went upstairs.

When I came back down, Hobie's hair was still wet, and he looked adorable. Gigi was sweeping the floor.

Fifteen minutes later, he was fully dried.

It had shrunk.

"GIGI!"

She came running.

"Why is it so short?"

"Oh, Molly. He looks like a little boy. Oh, my little Hobie," she turned toward his open-mouthed grinning face. "Look! We can see your eyes again."

I could see his eyes.

"Oh, Hobie . . . we can see you." She went on. "No need to for you to fumble trying to push your hair out of your face anymore!"

He laughed. As if he wanted to reassure her he, too, was pleased.

"Molly, look at him. Your baby boy." I looked at him. His hair was swept to the side—as you see in the middle photo in the collage. He was looking at me side-eyed. It felt like he was staring into my mind, asking for approval.

Then he raised his arms up to me, wanting to be held.

I swooped him into the air. He laughed and fell back down into my shoulder. Put his little head in that space where it still fits so well under my chin. He was still my baby. Still my exact same Hobie, despite looking less baby and more boyish.

☙❧

A day later, I was used to and already liking his shorter hair. Mostly because he was thrilled. He'd stopped shaking his head around, which I used to think was a cute baby move, but now see it was a functional action to help see out of the front of his face.

"You were right, Gigi," I said. "He needed the haircut."

I was dropping her off at the airport so she could head back to Florida. She smiled and hugged me, saying nothing. Not a word. Just a strong hug, full of love. Very Gigi-like. She pulled away and grabbed her bag and started walking into the terminal. I turned to head back into the car. Before I grabbed the door handle, though, I looked back at her. She had turned around as well and was looking at me. In that moment, I saw it. Her bad poker face. She had a little side smirk with happy eyes that silently screamed: "I was right."

She was right. I had let something become a bigger thing than it needed to be.

In other words, I just had to get past myself. Had to recognize that what seemed like a good idea at one point wasn't a great idea forever. Ideas evolve. Things change. All that is okay.

ↀ

It has now been a month. Hobie's hair grows like weeds. It's getting back to being a nuisance to his vision. See the final picture on the far right in the collage.

This time, I know what to do.

COMMENTS:

Carrie S. I remember my spiral-curled boy's first big cut. I sobbed. I blame hormones.

Melanie L. Your description of Gigi perfectly describes my mom, known as Mimi. Thank you for sharing this story. I love every part of the mother and child point of view, but for me, the mother/grandmother aspect was especially poignant.

Stokley J. This story brought me back to a moment in my son's nursery when I felt sad how quickly he was outgrowing his baby clothes. I realized he wouldn't get to wear all those adorable little outfits anymore and those precious baby days were slipping by.

Suzette B. Nothing better than a "little man" haircut.

Elizabeth Mc. I felt the same way about my baby son's long hair. Now after reading this, I'm reassessing whether I should cut it...

OCTOBER

Birthday Boy

This now seven-year-old is always a good time. Hutch: Your dad and I love your style, vivid word choices, colorful thoughts, endless accessories (like a pirate bandana head scarf at the bus stop), tender way of snuggling, and I even love your wicked-smartness in getting under your sister's skin. It's never the same tactic and always creative. You are all 360 degrees. We adore you. Happy birthday—you wear #TooMuchHutch well.

MONTH EIGHTY-FOUR: New Family Member

We have a puppy. She's twenty-four weeks old, and a mutt. We rescued her. I think she looks like Hobie, if Hobie were an animal. Parker named her as soon as she met her. "Mom—her eyes look like the ocean. Let's name her after the beach."

We've had Kure in our house for six weeks. I haven't mentioned this until now. Not mentioning a real-life addition felt . . . I don't know. Bizarre. I wasn't lying, but withholding a piece of important family dynamic felt like a contradiction to the open-book environment we have created in discussing real life. This is an accepting, truth-telling platform, and the grace you guys (generally) show for telling the Good, the Bad, and the Always Real is appreciated.

But, I also wanted to be smart. When we first got Kure, we didn't know how things would go. Not every pet is a good fit with every family, a tough lesson we'd already learned with Rudy. (Update: Rudy remains happy with his adopted family in a fenced-in yard.)

Teaching Parker how to handle the brokenness it feels on letting love go added great cautiousness in announcing Kure's arrival in our home. As a mom who had watched her daughter during the Rudy saga, I felt compelled to give it time before sharing publicly.

Time has passed. Kure is a perfect fit.

At twenty-four pounds, both Parker and Hutch can walk her. She's gentle with Hobie, housebroken, and likes to be around us. She won't run away when off a leash.

We do laugh, though. A neighbor walking by the bus stop looked at our entourage that first week and said, "Are you gluttons for punishment?" I had a stroller, Hobie, Hutch running around screaming for Wes to help him tie his shoes, Parker standing tall trying to boss the other kids around, and now Kure pulling at the leash wrapped around my wrist making my coffee spill. The neighbor wasn't wrong to ask.

Life is full of risks. You take them, watch some work, and some fail.

The rescue folks said that Kure was found under a trailer as part of a litter. Her blue eyes were stunning. Coworker and friend/

reporter Ron Lee fosters dogs. He and his wife Terrie have a heart for animals. Ron knew our personal hurt in letting Rudy go. He came into the station one day months ago and held out his phone with photos visible.

"Molly, look at our new foster. Think your family is ready?"

Her eyes got me.

From there, Ron brought Kure to meet the kids. Wes was adamantly against getting a puppy, but when your ten-year-old daughter begs you with promises of responsibility and continual hugs, dads have a way of softening. Ron kept her for us, for weeks until the school routines began. By then, Wes was on board.

Nothing about adopting a puppy is logical. I mean, the neighbor took one look and rightly questioned our sanity. Yet, Kure has turned out to be a great decision. Parker and I were playing with her this morning, and I said something along those lines. You know how she replied?

"It's like Lady Gaga. We had a hundred million reasons to walk away, but we found one good one to stay."

Lada Gaga. Not exactly my muse, but it made sense to P, which therefore works for me. (I'd looked into Kure's eyes and thought more Taylor Swift: "Oh my God, look at that face—you look like my next mistake.")

Anyway, Month Eighty-Four: meet our half Husky, half Basenji mutt we now don't think we can live without. Welcome, Kure.

Happy Halloween

Hope you had an *Incredible* night.

NOVEMBER

"Our Baby"

The second we take Hobie out, Kure hops in.

COMMENTS:

Marlene S. She just wants to see out the window.

Elizabeth Mc. Our little dog, Freckles, does that too, so eventually we just buckled her in.

Mammogram

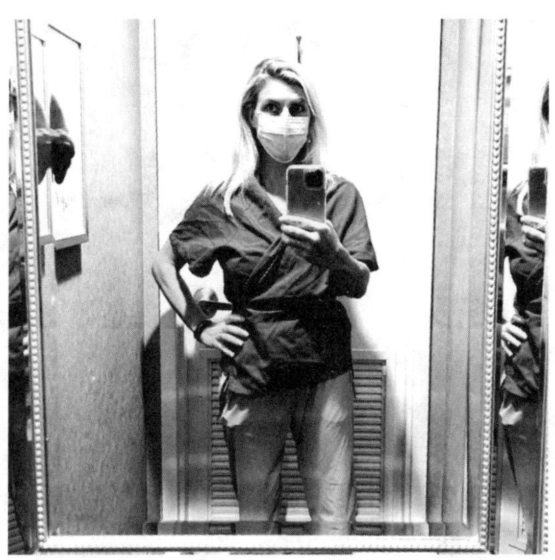

Feeling fierce before my mammogram today. Annual photo reminder to any woman age forty and above, or any woman younger if they have family history, please get checked. For your sake. With my family history, I got my first mammogram at age thirty as a birthday gift to myself. It's easy, doesn't (really) hurt, and either can bring you comfort or save your life.

If you see that lump protruding in my pocket in this photo, it's Hobie's binky. I couldn't find it for an hour this morning. Just saw this picture, wondered about the odd shape, and checked the right hip zipper. Voila.

If Hobie had Four Legs

Swear they look alike. Same mannerisms too.

MONTH EIGHTY-FIVE: Trip Versus Vacation

Parker's eyes in this photo match the trepidation in mine. She knew without knowing, while totally knowing, what the next two hours held in store for our row of seats.

Don't let this photo imply differently: our family traveling to the Caribbean over Thanksgiving with my brother, sister-in-law, and their three kids was a dream come true. We'd been in planning mode for a year; COVID almost derailed the trip more than once. The fact we pulled it off is reason alone to celebrate.

But . . . (breathe) . . . children + travel + passports + customs + protocols + pandemic = swirling stress. Then, throw in the first flight having a 5:46 a.m. take-off, after being on air until nearly midnight the evening before. I went from this photo you see to the right to the one at the top of the chapter, on less than two hours sleep. Felt like a doable idea until I was actually in the middle of the process.

My brother Jay was in charge. He's a good project manager. Every year, we plan to have our families meet to help keep cousins close. This was the most involved yearly get-together, ever. Jay found a travel deal that seemed worth the risk of not knowing where our world would be by this year's Thanksgiving, and we used a bazillion credit card points to book a getaway to the Bahamas.

Pro tip: Just because you're going somewhere tropical and unbelievably gorgeous does not change the makeup of your life. If you have three kids, don't forget you have three kids. If one is a baby, do not forget he is a baby. If you have visions of book-reading, beach-laying, and endless food-and-drink-consuming under sunshine-y skies, snap out of it. Those things were you twenty years ago. Not *now*.

Now means packing an entire suitcase that includes diapers, medicines, butt cream, and inflatable flotation devices for a child who can't talk, let alone swim. *Now* is making sure your seven-year-old takes pairs of shoes and not a left-foot sneaker and a right-foot flip-flop, because he likes to "mix them up." *Now* is ensuring your ten-year-old, who independently packs for herself—with the largest suitcase—doesn't take her entire Caboodle, value-sized bottles of body lotion, and every toiletry you've ever bought that combines to weigh eighty-five pounds.

Once suitcases are packed, unpacked, repacked, and zipped, also remember your *now* life means any normal airport stress is multiplied by fifty. I am a pretty adaptable person, but being calm in an airport is not possible when carrying a baby, bags, and watching your older children walk side by side lovingly before flipping an internal switch and challenging each other to race backward on the moving sidewalk in the opposite direction of you.

It's high-tension, even for a laid-back soul. Two adults with three kids, means you're outnumbered. Airports hold great potential for parents to absolutely lose it at any moment.

But at some point, you do take off. You do arrive. You do bumble through customs and rental cars. You get to the place you're trying to go. And, in our case, we did meet up with my brother's family.

So, I now stand here, on a gorgeous deck, and am looking at sparkling water.

The ocean is an indescribable shade. Turquoise? Azure? No blue word works.

It is here, when you finally get somewhere, that your mind begins to slowly slow down. It unpacks itself, just like you know you have yet to do with the bags inside. But, if you're like me, you try to take a minute to . . . stare. *How many words mean "blue"?* Off in the side of my head, I dream-wonder about the level of difficulty in marketing a new adjective for a color.

"Mooooooommmmmmmmmmmmmm!" Just like that, dictionary thoughts go poof. The screeching voice shakes reality into place: You are not alone. You brought kids.

"Where is my swimsuit? Mom! Did you forget suntan lotion?"

No, my love. Mom didn't forget lotion. Mom preemptively packed five bottles in different bags to not have too many liquids in one place and set off TSA alarms. In fact, if you must know, mom not only didn't forget suntan lotion, she thought about how to best pack it for two weeks.

Before turning around to find the lotion (which is guaranteed visible to their eyes if they looked first before screaming your name), you gaze at the water, again, and inhale deeply, again. Tell yourself that view isn't going anywhere. Then make yourself turn 180 degrees, and let your back face that blue as you walk away from peace, toward kids.

After getting them sun-protected, you smile again. They're

outside playing, happy, and children's joy is contagious. Who doesn't love to hear young cousins laugh? And the view, that view—you'll never get over that view—it's spectacular. You are back to directionally gazing. The tropical beauty is breathtaking. There is no noise, except the sound of a gentle breeze. This is the tranquility you've worked hard and traveled long to see.

Two breezy minutes. That's what you get. Two minutes before you hear a baby. Your baby. He's screaming. He is the youngest of the six cousins, and I'd loftily stuck him with the older kids, hoping that I could watch water. But, he is starving. The airplane snacks have worn off. It is time, Mom, to figure out food.

An hour later, same thing for the older kids: they're famished.

While coordinating meals, that perfect sky surrounds you. Sunrays reflect with no end. Your eyes see crystals dance on the lid that covers the endless ocean.

But your ears? They hear kids.

For five fantastic days, you ride that seesaw. Peace, shattered by child needs. You love every minute of the memories, being that it is a glorious family trip, and one you'd do again in an instant.

Note that word choice: trip.

You are on a trip. You are not on a vacation.

My very clear line of demarcation between the two came when Hobie threw a Nerf football into the pool for me to retrieve, like I was some sort of dog. When I got into the pool to get it, then out of the pool to give it back, he laughed maniacally and threw it right back in again. We played this game for fifty-two minutes. We had nothing else to do and he needed to be entertained before naptime. We only stopped because he pooped his swim diaper so badly it was leaking down his leg.

Trip, not vacation.

I'd click heels right now if a genie came along and offered to take our two families back to the Bahamas. Seeing your children have outside fun and live remarkable experiences is rewarding in many, many ways. I am grateful. I am blessed. None of that is taken for granted.

But chasing a Nerf football for fifty-some minutes before cleaning up swimming pool diarrhea is not what I call relaxing.

Trips have kids. Vacations do not.

COMMENTS:

Laura H. Brave mom to take that kind of *trip*. Nothing beats even a few tranquil turquoise views, but I'm dying laughing at "Mom," "Mommy," "Mom, Mom, Mom, Mom," "Mama," "Momma . . ." Even as my kids are adults I still hear it. Difference is I can now ignore them, for a moment anyway.

Stephanie F. This is exactly right. My kids are almost exactly the same ages as yours and we just took them to Disney World for five straight days. I feel every word of this. Great job on your *trip*.

Jill H. Mothering small children was always a bittersweet mix of sheer joy and small aggravations. (Poopy diapers at the most inconvenient times.) But, totally worth it. It was a mix of mom guilt and dogged-determination to be the best mom in the moment.

DECEMBER

Elfie's Letter

Parker, Hutch, & Hobie,

I'm sorry I was in the same place when you woke up yesterday morning. My magic still works, but IT IS HARD TO TRAVEL RIGHT NOW. I have to get COVID-tested every night I cross into the North Pole. Those tests take extra time. Santa still wants to know how you're acting, but this year I can't go roundtrip *every night* because of COVID. If you wake up any other morning this month and I haven't moved, that's the reason why.

But, I am watching. I am always watching. I love being part of your family during the holidays. Parker and Hutch, I'm watching you be a great help with Hobie, but please work on cleaning your Mermaid Academy desks better. You know your mom hates clutter. The countdown is on!

Love,
Elfie

Despite the best intentions, I've already forgotten Elfie twice in four days. Rather than kick myself, I got smart, and built in a future "I forgot" pass. Hello December. Hobbling in, but ready to play.

Not A Cat Fight

Well, this was new. Morgan Fogarty, the main anchor at a competing TV station in town, and I spoke to a group of women today as a joint keynote.

The group asked if we'd talk about the benefits of women supporting women. Earlier this year, they'd seen an article *The Charlotte Observer* wrote about our friendship, calling it "unlikely," because we should be, the paper said, competitors.

"It's like Coke and Pepsi being friends."

We've never been asked to speak together before; I hope it becomes a thing. Morgan and I go way back and did compete at some level for many years. Both of us came to this city in the early 2000s as young, hungry, bulldog reporters going after the same type of stories. A few years ago, we realized it was more fulfilling to lean on each other than battle back and forth.

Posting this at night. Good evening, Morgan. Good luck with your show.

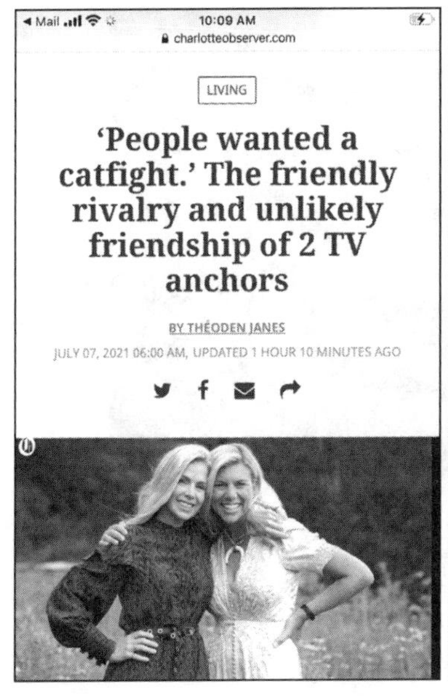

◂ Mail 10:09 AM
charlotteobserver.com

LIVING

'People wanted a catfight.' The friendly rivalry and unlikely friendship of 2 TV anchors

BY THÉODEN JANES

JULY 07, 2021 06:00 AM, UPDATED 1 HOUR 10 MINUTES AGO

◂ Mail 10:09 AM
charlotteobserver.com

LIVING

'People wanted a catfight.' The friendly rivalry and unlikely friendship of 2 TV anchors

BY THÉODEN JANES

JULY 07, 2021 06:00 AM, UPDATED 1 HOUR 10 MINUTES AGO

COMMENTS:

Callie D. I love this so much. Women can be friends even when their day (night?) jobs compete.

Wendy M. A great example that women don't have to knock each other over while they are climbing.

Kerri M. We watch Morgan at 10:00 p.m. and Molly at 11:00 p.m., so technically, not competitors. You ladies are both the real deal.

A Girl and Her Dog

They watched a movie. I mostly watched them.

COMMENTS:

Coggins M. Doesn't get any better than this.

Avery D. She is growing up before our eyes.

Kathy M. I still remember the fancy black dress she wanted for Christmas years ago. One of my favorite stories you've ever told.

Molly. Your memory is a good one. #Month25 #Small-Victories

Before Bedtime

They're now all in bed. And so begins the night.

Three seventy-five-pound boxes. Starting at (hold please, let me check) 8:57 p.m. By 7:00 a.m., we hope it'll be a seventeen-foot trampoline. Mrs. Claus and Santa might have bitten off more than they could chew this year . . .

December 25

Sunrise success. Merry Christmas. Here's to finding joy (maybe not serenity) in the day.

MONTH EIGHTY-SIX: A COVID-Christmas, Round Two

Santa brought a gift that keeps kids active, off screens, and somewhat isolated. (Moms, too. Thank you for this toe-touch.) A family trampoline felt like the perfect COVID-world gift. We could have appreciated it before COVID, will appreciate it post COVID, but know it's extra-excellent during still-here COVID. An outside place to send kids.

COVID is everywhere. Again. Twenty-two months later we're more educated, and fatigued. Feels impossible to keep track—who was sick? Were you around them? Does an at-home test count? Someone was asymptomatic but tested positive? Who were they around? How long is quarantine now? Five days and then a mask? Okay. Got it. I think.

Christmas 2020: "Hang in there."

Christmas 2021: "You've got to be kidding me."

This go-round is a different strain. We went from COVID to the Delta variant, and now it's a version called Omicron. This strain is less severe if you're fully vaccinated. Numbers fluctuate daily, but somewhere between 94 and 99 percent of people hospitalized with COVID are unvaccinated. Pretty solid proof the vaccine protects you from death.

But, frustration is also real. It's exhausting to be double-vaxxed and boosted, yet still susceptible to sickness. Omicron's contagiousness started sprouting in our consciousness sometime after Thanksgiving, and now, on this final day of the year, it can't be ignored. Charlotte testing lines are currently four to five hours long.

That's absurd. Five hours just to get tested? But people want to know.

Add to that, testing shows high numbers of positive results. Not knowing what's ahead, I'm going to relay some current-day facts. On December 30, North Carolina had over 18,500 new cases reported, with over 2,200 people hospitalized, and a percent positive rate of 22 percent. For perspective, that rate was roughly 7 percent a couple months ago. Even more chilling, the highest number of new recorded cases on any day *last year* in North Carolina was December 18, 2020, with over 8,400 people confirmed positive. Yesterday, we had ten thousand more. With a vaccine.

Before throwing your hands up in the air—something I've wanted to do a few times this break—remember: *the vaccinated aren't dying and a vast majority aren't hospitalized.* The vaccine can impact the severity of your case. That's a strong silver lining.

At this point, most of us have personal stories about our encounters with COVID. Maybe you got it. Maybe your family did. Maybe you're going through it now. At the end of 2021, a total of 19,426 people have died from COVID in North Carolina since this pandemic began, and many are hurting. Social media feeds are filled with anecdotes. Business owners are announcing temporary shutdowns. Twenty frontline workers at a testing site got it. My sister-in-law's entire neighborhood was positive in Atlanta. Half of my fourteen college girlfriends in ten different states on a large text string tested positive.

The unexpected flashlight into a true understanding about this new strain was when a ten-year-old boy who was visiting our house three days before Christmas—fully vaccinated, as was his family—felt tired and laid down on the couch, which was unlike his usual high-energy self. Bam. He was like a light switch. One minute fine, ten minutes later bundled in blankets. His mom packed their whole family fast and bolted. That's how we're now trained, isn't it? To instantly react to odd behavior? Even an innocent cough next to you can make you wonder.

This mom was smart, though. Her ten-year-old tested positive the next day. She had to cancel their trip to see her parents in Ohio.

Absorbing COVID information daily for twenty-two months is part of my job. I take in information, process, relay it in ways understandable, and yet, still don't feel like I know the rules when a ten-year-old visiting my house had it lying on my couch. His mom called his pediatrician. I called my doctor. Both said the same thing. The ten-year-old should quarantine, but anyone who'd spent time around him didn't have to *if* they were fully vaccinated. That included his parents, brother, and our family. None of us were showing symptoms, so doctors said we could live our lives. Made it less scary, since kids age five and up are now allowed to get a vaccine, and Parker and Hutch have theirs.

But the unvaccinated have different rules. We've been watching Hobie. At eighteen months old, he was asleep in his room and unintentionally isolated when the sick ten-year-old was in our home. We think he's going to be okay.

The fact COVID is back to being top-of-mind can make you crazy if you let it. At some point, I assume this will feel like a no-big-deal flu shot and the wacky surrounding this virus will wane. Until then, we're back to last-minute trips being postponed and New Year's Eve events suddenly canceled. No one wants it this way. No one wants to be sick. No small business wants to sustain itself through another shut-down, and many can't. But here we are.

Our family went to the place that always feels good: Kure. Wes and I looked at each other and just decided: Go. Be. Live. Try to enjoy these last couple of days in a rollercoaster year with plunging drops, breathtaking highs, and loop-the-loops. It felt important to us to have clear minds to start the new year, while not being around a ton of people. It was a good call. Hutch woke me this morning to see the sunrise. Together we scurried down the rickety wooden staircase to the coast. Looking up felt glorious. It is my favorite place in the world. And his. Seeing this spacious sky was a reminder of the expanse out there.

I know we're living in an inconvenient world. I also know it's important to find joy where you can. But where does it all go? I dunno. I do feel positive. I feel like we'll figure it out and by Christmas of next year, we won't be in four-to-five-hour COVID-testing lines and trashed family plans. Beyond that? Your guess is as good as mine. Just grabbing life how we can now as the days move on.

Happy New Year. Reflect. Renew. Recharge.

JANUARY

This Year's Resolution:

Find seats with a view. All four in perfect frame.

The Best Gift

While taking down our family stockings after this year, I was struck with the awesomeness of Hobie's. My sister-in-law, Amy, gifted it last year at his first Christmas. She had taken my mom's old clothes, recognizable fabrics very particular to Grammy, and had a seamstress make a patchwork stocking with his name.

Hobie's stocking matches stockings my mom made for Wes, me, Parker, Hutch, and even our first dog, Fisher. Every year we hang them together. They're totally my mom: kinda hippie, mismatching, and filled with love.

If you read the beginning of *The Juggle Is Real*, you know its first chapter, Month Thirty-One, began from the hospice house as I debated whether to let my kids see their Grammy that way. They were six and two. Mom knew them, but didn't know we'd someday have a Hobie. When Christmas rolled around in 2020 and the Tupperware bins of Christmas decorations came out, I realized Hobie didn't have a personalized stocking from Grammy. We were living in a daze back then, even more so than now. I could tread water, but I wasn't swimming. In between having a newborn, working, homeschool, and sheer survival, the fact that he didn't have a homemade stocking was the last thing I was worried about in 2020.

My sister-in-law, Amy, however, did think of it. My mom had made stockings for their family too. She knows the spirit running through them.

I was touched when opening Amy's present last year but didn't study it the way it deserved. While packing up today, I did.

That top material, with the hot peppers? That was one of Mom's chef coats. She was a culinary mastermind and had a catering business out of our home in Pennsylvania during my childhood. Later in life, she went back to school for advanced cooking lessons and interned at great restaurants. She was an artist. Food was her canvas. The second I saw the hot cayenne, I remembered her wearing that coat.

Love the little patch at the bottom that says, "Wilsie." My mom's name came from her grandfather Wilson, only she was a girl, so it was changed to Wilsie. She liked to get it embroidered on her cooking items, identifying them as hers, and had sewn that patch onto her own apron.

Some of the other baby fabrics on the stocking are from blankets she made for grandchildren. She'd always stitch "Handmade by Wilsie" in the back. Both Parker and Hutch have one. They're priceless.

The letters "H-O-B-I-E" are from Amy herself. The lady she'd hired told Amy that it would make it look more handmade if she cut out the letters and sewed them. So, Amy—not a seamstress—figured it out. My mom would've loved that font and loved Amy trying to make this stocking resemble the others.

Amy's foresight will help Hobie someday. Without it, he'd be aware his stocking looked different. Amy's gift assures her nephew will feel included for decades to come. In part because of this stocking, Hobie will know Grammy loves him and he is an equal grandchild, despite never meeting her. He'll also know he has an aunt who adores him.

Little things make big differences. Thanks, Aunt Amy. Love you.

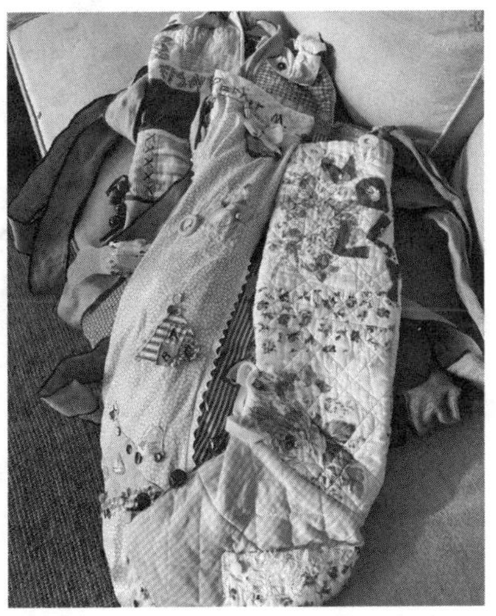

All stockings

Text from Preschool

He fell asleep on the wall.

Bubbles

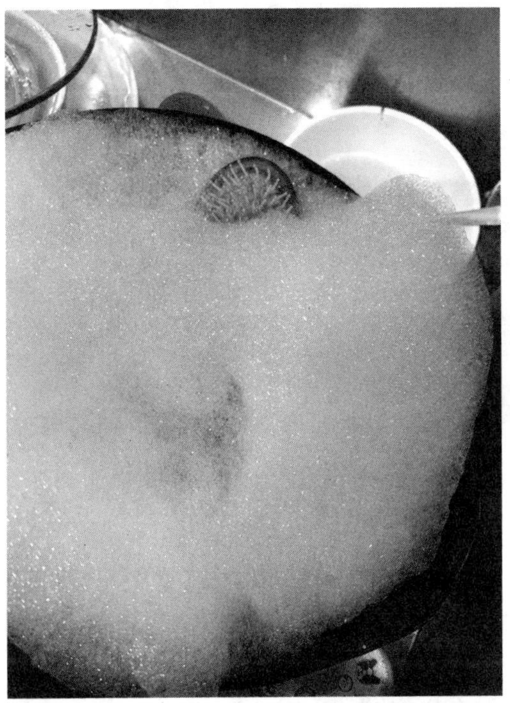

Morning: Parker overslept and couldn't find her brush. Hobie likes to give her brush to the dog (stop judging), so we looked everywhere Kure could've hidden it, gave up, missed the bus, and then I was yelling. Hutch was mysteriously quiet. I piled everyone in the car, drove to the elememtary school, got Hobie to preschool, came back home to start dishes, and voila. Hobie and Kure can't reach the sink, so, I think I found who thought it'd be fun to hide his sister's hairbrush in soap.

MONTH EIGHTY-SEVEN: Mom Shaming

Documenting the unplanned. You guys know by now: kids grow, life slaps us, I learn, and you share your raw truths in response. Through your comments and messages, we build a community.

Most months I write about what is happening. A funny story, an ongoing question, possibly an observation.

Not this month. This month was muddy. I thought—probably too much—about how to document January. The days felt cold and slow. To add to the fun, I could've written humorously about Hobie eating blue slime glue or Hutch's mindset on summer camps. I could've written about Parker looking ahead to middle school.

The more I thought, the more of what hit wasn't about the kids.

Rather, it was about moms.

Specifically, moms who judge other moms.

There are plenty out there. There are also plenty of amazing women—people who see silent struggles and stop to be a crutch. The truth is, in different moments, we all have a capability to be both: judgmental on some days, soft and kind on others.

Judgment about an outfit or appearance, while still wrong, feels very different than throwing personal opinions around about how someone else raises their kids. I'm particularly prickly to these parenting comments, and getting more so. I don't think it's hard to figure out why—our whole world feels a little more prickly about everything. We are nearly two years into the unthinkable, and most of us feel fatigued from wondering about when disruption will end. For parents of young kids, our only goal, really, has been to keep the train on tracks. One day at a time. Keep going, Momma. Keep going, Dad. Keep going. Do the best you can. The best you can is good enough.

That's all we keep saying.

So short of a child being in danger or abused, why would one parent tell another parent what they're doing is *wrong*? In what world—especially this one—is it okay to shame someone into thinking they don't love their kids enough? I can't think of one instance where that seems acceptable.

Buckle up, friends. I'm stepping on the soapbox.

᪥

Women have an unmatched ability to support other women in wonderous ways that feed our souls and give us hope. Need to organize assistance? Call a woman. Female-driven networks of love are efficient: women will generally have help delivered before a group of men can even find the address of where something should be sent.

But the flip side of this beautiful power that women have to unite is an unattractive underbelly. Some women in some moments feel justified in proclaiming their perfection because they think they do things better or best.

Someone doesn't like my look? Fine. Someone doesn't like my new haircut? Whatever. You think I look "sleazy" on TV (an actual voicemail I received last week)? Noted. Oh, wait! You also detest my shoes (that was at the end of the message—how do you even see them behind a desk?) Got it.

I've learned to let nasty comments roll off my back. Ignore, ignore, ignore. Being in front of the camera more than twenty years has taught me that everyone will have an opinion about you, no matter if it's what you consider your finest day or your most sloppy. The daily feedback has made me impervious. I know through life experience that appearance standards are entirely subjective and I can't wear the criticism tightly.

But judgment about how someone parents? Uh-uh. Those comments should be rejected.

I'm saying "parents" but, okay . . . do you hear much Dad shaming? In a twisted way, I wish I did. I might feel less disappointed if this ugly act wasn't practiced predominantly by women. But the truth is, Wes doesn't get attacked with pithy, snarky comments from other men about how far away he dropped Parker off as she ran into school (and yes, Wes is an involved father who often does carpool). He is never asked why Hutch doesn't have on a coat when it's cold outside. He is not looked at with a side-eye when he's out with Hobie, and Hobie poops and he has no diapers. I get those looks. Moms stare at me like, "You are going to just let him *sit* in that *poop* and not *clean him now*?" Wes certainly doesn't get questioned if he goes out of town for a weekend. No one says to him: Did you really leave your kids with someone else?

But I do. I hear all of it. Mom Shaming. Alive and (un)well.

That last example—a weekend away—was on full display this past month. We often travel with our kids and dream about family trips to Kure. But a friend got married in Savannah a few weeks ago. Wes and I went for the weekend, kid-free. I returned to work on Monday and posted a picture about being back in Charlotte, ready to cover the bad weather. One woman immediately responded: "Do you always look for a reason to go out and celebrate and leave your children? I never left mine for a night."

This was an instant assumption mixed with dismay.

Not much gets through my armor anymore, but I had to take a breath reading that one. It made me pause. If you comment on how I choose to love my children, Momma Bear claws are out fast, ready to protect them and my relationship with all three.

Two weeks after reading that comment, I write this more calmly: it's great if you never leave your children for a night, if that's what you want and what works best for your family. That is not what works best for us. That weekend, Wes and I left our kids with a loving caregiver for three days. We appreciated the getaway. Small breaks from our jam-packed days make me a better mother and more excited to enter the big top upon return.

What works for one parent might not work for another.

All moms have thoughts and questions about how to best care for their kids while keeping themselves sane. We parent children differently, much in the way a manager manages people differently. What creates productivity in one employee might not work for all. The tricky part is, parenting doesn't have a boss above dictating guidelines. Questions about "how to" can haunt a mom or dad. How to be fair? How to teach kindness? How do you, as the adult in charge with no time off from that role, not lose your own sense of self? There is no employee handbook with black-and-white procedures, or one-fits-all answers. We each find our own ways.

Motherhood is indescribably rewarding. Ten years into this journey, I find big gifts in the simplicity. Sunday nights are a favorite. Parker, Hutch, Hobie, Wes, and I watch a silly sitcom, cuddled in bed. I mindlessly brush my fingers on their arms, while Parker's clean, wet hair dangles on my shoulder, and our toes touch under the blankets. Every Sunday night, in that protected calm, I hope Monday never arrives.

But on good Mondays—or Tuesdays, Wednesdays, Thursdays, Fridays, or Saturdays—new rewards shoot through the busy-ness. This past week, Hobie started raising his arms in the highchair, and with all the authority and cuteness of a toddler learning to talk, says the word, "Up!" (It's only, "Up!" He has yet to learn "Down!") Days later, this still makes me want to brag. I am his mom. My level of pride in his new sounds are unmatched. Other moms have their own gems, which make their mazes of motherhood worthwhile. There is no map. No Cliffs Notes. No recipe on how to cook your creation. Along the way you watch your kids fail, or not handle something the way you would, and you learn to keep your big mouth shut. You try to teach kids not to fight, how to build personality, find good friends, love deeply, take advice, and become contributing humans in a currently upside-down world.

The exact journey of how to do all those things is different for each child... and each parent. The only thing we know for sure is that there is no right way, and rewards and battles can happen within minutes.

Let moms mom how moms will mom. Think before you speak. Or, before you write. Guide and listen before declaring what you think is correct. Look for laughter and relatability in what others weave, even if it's different than the tapestry you create.

COMMENTS:

Becky J. I was a working mom. My husband used to say, "You just have to know you are doing the best you can and not worry what other people think." Wear the cape proudly. It's a role to own.

Brandy B. Truth be told, our kids need a break from us too.

Beverly A. I read that woman's hateful post and was so very disgusted. It's great to see your post now and for us to realize it felt judgmental to you too.

Katie G. This is one of the best things I've read in a long time, and I don't even have kids.

FEBRUARY

Valentine's Day

A one-hour pizza dinner break after swim lessons (Hutch), soccer practice (Parker), and a babbling conversation (Hobie). I don't feel calm, but do feel loved.

COMMENTS:

Elizabeth Mc. And I thought pacifiers were supposed to be calm.

Old Mixed with New

If you've ever been to Kure Beach, you've probably walked by the strip of businesses leading to the Kure Beach Pier. The building on the very end has been multiple breakfast/lunch restaurants, most recently Kure Beach Diner. Originally, many moons ago, that spot next to the pier was called Ocean View. It was almost ruined multiple times over the decades because of various hurricanes hitting the coast, but the building never fell.

Memories of Ocean View lace my mind. My dad would walk me and my brothers there from our cement-block family shack on oceanfront Atlantic Avenue. The sun would be rising. He wanted a sausage and mustard toast sandwich, with a side of grits. Fishermen coming in from their overnights on the pier ordered heaping plates of food, and at five, ten, or fifteen years old, I saw it all. Remembered it all. The cracked linoleum, the old black-and-white photos on the wall, the sun-creased wrinkles in the foreheads of virtually every customer who walked in and made the bell ring on the door.

My dad loved Ocean View. After he passed away in 2006, we didn't go as much to whatever spot sat in its place. It just wasn't the same without him.

So imagine my surprise when I saw a sign in the window late last November that said Kure Beach Diner had been sold to new owners, was under construction, and would reopen in 2022 under the name, "Ocean View Restaurant." *That's intriguing*, I thought. *I wonder if the new owners know about its past.*

I started following the place on Instagram (@OVKB22) to see if I could get the backstory. They never said anything about who had bought it. Just kept promoting its grand opening. With nothing to do the weekend it was set to open and the kids off school that Monday, Wes and I threw everyone in the car. Any excuse is good enough to go breathe beach.

Once inside the restaurant the following morning, while eating omelets and French toast, the owner stopped by the table. He was checking on the thirty or so customers. Most seats were filled, and he was setting the tone, showing he wanted to interact. When he got to us, I asked about the name.

"Oh, it used to be called Ocean View a long time ago," he said casually. "Back then my dad owned it."

"I bet he and my dad were friends," I replied.

He stopped short, and I smiled. We got to talking. Turns out the current owner, Charlie, and I are the exact same age. His dad, Charles Smith, and my dad were both lifeguards on Kure Beach, presumably around the same time. Charlie said his grandfather, Howard Wilke, used to be the police chief forever ago for the Town of Kure Beach.

He pointed to one picture on the wall.

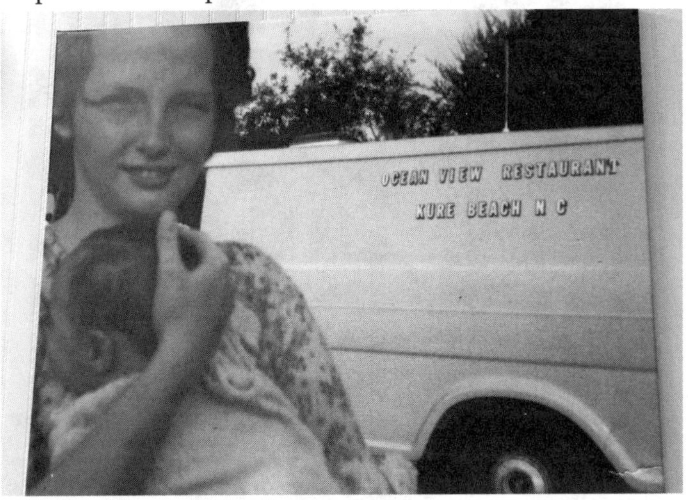

"That's my mom holding me as a baby in front of the van my dad used for the restaurant."

Behind the baby in a mother's arms, you see old-school block letters on a 1970s-looking yellow van: "Ocean View Restaurant."

It was worth the long commute to enjoy a meal at Ocean View. History is personal, and it's fun to stumble into someone else who shares pieces of yours.

MONTH EIGHTY-EIGHT: The Sauceman

Parker loved mermaids. Hutch loved work passes. Hobie loves . . . condiments.

We all have a personality at birth, and that personality evolves. Some is what DNA dictates, and some is learned. We are nature and nurture. That's why siblings can have similar mannerisms, but opposite personalities. Look at Parker and Hutch: they both cling to unique obsessions with stubborn Gorilla Glue-like grip, but focus on wildly different things.

Of course they do. They're mine. Daily Dunkin' coffee, pretzel M&M's—even this constant need to chronologically document history. If Parker, Hutch, and Hobie have patience, they got it from Wes. But odd, harmless addictions and an ability to deeply fixate? That's passed down from me.

Parker's first obsession was the easiest to understand. She'd be in diapers and make us walk far out on the pier, look down, and see if we could spot a mermaid beneath the surface. As a beach baby who fearlessly wanted to go farther in the ocean, under bigger waves, she's now a ten-year-old surfer who carries her own pink surfboard over wooden stairways and chases her dog on a hard-packed beach. She used to wear long dresses to climb the beach lifeguard stands and jump barefoot into sand dunes with her unbrushed hair flying. One summer, tiny sand crabs got caught in her long tangles. Rather than freak out, she giggled as I grabbed them. She was my little sun goddess who loved the sound of waves, and though she's older now—just ask her—she still loves the thought of female fish wearing sparkly scales to swim under the ocean. I do too. I get it, and get her.

Hutch's obsession was harder to understand. All the humor, sensitivity, and out-of-box thinking you can ever imagine is wrapped up in his unpredictability. At two years old, he became obsessed with my WBTV work pass and addicted to access. With an older sister always in charge, I think he wanted to find power in small ways. Work passes. Key fobs. Codes. Anything to do with security clearance. Any toy with a lock or password or thumbprint. He wanted lanyards with badges to jingle loudly. We couldn't leave the house to go on an errand if he didn't have a work pass on his neck or in his fist. Some kids take a beloved stuffed animal on a trip: Hutch would pack pretend IDs. As he has grown, that obsession has matured into him wanting—needing—to be the person who swipes credit cards at checkouts and press buttons on the card machine. If we're out to eat, he has to be the family member to add the tip on the receipt (in first-grade handwriting) and sign the name. Wes and I let him. It's his undeniable thing.

Despite raising Parker and Hutch through these moments, I hadn't consciously thought about the possibility of what Hobie would love.

He's just . . . you know. Third child. He rolls with the punches. Most lovable baby around. Who Hobie might someday be didn't consume me because I know he'll be great. I subconsciously assumed we'd learn his fixations whenever they made themselves visible.

That time has come. His obsession emerged this month during family dinners.

Being nineteen months old, Hobie points to what he wants. That's pretty typical for young kids with limited vocabularies. This past month, Hobie's game got intense. He began to throw his entire being toward something in his line of sight. Half grunting, he'd shake his outstretched chubby hands in a direction, and we'd guess. Someone else's cup? No. A saltshaker? No. The asparagus on Hutch's plate? Nooooo. He'd shake his head harder because we—the idiots!—weren't able to discern what his baby fingers wanted to hold. The more we guessed wrong, the more his highchair straps would strain and he'd yell unintelligible noises. For weeks, we couldn't figure it out. He'd have his sippy cup and cut up food and, ultimately, we'd ignore the tantrum. We'd eat fast, clear the table, and carry on. No use giving a nineteen-month-old the power to control dinner.

Recently, this routine happened when we were out to eat at a casual restaurant. Nachos were in the middle of the table. Beside that, Hutch's favorite food: mozzarella sticks. Hobie's highchair was at the end of the booth. We'd taken chips, chicken, and corn from the nacho plate and put them in front of his highchair in pieces.

He wanted nothing to do with his own little smorgasbord. He began to yell. We added a torn-up mozzarella stick. He kept yelling and pointed to the big plate with loaded toppings.

Finally, because he was causing a scene, I put him beside me in the booth to get him closer to the nachos and whatever it was he was trying to reach.

It was the plastic container of sour cream.

And the side of salsa.

And the side of marinara sauce on Hutch's "cheese dippers." (Hutch's name for the mozzarella.)

Hobie wanted *all* the sauces.

Hmm.

I put the three small side bowls in front of the highchair and strapped him back. Now my little monster was agreeable. He took one of the chips still in front of him and dipped it in the salsa. He licked the salsa off and double-dipped that chip into the sour cream. Licked that off and did the same for the marinara sauce. He finally bit into the chip itself and chewed a bite, then put it down. Then picked it back up and repeated the whole dip-lick process.

"Moooommmm, I need my marinara." Hutch began to whine, highly annoyed.

"Wait, Hutch. Watch your brother. Let's see what he does."

We all stopped eating and stared at Hobie.

He repeated that same routine with his third and final chip.

Afterward, he began pointing again, this time I thought: *my utensil?* I gave him my fork. He snatched it—*good job, Mom!* He dipped the fork into the salsa, and shoveled the pile of mild tomato chunkiness into his mouth. No chip. Just salsa. Then did the same thing with the sour cream. Part of the thick white cream fell onto his lap. Same with the marinara. Now it was a peppermint-looking mural on his sweatpants.

He was eating the sauces straight. Shoveling them down his throat. Quiet Hobie. Gloriously focused.

Our entire family watched. Even Hutch had left his suffering over missing sauces behind to study the scene his baby brother was acting out with this liquid buffet.

My salad soon arrived. Honey mustard dressing on the side.

Hobie immediately started pointing.

I gave it to him.

He was now dipping his fork into the yellow, sticky dressing.

Before you report me to DSS, there were still pieces of chicken in front of him. Parker had also added some of her fries. But he didn't want to dip the protein or potatoes. He did like my salad croutons though; I think because they fit into the sauce buckets better.

By the end of the meal, a colorful array covered his lips, cheeks, hands, pants, and the highchair. He didn't care. He was joyful. Happy, happy Hobie.

Unbeknownst to me, the woman at a table behind him had been monitoring the debacle. She approached as she was leaving.

"I haven't had that enjoyable of a lunch in a long time," she said. "My sons are in their early twenties and watching your curly-haired boy eat has given me a great laugh."

ঔ

Since that meal, Hobie's obsession has intensified. I do get healthy vegetables, fruits, deli turkey, cheese sticks, noodles, and chicken in him, but he must first dip that hearty food into a messy sauce first. Ranch is popular, as is soy sauce. He wants smaller bowls next to his plate. His brother tries to borrow a spoonful or two—Hobie won't share. He mixes and matches. A fork in the ketchup, then the yellow mustard. If it's corn on the cob, he'll plop everything into melted butter. If it's breakfast pancakes, he'll get syrup everywhere. He has even tried hot sauce, and surprisingly, didn't hate the Texas Pete.

What is the meaning of this addiction? I don't know. Parker loved mermaids because she's imaginative and saw herself as a beautiful Queen of the Ocean. Hutch loved work passes because he wanted to gain power.

Hobie? Maybe he's just trying to tell me I can't cook.

COMMENTS:

Watson C. Maybe he'll grow up to be a chef.

Bobbi E. My nineteen-month-old loves sauces right now, too. Her current favorite is A-1.

Linda C. I wonder if the bright colors of the condiments are part of the attraction.

Francis P. I used to eat ketchup and mustard sandwiches.

Kristen B. My toddler loves dipping and also eats salsa with a fork.

Brenda S. What? No pacifier in the sauce?

Melissa C. I have the same obsession. My family refers to me as the condiment queen.

Jennifer S. I'm thinking back to your post a couple weeks ago. How anyone could say you're a slacker mom is baffling. The way you write about your kids is so full of love and empathy. It's fun to speculate on how your kids' personalities and quirks will translate later in life.

Why Not?

A love story.

A year ago, the girl in this story saw a dress. She spotted the off-white satin softness on an app called Rent the Runway, where you get clothes shipped to you. You wear them, then ship them back when you're done. It's an unlimited plan, so there are no time restraints. This girl waited for the dress to become available. She'd patiently check to see if whoever was wearing it somewhere else, had returned it to the company. She waited and waited and waited, for months. When it one day became listed as "available," the girl jumped. Had it sent to her front door. The night it arrived, she tried it on. She felt pretty and regal, and then . . . she put it back on the hanger. She had nowhere to wear such a statement. It hung in her closet for weeks as a tease.

Week after week she'd let it hang, wasted, being unworn.

Until it hit her: she didn't need a reason to dress up.

We can wear what we want, when we want, and turn an empty night into an Uptown city tour. Eat, drink, and make people point. *Wearing all white in February? Why?* She imagined herself replying to anyone who'd ask: because I want to. Because happiness is beautiful. Because women get trapped in being what they need to be for everyone else, and to create an evening for no reason that feels smiling and strong isn't wrong, it's right. Eating the half dozen warm chocolate chip cookies to end the evening? Also totally correct.

Best night in a long time. There is a lot of heaviness in the world. Making simple things count seems more important than ever.

The dress is now back in the mail, heading to RTR and its next temporary owner. Lucky her. Hope she feels the magic.

COMMENTS:

Lynette C. You make me want to dance in the rain.

Phyllis W. My precious Aunt Nell passed away at age eighty-six. Several years earlier she sent me a poem entitled, "Dust if You Must." In part it says, "I'm reading more and dusting less, remove 'someday' and 'one day' from your vocabulary. If it's worth doing now, don't save it for later. Life is a gift that's why they call it the present."

Lori K. I just read this to my husband. Living and loving life is incredible.

MARCH

Smart Babysitter

Walked in on Wes changing Hobie's diaper. This is how he opted to keep Hobie focused and still during the process.

COMMENTS:

Logan B. Wes is awesome.

Amanda R. Way to a man's heart is through his stomach.

Bridget K. That slice is as big as Hobie. I'm a germaphobe—this is freaking me out.

MONTH EIGHTY-NINE: Parker

World, help me raise her to know her worth.

Our days are funny. They fill up. Fast steps, meetings, new dominos, a thrown grenade, a fire that needs put out, high stress, ASAP emails, hugs, what-are-we-having-for-dinner thoughts, and bed and bath routines. Good ones and tough ones. One thing to the next. The pace can be oddly comforting or bring on a headache.

Then the weekend arrives. We enjoy taking normal breaths and more laid-back hours. The busier the week, the more appreciated is the silence. Working parents love their children just as much as those who don't work, but I've always confessed that being out of the house fifty hours a week (including every night) does make me feel like I miss things. Weekends are used to catch up and take it in.

This past weekend, I had a moment where I looked at Parker and stopped short. Maybe it was the sunlight, or this new hairdo she tried, or the fact she grows taller by the day, but I saw her and wondered—was struck dumb wondering—how she got so old.

That was Saturday. On Sunday, I watched her play soccer, rush the goal, guard the goal, and laugh with friends afterward, despite a loss. Competitive, yet happy.

Wes looked at me as she walked off the field, still far from us but heading our way. She was smiling and joking with a teammate. Her low ponytail was sweaty and her hands were full of gear as she helped carry an extra soccer ball for someone else.

"Does she look taller to you?" he asked.

He sees it too.

Next month Parker turns eleven. This summer she heads to camp for an entire month (her choice). In the fall, she starts middle school. It's going fast. I'm not complaining: I write this in awe. Parker's independent streak is a mile wide, as my father used to say about me, and getting this front-row seat as she figures out who she is, what makes her happy, and what doesn't feel as good, is the best stage of parenting I've experienced so far. There is more ahead, obviously. She's not even a teenager. I know struggles will come and, candidly, we've already worked through some. (Fifth grade isn't easy, you guys.) I do not wish this time away and don't want to rush to the landmarks ahead. But this past weekend I looked at her and saw everything in the future right there in front of me.

I thought this when she turned ten, but there's no debating it now: she is no longer my little girl.

P . . . if you ever look back and read about your own self here, I bet you'll have your own memories of what life feels like for you right now. Those personal thoughts of yours may or may not match up with what I see. That's okay. Your thoughts are your thoughts. My selfish part wants to know every single thing in your head, but I also hope you can learn self-analysis. I am getting more and more okay with you asking for advice but not leaning on me for every question.

If you really do read this—because why else write these monthly posts if not to document the truth for you and your brothers later?—let me add this: you, Parker Meade, are forever remarkable. Your dad and I are proud of you. We see your heart. We see your decision-making processes, your humor, your responsible nature with Hobie, your attempts—sometimes successful—to reign in frustrations with how much Hutch adores you, your excitement, your fearlessness, and how you dream big. Look no further than the fact you want to go to camp for a month. I already miss you and it's still three months away.

March brought lots of busy days as the world picked up after our sudden slow-down two years ago. Parker, you personify that pace. It's on. You're growing, learning, laughing, and full speed ahead.

This month turned into a letter to you. Going to sign it that way.

—Momma

COMMENTS:

Molly. Saturday.

Molly. Sunday.

Gloria H. I have two daughters. I am so proud of the women they became. As I see my three granddaughters grow, I feel what you feel and understand. Where did it all go?

Nancy O. Hard to talk about your oldest. Know that sometimes you'll be left in the back seat and on the outside. Then there will be a day when she comes and gets in your lap to cry when she realizes that growing up is hard.

Jessie S. I'm seeing firsthand how fast they grow. My first blessing is now eighteen and about to enter the Job Corps. On the cusp of her living her own life, I find myself wondering if I've given her the tools for this world. My fourteen-year-old is her own self, confident, never willing to settle for less than she feels is fair. I'm in awe of them.

Unwanted Art Class

Hutch decided to add some coloring to the mix with his brother's face as the paper. Didn't this happen years ago, only Hutch was the paper and Parker was the artist? Lessons flow downhill, and long periods of quiet aren't a gift: they're a signal. Go check and see why.

COMMENTS:

Burt B. Been there. Both the artist and the "paper."

Jackie E. I was driving years ago and thought my two were being good in the back seat because they were quiet. When we arrived and I went around to get them out, they'd covered each other in marker.

APRIL

Angry Note

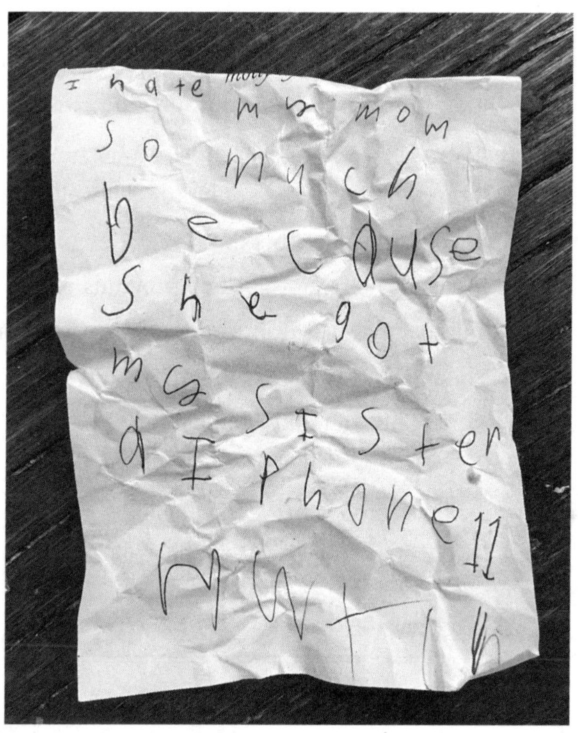

This morning, after presenting a "business plan" last week as to why she believed she was old enough to get a cell phone, and after signing a contract on rules she must follow, Parker got an iPhone for her eleventh birthday. She was thrilled.

Hutch was not.

Crumpled up and thrown into the middle of the floor—think the exact opposite of what a paper airplane looks like gliding into a room—here was the angry, jealous note my sweet Hutch hurled:

"I hate my mom so much because she got my sister an iPhone 11 Hutch."

Heart on his sleeve. Frustrated and seething but trying not to ruin her birthday breakfast by crying out loud. Instead, he slid from the room, then wrote out his feelings and threw them in our faces before heading to school. Parker handled it well, and defused his attitude by explaining that this means he'll be now able to get one when he turns eleven too. (Not our previous rule of turning twelve.) She explained *she* was doing all the hard work for him, to get it a year earlier. *She* created a presentation, and *she* helped "the parents" see that "it's not that big of a deal."

His ying, her yang.

Sorry, Hutchie. Take comfort in the fact that older siblings are always guinea pigs, while younger siblings generally have an easier path.

COMMENTS:

Nana L. Save the note, and the date. There will be more like it.

Julie M. Please keep us posted on how Parker does with the rule-following. Girls mature in that sense much faster than boys. My oldest grandson got his first phone at eleven as well, and honestly has probably not talked a full two hours on it and is now nineteen years old. The phone is only for emergencies in his eyes.

A Brush

We all know by now, Hutch's mind is wired to look for the more creative way. When he stares at a checkers board, he automatically sees blocks on which to play chess. Never the easy moves or basic strategy. Always the special.

Which is why with his chlorinated, salt-encrusted, surfed-out tangled hair this week on spring break, he decided he needed smaller prongs and more of a handle when working through the knots. So, he went to the kitchen utensil drawer.

A fork = a brush.

I will spend my entire life desperately trying to protect his thought process.

Trampoline Watching

To my friends who are exhausted . . . here's where I fell asleep last night while saying to the trampoline behind me, "Good trick. Yes, I'm watching. I'm watching. I'm watching. I'm watch . . ." and then, silence. Conked out while mindlessly reassuring a child. We had a jam-packed weekend with three soccer games in Concord, two different kid parties in opposite directions in the city, a summer camp tour, a chess tournament (Hutch's first!), and the best night listening to Billy Joel live in concert. Yeah. I crashed. All-over-the-place fun can do that to you.

Hutch took this photo to mock me. Or was it Wes? Either way, they were laughing. Who passes out mid-conversation in a chair? I'm glad to see it, though. Have we learned nothing from COVID? Now that the world is opening up and we're in-person with schedules and events and joyful reunions, are we jumping back into the rat race with no pause? Forgetting how through frustrations of isolation, "nothing" was also good in some ways, and we'd found peace in downtime?

You might have different details, but a similar feel. So, I remind you this Monday morning with the week ahead, pick a ball to drop. Pick a few if you need. Let the balls fall. That's the advice my own body gave me last night. Sometimes sitting is the best reward.

COMMENTS:

Elizabeth E. Sometimes we *need* rest.

Patty S. I was at the beach this past week. Was trying to cram everything into a short time frame. Then there was a "nothing" time. I really enjoyed that the most. Super-busy people always catch a nap once in a while. (Hutch took a good picture, too!)

Nana L. That chair looks comfy. I'd nap there too.

Lisa Q. Girl, that was me too! We had almost the exact schedule this weekend and I feel the same. In bed by 9:00 p.m.

Mike E. Spring break and kids out of school can be very tiring. Now you go back to work to rest.

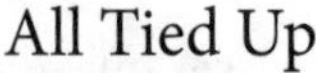

All Tied Up

Most of the time, we make the bus on time and the preschool drop-off is successful. Not this morning. Hutch handed me his booby-trapped, seventeen-knot shark sneaker ("Mom, it's like your double knot, but more!) and needed me to untie it for him. Took me twenty-four minutes. The bus left without him.

COMMENTS:

Tonia H. All day, every day, times eighteen. I'm a kindergarten teacher.

Brooks H. What happened to that fork he used weeks ago?

MONTH NINETY: Eleven, Seven, and One

The pendulum swing from the physical strain of chasing toddler Hobie to the deep mental strain of keeping up with Parker's quick wit—while never losing sight of Hutch caught in the middle—leaves me far to the left before leaping fast to the far right. Pieces of parenting get left in stages. It's hard to give full focus to one child because you have an awareness of the one you just left and the one you're going to help next. It puts the kids at odds: no one gets all of me, and few activities happily speak to all three.

Unless we're at the beach.

At the beach, we all have each other.

It has been a fighting few months between Parker and Hutch. She is cooler than most first-grade activities, and Hutch can't play her games. She likes sports, he likes art. She wants privacy, he wants to cling to and copy her. Add Hobie to the mix, and rather than create a bridge of safe space, it turns into an argument of which sibling he loves more. At twenty-one months, Hobie laughs. Somehow, he already knows he holds the power.

I watch. I enjoy. I appreciate. I yell, direct, love, hug, then fly on the pendulum as we fall in the opposite direction to the next diaper, distraction, meal, text, to-do checkmark. It has felt that way for months.

What is a pulled-apart parent supposed to do with three kids and an age gap this wide? Family walks work—Hobie is in a stroller, Hutch on a scooter, and Parker wearing her glitter roller-girl skates—but a family can only do so much walking. We usually get twenty minutes in before complaints arise, from roller skates being too tight to who's the line leader. Everyone digs the trampoline that Santa brought, but that also only buys us about a half hour.

Like many this time of year, we are feeling fried. Then—aha!—spring break approaches. A week with nothing planned, combined with our family needing a scenery change. This year especially, we needed something easy—no plane tickets or stress with a toddler. There is one obvious answer.

As always, Kure.

But suddenly, this time . . . Parker wasn't on board. She has never not wanted to drive toward salt water. Why was she saying, "I won't see my friends for AN ENTIRE WEEK!?!?" She sounded bratty, and she's not a brat. Rather than get mad, I tried to rewind myself decades. I gave pause and remembered how it felt to be eleven years old. Back then, it was cassette tapes on my Walkman instead of playing games on a cell phone, but I could recall feeling far from friends on family trips.

So I ignored her complaints and attitude, kissed her forehead, told her to pack her swimsuits, flip-flops, some long-sleeved T-shirts, and then to get in the car. Which she angrily did.

Once there, breathing beach, something notable happened.

Parker never once mentioned missing Charlotte, and got out her surfboard. Hutch ran through the waves chasing her on his boogie board. They both played with Hobie, and the fighting lessened. We all did the same activity: sand. Mom was shared equally.

On Easter morning, all three even wore bunny lips together.

Month Ninety: The simple reminder that Kure *can* cure.

COMMENTS:

Caroline W. My three are seventeen, fifteen, and thirteen. They all get annoyed with each other and with us (the parents) and sometimes whoever is around just because they can (teen years are fun). Let someone hurt one of them, though—even just being verbally mean—and the other two become personal bodyguards.

MAY

Tell Me I'm Wrong

Today is Superhero Day at preschool. He dressed like a working mom.

COMMENTS:

Molly. Make no doubt, whether you work in the home or out of it, as an entrepreneur, or an unpaid CEO of your household making sure things run, you are working.

The Murder of Lambie

In the middle of significant news headlines today—raw sadness in Ukraine, and, locally, a little boy fighting for his life with kidney failure—comes this ridiculous fact: Kure (the dog) just killed Lambie. Hutch left his precious partner on the couch this morning, and upon return from preschool drop-off, I walked in and gasped. Oh my God. Kure looked at me with puppy eyes and left the room, as if she knew that she'd savagely ripped apart her older brother's soul, and I'd caught her living in the guilt.

If you see Hutch, don't tell him. I cleaned up the scene. All of Lambie's parts are in a plastic bag until I can somehow find an emergency solution to surgically reattach his insides and little Lambie face. I'm unsure at this point what to say to him tonight on dinner break when it's time to go to bed. I'll cross that bridge when we get there.

Any ideas on professional and quick-working stuffed animal doctors are welcome.

The fact that Kure also mutilated my shoes is not even important right now. I'm just a swirling mess worried about how to resurrect the one thing Hutch needs every night. *Why* do these things get unexpectedly thrown into a day to make it exponentially harder? The emotions feel like a weight around my neck.

Going now to scour the city for stuffed animal seamstresses.

COMMENTS:

Molly. Here's what Lambie looked like "before," when Hutch went in for an emergency appendicitis and Lambie showed him how to be brave.

JDarlene B. Lambie was beside Hutch's side for surgery, so now Hutch can beside Lambie for his?

Donovan S. Thoughts and prayers.

Lambie Update

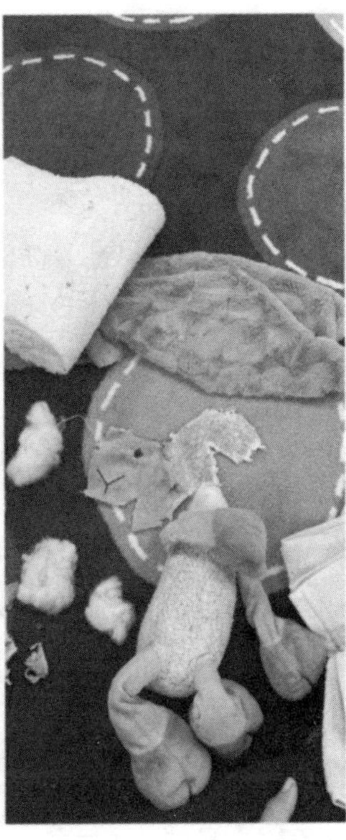

Ms. Linda is a seamstress. She's also a preschool teacher at Hobie's school. She saw the photo of murdered Lambie and offered to help. Today she showed me what she has so far: super-soft material for patches and some pieces already handsewn with love. Surgery continues, but he's looking better. Meantime, a friend found a new Lambie on eBay, and he is in my hands.

When Hutch finally sees what happened—

NO, I HAVEN'T TOLD HIM AND PLEASE DON'T START THROWING SHAME OVER THAT BECAUSE PARENTING IS HARD AND THERE ARE NO RULES ON HOW TO LET YOUR SON KNOW HIS SOUL WAS GNARLED TO DEATH BY HIS SISTER'S PUPPY AND YES I SEARCHED ONLINE TO FIND A SHORT VERSION ON HOW TO BREAK THAT TOUGH LESSON AND NO THE UNIVERSITY OF GOOGLE DOESN'T HAVE THAT COURSE AVAILABLE SO YOU'RE RIGHT I AM JUST A MOM POSTPONING THE AWFUL—

he might resent the puppy forever, but he will also have Lambie back with very soft patches of fur and lots of new surgical "cool" marks.

There's a chance, then, that Hutch can feel powerful once he gets original Lambie back, and can, maybe?, give new eBay Lambie to Hobie. He can show Hobie how war-torn Lambie was strong. just like Hutch himself. None of this will make sense to Hobie at his young age, but it might be a good big-brother moment for Hutch.

So, Ms. Linda, and Ms. eBay Gift-Giver, thank you. Because of you, I have hope.

Meantime, every night, Hutch looks for him. It's dreadful. Every night we're rubbing his back to sleep with dreamy promises that we'll find him in the morning. Not sure how many more mornings I can act too distracted to look . . .

COMMENTS:

John K. You could make up a story about how Lambie got out and had the most glorious and harrowing adventures, but because he was mauled by a rhinoceros in the Gobi Desert, he had to go to the hospital to get fixed up.

Mitzie M. Molly, this is our Lamby! She is twenty now and has traveled many places, on vacations, underwent five ear surgeries, dentist trips, and is now home for the summer, though otherwise lives with our senior at Liberty University. I kind of wanted to keep her here when my daughter went to school, but knew she needed her more than I did.

Kristy L. If Ms. Linda is able to do her magic, you could keep the brand-new Lambie to give to Hutch when he has kids. Put them side by side in a shadow box for safe-keeping after he grows out of Lambie.

Kim G. The all-caps made me laugh out loud.

Jerome P. If Ms. Linda does this, she's a magician.

Cynthia D. My granddaughter has had a Duffy Bear for thirteen years. He was left at Disney and had his face chewed off by the family dog. He was mailed back home by Mickey and patched together. She wouldn't even accept a new one bought off eBay because his style had been retired and he looked slightly different. He has been to every hospital stay, doctor's visit, and every sleepover.

Lambie Update 2.0

An hour ago, I wrote and posted a story about a principal who moved commencement up a week for one student, so he could graduate by his hospice bed. I quoted this principal as saying, "There are great people and stories of love always around."

After typing those words, I went to preschool pick-up. Miss Linda was waiting for me. She had finished sewing on the eyes of Lambie this morning at 1:30 a.m., and handed him back in a grocery bag. Lambie is back. He has added shades of blue on his face, but he is back and looks great. Now for the Hutch unveil . . .

Lambie's Back

He loves the brave scars and multi colors of new-old Lambie. Rubbed the soft blue texture on his new-old head, touched his battle wounds, and hugged him when I finally broke the bad news.

"Hutch: Remember when you once were in surgery?"

"Yes."

"It was years ago, but remember how you were brave?"

"Yes."

"So, a few days ago, you left Lambie out on the couch. Kure nibbled a little bit on him . . . Hutch don't look upset, it's okay . . .

Lambie had to go into surgery. The surgeon was a preschool teacher at Hobie's school, Ms. Linda. Look, Hutch! He's okay! Lambie is here for you. He's back!"

I pulled new-old Lambie from behind my back and Hutch grabbed him. Suffocated him in a hug.

A hundred pounds lifted off my shoulders.

Relief, relief, relief. Hutch instinctively reached for him, wanting a post-surgery Lambie in his arms. He willed the new eBay Lambie to Hobie and voila. We can do it all, if we lean on others.

COMMENTS:

Molly. The freaking culprit. Right there. Bottom right corner. Out on bond, I suppose. Staring at the recovered victim. Didn't even know this picture was taken and gasped when going through my phone. KURE: YOU STAY AWAY FROM NEW-OLD LAMBIE.

Sarah P. So happy Hutch wants his new-old Lambie and Hobie has his own Lambie to love, too, just like his big brother.

Sylvia E. Everyday miracles show in unexpected places.

Jax K. Think that's the biggest smile I've ever seen.

Sincerely Written

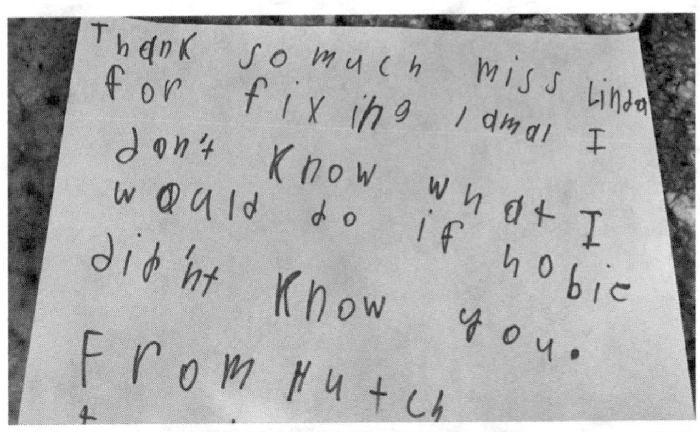
Thank so much miss Linda
for fixing lamal I
don't know what I
would do if hobie
didn't know you.
From Hutch

In the final chapter of our Lambie saga, Hutch's thank-you card to preschool teacher Miss Linda, that he wrote from his heart.

"I don't know what I would do if Hobie didn't know you."

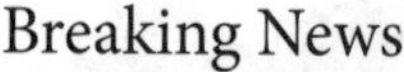

Breaking News

At least nineteen children and one teacher killed. Every hour more information emerges from Robb Elementary School in Uvalde. This small community is ninety minutes from San Antonio. The school has less than six hundred students in second, third, and fourth grades. Ages of those who died aren't clear. Tomorrow was supposed to be the school's awards ceremony. Thursday was supposed to be its last day.

They were just little kids.

The eighteen-year-old who law enforcement say acted alone shot his grandmother at her home (she's still alive), then walked into the school with at least one firearm (still not confirmed exactly how many weapons total) and killed the students and teacher. He was then killed as well. I could give you his name, but am not. I don't care. Whatever his name is and whatever proposed ideology or belief he had rattling around seems utterly unimportant. At least nineteen innocent people are dead.

None of us want to hear this, but tonight federal law enforcement officials told the Associated Press the death toll could rise. They spoke on condition of anonymity, not authorized to release investigative details.

This is the deadliest shooting at an American grade school since Sandy Hook in Newtown, Connecticut, where twenty children and six adults were killed.

Personally, I'm wondering if and how parents are talking about this tonight with their kids. I felt compelled to bring it up with Parker and Hutch at dinner, though I realize my job probably pushes me to address things not every parent chooses to discuss. But it's real. Guns are real. School shootings killing innocent people are real. In case it's brought up in school tomorrow, I wanted them to hear it from me first.

Parker's immediate reaction was anger. That struck me as interesting. Where I am breaking apart inside thinking of the parents and their loss, she is irate at the gunman.

"Why are there people who want to hurt other people?" she blurted, in her eleven-year-old unfiltered way. "It makes no sense! Why are they so stupid?"

Whatever you're feeling, let yourself feel it. This news is hard to process. See you at 11p.

MONTH NINETY-ONE: It's Too Much, Yet Again

Days after horrific facts emerged one after the other, we're still struggling: How do you explain evil?

Uvalde was a massacre of young bodies. Parents were asked to bring in DNA to help identify what was unidentifiable to the human eye. Mass shootings can happen anywhere at any time—as we are continually shown—and the carnage left in Texas earlier this week was grisly. Sanitizing that horror when talking to our kids makes sense, but we shouldn't sanitize it from ourselves. Pretending hard truths aren't hard only make them easier to forget.

We should not forget. We should not move on quickly.

Some parents chose to talk with their kids; others chose not to. I took the first route, pulling Parker and Hutch aside in separate moments, as I mentioned the night it happened. My goal was education and a tone of empathy, not fear. I never mentioned gory details. I didn't tell them how some surviving students are now talking about the sound of hearing their best friends' screams, or how those kids who made it walked through pools of blood, or how one child told a reporter he threw himself on top of other dead children to fool the shooter into thinking he, too, was dead. It worked.

Those things are true. These details make it even more important to face the truth.

But different ages need different things. With fifth-grader Parker, it was facts. I told her nineteen fourth graders in Texas were murdered in all their innocence after a school awards ceremony. Many took pictures with their parents who came for that ceremony before going back to class to finish one of the last days of the school year.

As I mentioned that night of the shooting, her reaction was rage. She had a lot of confusion over "the stupidity" of "stupid people" who "had guns" and "wanted to hurt others." My sadness and facts went into her ears, processed through her brain, and came out as anger.

I told Hutch far less. At seven years old and a child who feels the world around him, I told him that his dad and I love him and his brother and sister forever. I told him a person walked into a school filled with kids his age with a gun, and to always, always, always listen to teachers during lockdown drills, to know where to go, where to hide, and to know the plan if for some reason bad people come into his school. He hugged me, then asked to watch a cartoon.

I don't know if my words were right. It feels like I'm flying blind. Decades ago, we had fire drills and tornado warnings. I have no recollection of learning to hide from bullets.

You know what one local teacher told us today? She said she always keeps extra lollipops in her desk because that's what she'll give her class of young kids to suck on to keep their mouths closed and quiet, should a gunman come in.

Lollipops versus a mentally deranged, armed human.

Our US Constitution is a beautiful, brilliant document. But words written over two hundred years ago in a world wildly different from where we are now, by men in curly wigs with no concept of the twenty-first century or—imagine!—the internet, might need reassessing. Look no further than nineteen children and two teachers murdered in school.

Uvalde was ten days, mind you, after ten people were murdered in a New York supermarket.

Wait. As I write this, there's breaking news: The Texas Department of Public Safety just said in a national press conference that "mistakes were made." Authorities confirm nearly twenty officers were in a hallway outside of classrooms at Robb Elementary School for more than forty-five minutes before agents used a master key to open a door and confront the gunman. Apparently, the on-site commander believed the gunman was barricaded in a classroom and the children weren't at risk. There was no school resource officer on campus.

The officers waited more than forty-five minutes.

"It was not the right decision," Director Steven McCraw said. "It was the wrong decision."

All this while kids were calling 911 and asking for help from police.

Police were there. They heard the kids' calls.

They just weren't helping.

Hold on. Hold on. Please. I'll come back to typing.

ᴒᴒ

Stepped away from the computer. Needed a breath.

To those families in Texas, it is too much. Lean on those who love you. It is too much.

ᴒᴒ

There is something to be said for the public safety director copping to a complete failure of his department as opposed to standing at a podium and passing blame. But this new inexcusable information makes the whole situation even worse. What an added nightmare to know the adults tasked with safe-keeping didn't keep them safe.

These new facts, however, don't alter how we, as Americans, have also failed these kids. How we, as Americans, have been here before, yet we, as Americans, didn't force significant change.

Guns can serve a good purpose. I have friends—men and women—who own guns. I don't. But we talk about these things together, in calm ways. These law-abiding, gun-owning friends don't think high-powered assault rifles are necessary. They tell me having a weapon inside their home makes them feel more protected. For them a firearm, hidden from children, gives comfort. If that's how they feel, it's okay. That feeling of responsibility around a weapon is not the same as having assault rifles. The availability of ARs, many proud gun owners have said, is what's turning elementary schools, churches, and grocery stores into active battlefields.

The other part of this—the mental health side—is also real. There is no comprehensive way to check someone's mental health when they apply for gun permits. Ask current law enforcement, and they'll tell you that straight-up. Mental health and gun control are braided together, but their systems are separate.

Also, don't let anyone tell you mass shootings are *just* about mental health, *just* about gun laws, or *just* about a failure of law enforcement. Rhetoric and emotional talking points from all perspectives can too easily become political crutches. Especially on weeks like this, don't let yourself get convinced otherwise. It is always okay to step back and think about what you really think.

After the shooting Tuesday, I said I wasn't going to name the alleged shooter in my posts. For the record, I remain in that position. Whatever his name was, and whatever he thought doesn't matter. He killed kids.

So, now, back to that first question: How do we explain evil to our children?

I tried what I tried. I'd love to hear what, if anything, you said to your children. Post below if you feel comfortable. Finding age-appropriate words is hard. I doubted myself afterward.

There was something, though, that I told Parker that stuck with me these past few days. In response to her saying she didn't know why "stupid people had guns and wanted to hurt other people," I just said, "I know, honey. It's complicated."

I was wrong. It's not complicated.

It's actually quite simple.

Valuing the lives of people, learning from past atrocities, and putting compassion first isn't that hard at all.

ᴥ

The twenty first graders in Sandy Hook? They'd be wrapping up eleventh grade this week, preparing for senior year.

COMMENTS:

Talbert B. The world is changing, and not all for good. We used to have fire drills and tornado drills like you said. Maybe a bomb threat. We could've never dreamed the practices our kids now face.

Hoffman J. The things going through little minds and the ones calling 911 and no one rushing in to help them? The parents trying to get in to save their child? You're right. It's too much.

Erin R. I told my thirteen-year-old that it's important to recognize if anyone ever sends a picture of a weapon, that's not normal and to speak up. I also told him to always know where he'd go to hide.

Jennifer B. I stress to my son: hide, stay quiet, be small, and wait for Mama or your school resource officer at the school. I also stress to not to come out for anything or anyone no matter what lie they tell through a door. I've told him if something bad happens, I'm coming, baby. Just know I'm on the way even if I have to drive my car through the doors of the school. I told him I'm sorry that this is how things are, but my goal is to prepare him for the good and bad of life, because that's my job as his mom.

Sherry S. I'm a teacher. My daughter is fifteen. She is Asian. Her very first question to me after that detail was: Did they not help since it's a mostly Hispanic school? God, that question broke my heart even more. I told her I don't think so—the town is mostly Hispanic, as is the police chief. It is so hard at every age to discuss what you are currently processing yourself.

Annie E. I told my second grader. Recently he's been playing more pretend guns and I struggle with that, even if it's normal. He asked questions about why someone would do that, and asked if police "got the bad guy." We talked about lockdown drills. This morning he said he was still sad about the situation. I reassured him that was normal, and I'm still sad too. I don't know if that was alright, but I went there . . . and probably took some of his innocence with me.

Tim S. YOU are part of the problem, Molly. We know how to keep people safe. It's with security and more guns. YOU, and all media, are the problem.

Molly. I am reporting facts. You might not like those facts, but that doesn't make the person reporting the truth, "the problem." You are welcome to your opinion.

JUNE

Ring Bearer Alert

This morning, Hutch got an invitation to walk down the aisle to carry the wedding bands for former producer Maggie and her fiancé, Chris, this coming August. Hutch got to know Maggie once the news station relaxed COVID rules and outside family could again visit. Occasionally at night, if there's a childcare snafu or carpool-timing doesn't match perfectly, the kids have to come to my office for a small window of time—ten or twenty minutes—until Wes or a sitter can pick them up there. Hutch loves those nights. He loves coming into the newsroom. He really loves hanging around Maggie's desk and standing behind her chair. She always welcomes him with hugs and kind questions about his day.

Check the way she invited him to be part of her wedding: by giving him a security ID she made, to create "access" to walk down the aisle.

Mags, he put the temporary paper security badge in a toy safe where he stores his most valuable items. You made him feel like a million bucks.

COMMENTS:

Trayvonda C. Maggie couldn't have thought of anyone who will secure those rings like Hutch.

Avery D. What an awesome invite, Hutch!

Hurley P. Big responsibility, Hutch, only for the most trustworthy.

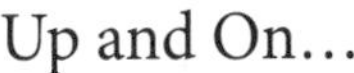

Up and On…

She's no longer in elementary school. Today her sass and free spirit moved up to middle. Her teachers said beautiful things about how this class left school in third grade for COVID and returned eighteen months later, in some ways like strangers. These kids are full of emotion, resilient as hell, and rolling with punches. Leaders of the way.

Love you more than anything, P. We are so proud.

ᴄɞᴓ

Because nothing is ever simple, Parker graduated at noon, and was in urgent care by 4:00 p.m. after shredding her toe on a door at a park. By 7:00 p.m., her big toenail had to be removed. She'll be fine, despite no swimming for a bit. Who writes this life skit? Do they not recognize there should be peaceful intermissions and calm pauses in between acts?

ᴄɞᴓ

Yesterday, Hobie wanted to steal the first-grade balloons from Hutch's awards ceremony. He kept disruptively yelling and pointing to the arch in the front of the gym. Hutch and I were both at a loss. Today in the same gym, he wanted to sit up front in Parker's lap, close to her as possible. She handled him. Deftly, and with grace.

I Was Trained in Full Sentences

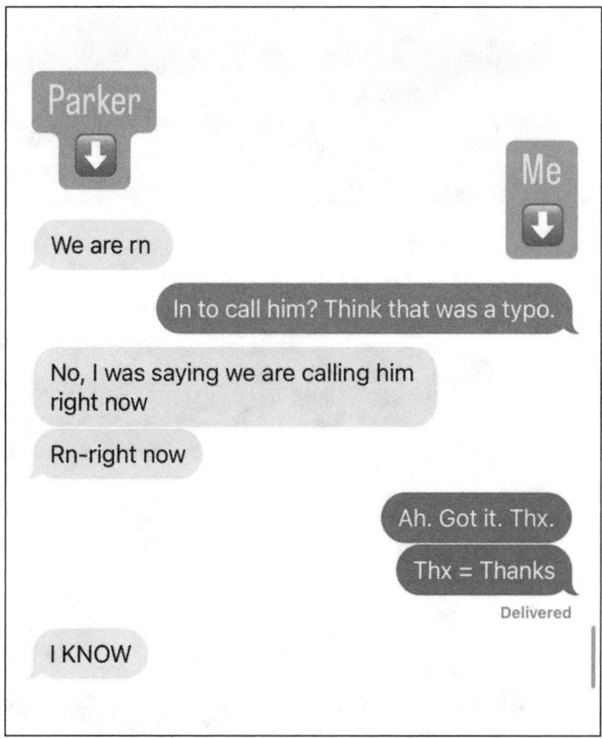

Maybe I'll start a new segment: Texts with a Preteen.

COMMENTS:

WBTV's Alex Giles (who sits across from me). "Maybe Parker having a phone will stop you from texting so formally."

Morgan F. God, Molly. You are so uncool it's cute.

Melissa W. I felt her eye roll in that text exchange

Annual Two Weeks Done

One favorite photo.

MONTH NINETY-TWO: Who, Me?

He's now stringing together short sentences. The talking is adorable because he has no idea how different from us he sounds. His current favorite word is "bulldozer." Multi-syllabic. Hard to sound out for new vocabularies, so when it falls out of Hobie's twenty-three-month-old mouth, it sounds like "Buh-DOH-zzza." He loves bulldozers as much as he loves dipping all foods in any sauce, and as much as he's starting to like balloons. The best is when you walk by a construction zone with him. Hobie will stare, addictively, as the machinery stills him. The *beep-beep-beeps* from large-wheeled contraptions backing over dirt piles quiets him better than any ceiling fan or mobile over his crib. He is my only child to adore construction equipment.

How lovely he isn't like Parker or Hutch. How beautiful Hobie is just being himself.

It's easy to compare kids, though not doing so seems important. The fact that Hobie already stands out on his own is remarkable. Part of me feels like the beginning of his life was so hectic with homeschooling and a world filled with pandemic concerns that I never focused on him in the way I did the other two when they were babies. Given he's already forming his own independent personality—a distinct one—keeps me from painting him with an already-used brush to raise him as an individual. As a writer, I am finding new descriptions for Hobie, because he does and says things the other two never did or said.

Yet, there is one certain familiar feeling that I felt with both kids before, like a carbon-copy parenting sensation: how much I look forward to The Nap.

The Nap is a set-in-stone two-to-three-hour part of a day that toddlers need, and that you, the caregiver, anxiously await. The

Nap gives you room to breathe. The Nap can be planned around. During The Nap, items on your at-home to-do list might get done. Phone calls might be made. Kitchens might get cleaned up. Your own two legs might, possibly, rest.

With Parker, The Nap ended the day she turned two. I had gotten used to her being safely asleep as I got ready for my afternoon/night shift at work, with no baby tugging on my skirt hem. Her transition from The Nap to No Nap was a nightmare. I battled inside my own self, feeling guilty over my anger that she wanted No Nap; I actively denied that it was now in her past. I'd fight to put her in the crib. I'd turn on the sound machine. I'd run out of the nursery and shut the door. Then, I'd listen to her scream. A few days in, she got smart. She stayed silent—sometimes quiet is scarier than crying—and then taught herself to catapult out of the crib like a diaper-wearing ninja. A baby monitor showed the whole thing. It would've been impressive had it not been so frustrating. Her determined mind decided The Nap was over, and, folks, that was it. Nonnegotiable. We were done.

When Hutch rolled around to his second birthday, he not only kept The Nap, he *loved* The Nap. He managed to keep The Nap through the ages of three, four, *and* into turning five. It got to the point where I'd spend half the time during The Nap wondering if he was even alive. Hutch contentedly and deeply slept, sometimes up to three hours a day.

For P and H, the release of The Nap fit who they are and have always been: Parker born six days early, fearful of missing out;

Hutch, born eight days late, happy to hang out where he was.

Where would Hobie fall? My heart had high hopes he'd be more like Hutch. *Please*, I've thought for months, *please let Parker be an anomaly and her own creature of habit. Most toddlers need sleep. Surely Hobie—who turns two in two weeks—will give The Nap another couple years?*

July 14 is his birthday. Surely, *surely*, he'd keep The Nap beyond then.

Instead, a devastating reality reared itself in June. Hobie would play all afternoon, unaware that he should be tired. The Nap to No Nap started at Kure, during our two-week family trip (at the beach! When the nap is needed for a parent more than ever!). We'd find Hobie cruising through days at a time, happily skipping The Nap. No tears. No worries. Just alert throughout the afternoon, laughing, laughing, laughing. No cranky crying. No bratty temper tantrums. All day awake, requiring adult attention. If we'd be at the pool, he'd put his toes right on the edge, jump in with his swimmies, whether I was in the pool to catch him or not, doggie paddle to the steps and walk himself back up to the deck to do it again. He spent hours of alert and awake time jumping, doggie paddling, climbing out, jumping again. Not even two years old, and not tired. The cycle never wore him down, showing Wes and me that afternoon sleep-time was no longer needed.

Worst part is he was as happy at 7:30 p.m. bedtime with The Nap, or No Nap. It wasn't like we bought time later. His body didn't care either way. There were times I wanted to temporarily stop being a mom and soak in sunshine and read alone. I'd dream of opening him up and magically speaking to his insides: *"Earth to Hobie: The Nap isn't actually for you. It's for me. You need sleep for my sake."*

I'd be ripped out of this dream state by a big splash. His toes had left the edge and those swimmies would be flying at me.

Since being back home, Hobie has hit The Nap a few days, but it's not regularly scheduled anymore. He is definitely not on Hutch's path. He, sadly, seems to even be beating his sister's record of when she shed The Nap for good.

I am disappointed. I selfishly want that time. Then I look at him. My happy little wild man. Can't stay mad at him for long.

At least I know where he gets it from. Little sleep, full days.

The apple doesn't fall too far from the tree.

COMMENTS:

Dora A. If only they understood at two years old what we know as adults: The Nap is the greatest thing ever.

Nina C. My baby shed The Nap early. His kindergarten teacher even mentioned it during our parent conference, how he wouldn't sleep at nap time. My little boy shrugged his shoulders and said, "I sleep at night, not during the day."

Suzanne K. My brother loved bulldozers at that age. I remember a long drive to Maryland where they were working on the interstate almost the entire trip. Best way to keep a two-year-old entertained for six to seven hours.

JULY

Costco

Emptying out a cart in a Costco, ignoring Hutch whining about wanting pizza, getting bumped by pushy people brushing by, bending down and up, down and up to get everything . . . *Where the heck is my Costco card? Where did I put it*? And in the mind-numbingness, I realize I'd taken Hobie out of the cart and put him on the conveyor as if he was an item to purchase.

Following in Footsteps

Cleaning out garage. Different dog, different son. But who else remembers?

COMMENTS:

Lindalynn R. He looks just like Hutch in the ice cream truck!

Cruz V. He's going to need an ID badge soon enough.

Robbin W. I remember you at the Panthers stadium that day. Hutch in the ice cream truck and your daughter on a hoverboard. #TheJuggleIsReal #DuringMonthFortyNine

Under Construction

A weekend met with approximately a hundred million pieces. Parker is getting a new preteen bed. But baby, it's done. I learned how to use electric tools, and finished the bed and headboard with cabinets. I don't run marathons, but this might be how marathon runners feel. Bring on the week.

COMMENTS:

Tony M. Been there, done that. It really is a sense of accomplishment to get through. There can be a gazillion screws and brackets.

Sandi A. I love my power tools.

Jenny A. My husband calls them adult Lego sets.

Hobie is Two

Exactly two years ago, the world gave our family the best gift. You make us complete, Hobie. Never lose your natural charm. Happy second birthday to our magnificent surprise.

Garth Concert

I don't know. I don't know. We had Garth Brooks tickets for tonight. Saturday. July. Hot. Southern humidity. We walked into the stadium—upper deck. Not good seats. Four of us walking together and a guy says, "I work for Garth. Do the four of you want row 1?" I swear. For no reason. He was legit. Had a walkie-talkie and fanny pack holding multi-colored wristbands. He said Garth never sells the first two rows so that he can instead give the seats out to random fans. Tonight, we were the random fans. Posting from front row now before show starts. Ready for whatever happens.

We Asked a Guy for Directions—He Pointed Us to the Front Row

Before July 16, I was no Garth Brooks superfan.

Country music wasn't big where I grew up in Pennsylvania. I'd never heard Garth sing until my college roommate played him on repeat in our small Chapel Hill dorm room. I learned his song lyrics through osmosis. In comparison, my husband Wes—from Kentucky—loved Garth as a kid.

When Wes got the tickets, he asked if I wanted to go, or should he find other friends?

"I'll go," I said. It'd be fun to see an artist touted as one of the greatest entertainers of all time.

On the Saturday evening of the concert, we walked up a large, mostly deserted concrete ramp inside Bank of America Stadium in search of section 252 with our friends Raile and Steve. Raile saw an official-looking guy with a walkie-talkie. Another group of women were walking away from the man; I remember thinking they seemed giddy.

Our husbands were with us but weren't interested in asking for directions. No surprise there. Raile and I approached the man anyway to ask if we were going the wrong way. He looked at our tickets and said we were. Then, he asked if we knew the legendary country superstar doesn't sell his front two rows. This guy explained how Garth gives those best seats away.

Instead of directing us the proper way to section 252, he then handed us wristbands and individual tickets with the words "Row 1."

We told him we were a group of four and waved the guys over. Wes didn't believe him. Looked at him when he offered and said, "This is a sham." So, the Garth guy, who emphatically declined to take a photo, opened his fanny pack to show colored wristbands and a stack of tickets wrapped with a rubber band. Wes, gratefully, shut up.

Moments later, the four of us skipped down the ramp with neon paper attached tightly to our wrists, Raile and I squealing like the eleven-year-old daughters we both have, and it hit us: the man cleverly avoided a photo so his face wouldn't get posted and future concertgoers wouldn't comb venues looking for him.

We arrived at our seats to find they were even better than unbelievable. With a 360-degree stage, we could've been front row, but in the back of the stage. Or front row, to the side of the stage. *Our seats were front row. Middle of row. Middle of front of stage.*

What is there to say about seeing a megastar performance on a sold-out stage in your home city from a vantage point so close, you can touch his shoes? Nothing. It's not about words.

We let go, didn't worry about how we looked, danced, sang, and stomped the night away.

In fact, Garth said as much himself in his Facebook Live to millions of followers the next day. As his producers were showing Charlotte concert photos, one popped onto the screen of the moment he leaned down toward me. He said, and I quote:

"Shhhhhheeeee was fantastic. She was so . . . lost in the music, having a great time, and finally at the last second, I didn't know what she was going to do with the pick, but she finally reached up to get the pick. It was a cool moment."

"Cool moment." Also known as: best live music memory for life.

The series of circumstances that fell into place for July 16 to play out the way they did could never be scripted, and will never be repeated. The evening is further proof that the best life moments are the ones you don't expect. We didn't know front row, middle of row, middle of front of stage was going to happen, so we had no time to envision how awesome that should look. We took the gift, and ran to live in the present.

Thank you, Garth. Thank you, Lady Luck, appearing in the form of a man with a walkie-talkie. Please let the debate forever be silenced: it's okay to stop and ask directions.

COMMENTS:

Katie Mc. When one of the best stories happens to one of the best storytellers.

Tina S. Bought the tickets two years ago as a graduation present for my son. After two rescheduled dates, COVID and disappointment, last night finally came. It was worth the wait. We laughed, we danced, we sang. My cheeks literally hurt from smiling so much. Thank you, Garth, for these memories with my son.

Misty F. I saw you walking through concourse last night and almost yelled, "Hey Molly!" out of thinking I know you from your writing, but also think it was before the ticket switch, because you were smiling, but calm. No way to stay calm when given front seat, front row!

Kaydee H. Saw the post about this first last night when you were there waiting for the show and couldn't believe THE LUCK.

An Exhausting Success

"Let her sleep for when she wakes, she will move mountains."

Haven't seen her for a month. I can't stop turning around to stare.

COMMENTS:

Beth M. Nothing sweeter than a sleeping child.

Julie P. She is beautiful. She'll be going to college next time you turn around to look.

Tammy K. Brown Bear survives, still. (I remember when he was lost in Walmart years ago.) #SmallVictories #DuringMonthEight

MONTH NINETY-THREE: Gone a Month

Growing up, sleepaway summer camp passed me by. I never went as a kid. Never even knew about it, really. My cluelessness can be due to (A) not having the opportunity, (B) it's more popular in the South, and I grew up in Pennsylvania, or (C) I was so happy life-guarding and being a pool rat, I wore blinders to other activities.

Camp is, however, a huge part of my kids' lives.

Parker has been going since the age of seven, starting even then with two full weeks overnight. Writing this now five years after that first year, I'm used to the process. (First-time camper parents: do not worry if you feel overwhelmed.) It is consuming. There are tedious packing checklists, online forms that start coming months beforehand, a long single-file line of cars on drop-off day . . . and then . . . the pulling away after they hop out. COVID stopped parents from setting up their bunks for them. That meant this year, I stared out the sideview mirror while trying to keep the car on the windy exit road. Her back skipped away with her head moving; she was already jabbering to her teenage counselors. A pillow stored under one arm and Brown Bear in hand. Even this summer, at age eleven, Brown Bear was there.

I came close to running off that narrow road. I couldn't grasp how one child could look both fifteen and five at the same time.

Driving away was easy *and* hard.

Why easy?

- I know she's cared for.
- I know she's thrilled with what's ahead.
- I know she'll have lots of chances to spread her wings and fly in a safe, protective bubble.

Why hard?

- I know she's cared for (but not by me).
- I know she's thrilled with what's ahead (that has nothing to do with me).
- I know she'll spread her wings (without me there to watch).

The only contact I knew we'd have would be from letter writing, unless you count how I stalked online camp photos, zooming in to see if I could identify her ponytail in the mix of hundreds of girls.

This summer, she requested to go for a month. It was a request that came out of nowhere, on a morning back in January. She mentioned it while grabbing her school backpack. Her saying it six months in advance indicated that camp might be once a year, but it had set up shop year-round in her mind.

All-girls camp, no "screens" allowed (e.g. cell phones, iPads, laptops), and big-time fun. Win-win-win. Wes and I decided on the spot that we'd figure out the how to make a month work.

Fast-forward to the end of June and we dropped Parker in the North Carolina mountains. Because of these COVID changes, we just gave her a big hug over the car seat, and I handed her a sealed letter I wrote filled with family photos. I gave verbal instructions to open it that night and sleep with us under her pillow. Then, a wave, an "I love you," and we headed back down that winding road with conflicting feelings washing my insides.

Wes and I didn't pick her up until last Friday. Four full weeks later. A full four weeks for her to grow without my eyes witnessing a thing.

Hutch, and more recently, Hobie, have watched the camp process. Younger siblings live life much by the paths their older siblings lay. I say that knowing each child is different. Though Hutch is seven this summer, the same age as Parker when she first tried overnight camp, he had zero interest. But he did want to try day camp. One week. Drop off morning, pick up at dinner. A co-ed camp closer to home.

After that first day, Hutch was smitten. He'd crash at night, whipped from the constant running, joy of being on the lake, and meeting new people. His personality of wanting to be in the midst of whatever is going on meshed well with his surroundings during his long days. Camp is designed for kids. He swam. He went boating and did swing drops into the water. He learned archery (like his sister) and got to walk into the canteen to pick out his own lunches from what he referred to as "the chow line." He loved every minute.

I had taken a massive risk, because without his approval or knowledge, I'd signed Hutch up for one week of overnight camp later in July. Despite his proclamations he didn't want to go away, history has shown that pushing Hutch is a good thing. I assumed once he experienced day camp, he'd be all in. He was. When I surprise-announced a planned week at overnight camp, he pumped his fists and said, "YES! The Banana Boat Bubble Blob again!" (It's a big raft trampoline on water; I don't really get it.)

So while Parker was still in the mountains, we did the same camp process for Hutch: tedious packing, single-file car-line drop-off, handing over a letter to put under his pillow, staring as he exited the car with a pillow and Lambie, then driving away, feeling even more conflicted knowing he's younger and more shy than his sister.

This past weekend, both were back home. Everyone was together again.

Parker, four weeks away. Hutch, a very large one.

Mostly, it's Parker who has grown. In ways you see and ways you can't. She's taller. More independent and well-spoken. She was wearing a new T-shirt on pick-up day. I didn't recognize the shoes on her feet—turns out she'd swapped footwear with a fellow camper. Going through her laundry, I saw other last names written on clothing tags in Sharpie. When I asked, she said casually, "Oh, some of my bunkmates and I traded clothes."

Bunkmates. A term and concept to which I was unfamiliar. I wanted to ask if "bunkmates" were like college dorm roommates, but caught myself. She is eleven, I reminded my mom mind. She doesn't yet know about dorms. Then, I wondered, is sharing clothes like having a sister? I don't know. I never had one. Neither has she.

There were other changes too. We went out for breakfast, and instead of ordering French toast or a sausage biscuit (her always and only go-tos), she ordered Greek vanilla yogurt with fruit, almonds, and sprinkled cinnamon sugar. And when we got home, she asked if I could teach her to do laundry.

What? Why, yes. I can. Thank you, camp.

In comparison, Hutch is still gloriously just Hutch. He ordered his same breakfast as always, was wearing the same outfit we dropped him off in, and had left his dirty clothes in his trunk the entire first day home. A seven-year-old boy does not think or worry about stinky T-shirts.

But he did have a blast. He told us lots of stories. Counselors also gave their impressions of him at pick-up, and online camp photos filled in more holes. Though there might have been some homesickness in the beginning, he has been talking about camp since. He said he wants to go back next year for two weeks.

Parker wants to return for a month, again.

I'm not sure I like this lesson of learning to let them grow. I want my kids to mature, but also want to know everything they think and do. That contradiction is especially evident when looking at Parker. I want her to be the most awesome version of herself that she can create and our family can realistically provide, but I also want her to miss me terribly and never let go of Brown Bear's hand.

Hutch still feels young and needy. In a few years, I'll look at him and feel the same pathetic need to want him to never leave me—or Lambie—behind. Maybe by the time Hobie rolls around to these stages, I'll be cooler. Maybe I won't stalk online camp photo albums looking for his curls, or count down the days until I see him again. Maybe by then, I'll be used to it all.

Something tells me that won't be the case.

COMMENTS:

Molly. His world was back.

Betty N. I'm a little speechless, actually. Reading this thinking how fortunate your children are to have guidance. Not necessarily all the items, but love surrounding them.

Debbie D. I never got to go to camp when I was younger, but am a counselor now at a church camp. I love it! No TVs or air conditioning; just ol' fashioned mountain air.

Rhonda C. When it's Hobie's time, you'll be worse. For some reason, we cling to the third and final. I talk to my baby boy almost daily, or at least text, and he's twenty.

Martha B. My kids are older than yours, but those feelings never change. The cause of emotions change, but concern never leaves.

Numbers Boy

He thinks he is winning tonight's Mega Millions billion-dollar jackpot lottery, and has been begging to stay up until 11:00 p.m. to see the numbers, the same way he begs on Christmas Eve to stay up to hear Santa's sleigh hit the roof. Of the five tickets sitting on our kitchen counter, he deliberated for an hour over the combinations trying to choose "the best one" as his own. He also decided one thing he'll buy for each person in the family when he takes the billion. At our dinner break, he announced our gifts. I'm apparently getting a nail salon (?).

My numbers boy. Wish him luck, and maybe some peace in what's sure to be a little late-night disappointment.

We will air the winning lotto numbers at 11:00 p.m. For the first time in maybe ever, I might have my seven-year-old watching.

AUGUST

Pedicures

Special pedicure appointment with my girl because I thought it'd be good mommy-daughter time . . . only Hobie is making sure it's not about us at all.

COMMENTS:

Shantella R. From the time you were doing news at home with Parker in the background during COVID to now, she has grown at least a foot.

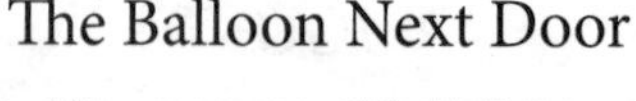

The Balloon Next Door

Tonight we met this smiling woman, Andraya. It's her birthday. She was celebrating at the casual restaurant at a table near where our family was seated for dinner.

Though Andraya was having fun with her friends, Hobie wouldn't leave her alone. Rather than eat his food, he spent our entire dinner walking to her table trying to touch her Happy Birthday balloons. He loves a balloon, now almost as much as he loves a bulldozer. He'd enter her space, stare, point, and goofily yell, "BALLOON!"

The entire patio was starting to notice. I tried. I promise. I'd pick him up and bring him back to our table and sit him in my lap and attempt to keep him still. He'd cry each time, screaming, "BALLLLOOOOOOON!" loudly, while wriggling out from under my arms. Trying to keep him away from Andraya became more of a scene than just letting him run back to this beautiful birthday girl, with multiple strings tied to her chair, attached to helium balloons.

She eventually gave Hobie this blue balloon. Parker helped tie it to his wrist and he walked around with dried tears, showing everyone who'd even half look his way, "BALLLOOOOON." Even in this one picture, he's clinging to it with a death grip.

Andraya: Understanding makes the world go round. It was nice to meet you and so sorry you had to sorta celebrate with a two-year-old. Happy, happy birthday.

Andraya's Balloon Stays Inflated

He slept with it in his room—tied to furniture far from the crib, but still visible—and hasn't let it go since waking up. He grasped it on the morning neighborhood walk and insisted on bringing it to Miss Tiffany's chair for the kids' back-to-school haircuts.

COMMENTS:

Evonne C. It really is the little things that make kids happy.

Patricia I. His expression. He's like, "Okay, I have my balloon, I'm being good. But when is this all over . . ."

Alice A. Crazy, isn't it, what children zero in on?

Andraya's Balloon, Still Going

Still going strong. Best toy ever. Death grip remains.

COMMENTS:

Joseena B. Oh, hope Andraya is seeing all this!

Synthia H. You need to have a spare in case it blows away.

Angel M. That's some good helium.

Ring Bearer on the Way

Special weekend ahead with my seven-year-old date. He's got ring bearer duties, and I can't wait to celebrate former producer Maggie. We're coming to get you, Mags. Our first trip to Indiana.

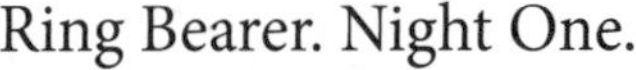

Ring Bearer. Night One.

Rehearsal dinner. Mutual pride.

COMMENTS:

Kathy B. He looks so handsome!

Bonnie W. Seersucker. The South hits Indiana.

Brenda W. He's a great age.

MONTH NINETY-FOUR: An Unplanned Gift

I knew that invite a few months ago from Maggie asking Hutch to be her ring bearer with the "ring security" paper badge was thoughtful. I didn't know how the weekend would turn into something more than expected.

While the whole family was invited to Maggie and Chris's wedding in Noblesville, Indiana, only Hutch had a special role. Imagine. Something for just Hutch. Something that didn't include his older sister, who by birth order and being the only girl ends up with attention, and didn't include his two-year-old brother, who, by being the baby and perpetually adorable, ends up with plenty of attention as well.

Just for Hutch.

Things got even more special when Parker's soccer schedule showed a tournament that weekend in Chapel Hill. Wes and I both couldn't be in two states at one time, so we divided to conquer. I went with Hutch, and he'd go with Parker. Hobie, as always, would roll along happily with one of us, but it was easier to throw him in a car than buy a plane ticket, so circumstance delivered to Hutch and me a whole weekend together.

I learned a great lesson these past two days. Taking a trip alone with one child—no spouse, friend, other family, or other kids—is a rewarding, memorable, and remarkable gift. We had a blast.

When you have multiple kids, it's easy to group them together as a unit. On a trip I pack for "the kids." I refer to them often as "the kids." If we get snacks at a gas station stop, "the kids" each get one. They'll make different choices, but "the kids" know they can only each have one item because, tit for tat. Everything is equal. If someone got two things, then all "the kids" would have to get two things.

It also becomes easy when referring to "the kids" to naturally assign each kid in the unit a specific role. Parker is my leader. I give her responsibilities. I trust Parker to take Hutch into a gas station bathroom and wait for him outside. I trust her to make sure she has "the kids" ready on time. I trust Parker to know our schedule. With the addition of Hobie in the mix, I lean on her even more. Wes and I are the parents, but she's the backup. She's the oldest, and now has a phone. She's my go-to.

What this weekend helped me to see, and what I didn't necessarily realize before and what isn't very pretty to admit, is how my leaning on Parker inversely impacts Hutch. He absorbs everything I say and sees *her* as my helper. I rarely ask him to be the responsible one or the leader. We build him up in other ways, but he doesn't usually get to be my sidekick.

This weekend, that changed. This weekend was only him. Him with me. I let him lead us to the airplane gate. I let him hold our boarding passes. I tasked him with looking for the rental car signs in the terminal. Driving away from Indianapolis, I gave him my phone in the back seat to follow the GPS. Hutch told me when to turn and what navigational directions were coming next. He helped check us in to the hotel. He got to wear a new suit we got just for him—not one new outfit each for all "the kids"—and when he wanted two snacks to keep in our room and couldn't decide on just one, I let him get both.

I gave him all my attention. We talked about the difference in gas prices, why you rehearse before a wedding, how to use your manners in a buffet line. He talked about his friends, and I got to ask more questions about his thoughts before he enters second grade. All of everything was about him. Me and him. Hutch and his mom.

And the wedding? Oh, Maggie outdid herself. As would be expected. Though she no longer works at WBTV, she is a producer at heart and a darn good one at that. She doesn't miss details. Her wedding was her finest piece of work. She was gorgeous, happy, and she and Chris couldn't stop smiling at each other.

Add the twinkling lights and music, and Hutch's already bolstered ego, and he was the happiest #TooMuchHutch I've ever witnessed. He happily dressed for Friday's rehearsal in a hand-me-down, slightly too big blazer and pink bowtie. He was giddy to wear his new suit on Saturday. He hugged Maggie a hundred times, and propped his hand in his pocket to take pictures with the groomsmen. By the end of the night on the dance floor, he was barefoot, belt-less, jacket carelessly thrown on a chair, and had drink stains all over his untucked shirt. The only thing still intact was his hair, which he'd proudly sprayed before the ceremony with lots of hairspray. As someone there said who'd never met him, "Your seven-year-old is a vibe."

My favorite part about Hutch, though, might be the note he wrote Maggie before the weekend began. He called her his "favorite person" and he "couldn't wait to be the ring bear." (He did write "ring bear," like an animal.)

How do I know Hutch felt all the same things about our time together? (A) He told me. (B) His actions showed me. There were two beds in our one hotel room. When we first arrived, he was overjoyed to have his own bed and not be with all "the kids" sharing one. But this morning, when we both woke up in our individual beds, he asked if I could crawl into his to cuddle. He knew the weekend was ending. Though he wanted freedom from Parker and Hobie, he didn't want full freedom from me.

The wedding was beautiful and the party really fun, but it was the lesson this weekend Maggie and Chris unintentionally taught that I'll carry forever: make time for significant one-on-ones with your children as individuals. Each parent. Each kid. I can't wait to do something like this with Parker, and then Hobie, and have Wes have individual weekends or nights with them too. I'm already brainstorming about what might be next. Give your child time to be a superstar. Your only superstar, even if temporarily.

Month Ninety-Four, a good one. And hallelujah: school starts tomorrow.

COMMENTS:

Maggie C . . . wait, a now married Maggie W. I loved every one of his hugs and notes. My favorite part—standing about to walk down the aisle. He turned and said, "I can't stop looking at you." He is my favorite little guy. I'm so glad both of you were with us.

SEPTEMBER

Hutch's White Folder

This one's for all the moms, dads, guardians, older siblings, grandparents, etc., who get handed a long list of specific school supplies before school starts. The list gets shorter as kids get older. Hutch is a second grader, and his list was extensive.

As one line item, he had to have nine different folders, all with a three-hole punch. The nine exact colors were listed. Before school began on the first day, we had eight, but I couldn't find a white folder. I tried multiple stores when they were stocked with back-to-school items. No one had white. Green, yellow, blue, black, orange, pink, red—you get the picture. I was not concerned, though, because I figured he has too much of everything else and, honestly . . . whatever. I tried. That, in my mind, counts.

Hutch came home on day two of school: "Mom, I need a white folder."

Mm-hmm. Okay.

He came home day three:

"Mom, I still need a white folder."

Fine. I took Hobie to three stores yesterday looking for just one white three-hole-punched folder for Hutch.

Nothing. None at Walmart, Target, or CVS.

Let me tell you, driving around town looking for one ninety-nine-cent item for your second grader in a specific color while toting around your two-year-old is not calming. Finding every other color in the rainbow but the one you need ramps up the frustration factor. At the last store, I saw this lilac version, and a light bulb turned on. I decided to do arts and crafts myself.

With apologies to his kind teacher, Hutch took in his homemade version today. She might be appalled. Hopefully she'll see the humor? Maybe use it as an example of resourcefulness, or thinking outside the box?

I'll keep looking, Mrs. B.

COMMENTS:

Michelle L. In our district we have to provide a statement on school supply lists that lets parents know buying supplies is optional. We have to keep lists under $20. I was overwhelmed to tears to see how generous my students' families were this year, especially with cost of living so high, and we are a Title I school. We teachers appreciate the efforts families make.

Lisa B. In all my years of being a teacher's assistant, I've never seen a white folder. Does anyone know where to find a white folder with three holes?

Donnie J. This is why Amazon succeeds. No one wants to run around anywhere looking for one item. Type it in, and it's there.

Kimberly S. My daughter needed a blue folder. I didn't have time to get one but had a green one and blue duct tape.

Carole A. Love this remedy. Do this for all of them.

Bob G. We also had an elusive item: seven college-ruled composition books with holes. Can we drill holes into the composition books? Because they do not exist.

Meredith P. I was in school when I read this. Passed it to all the teachers and all the second grade teachers then read it. We were laughing out loud! Bravo on the creativity. (FYI: we only asked for four different colored folders.)

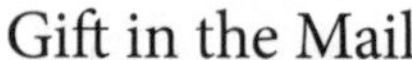

Gift in the Mail

A large Amazon delivery to the station today under my name. Imagine my surprise when the card is signed, "A mom who understands. Christine G." I already let Hutch's teacher know I'm donating all fifty to her class for anyone who might need one now or in the future.

I love us. As in, you guys.

COMMENTS:

Christine Garris. I sent them because the real-life struggles are ones we all face. You writing about them helps us.

Mark V. Maybe keep one or two at home just in case he loses his?

Lori C. Don't change out his original white folder though; I loved that idea.

New Balloon

Got it two days ago. Hasn't let go since.

COMMENTS:

Bobby H. Guys are simple people.

Still Going

Asked three dozen times during a weekend morning walk, “Is it his birthday?” Nope.

Day five and it remains semi-inflated.

COMMENTS:

Gloria H. It’s so adorable how he relates like it’s his real buddy.

And . . . Still Going

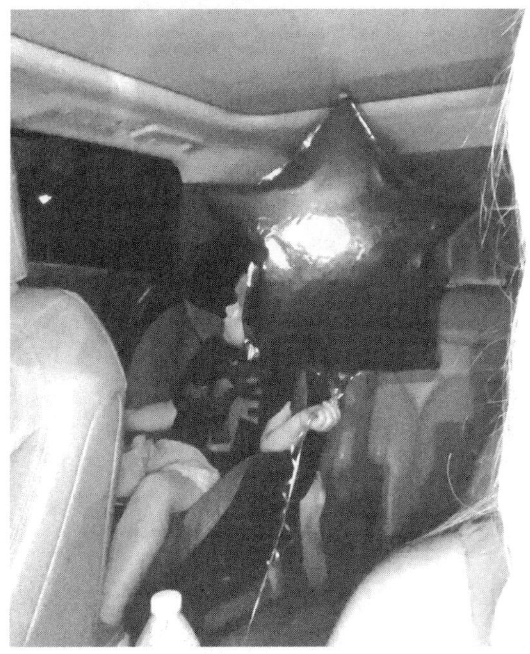

Dinner break. Green Balloon is like my fourth child.

COMMENTS:

Betty N. Oh, how I dread the day it deflates.

And, Yes . . . Still Going

In this morning's episode of "What is Actually Happening," while coordinating a million weekend cancellations, family evacuating from Florida because of the pending hurricane, planning to work now for big weather coverage, and figuring out the right words for a keynote tomorrow morning, Hobie and best friend Green Balloon drag Potty to the kitchen, pull down Pull-Up, and sit to practice.

The most remarkable $3 purchase in history. It's on day ten of life.

COMMENTS:

Bradford L. You live an interesting life. Or you just notice what's interesting in it.

MONTH NINETY-FIVE: The Little Things

We knew Green Balloon would die at some point. It happened this past weekend. Its helium expired on day eleven, and Mr. Balloon fell flat. Hobie dragged him through the house, still clipping him to his belt loop, and at one point, Kure pounced on it. At sixteen months old, she's still a puppy, and she ripped into Green Balloon because it was floor-level and she could. It was over. This girl has clearly learned nothing since doing the same to Lambie.

Happy Hobie's sad reaction to Green Balloon's demise surprised us all. We knew he was obsessed, but none of us dreamed he'd take it as if an actual friend had been gnarled in front of him. We all wrapped our arms around our littlest nugget as he wept. P and H, and Wes and I, promised him a million other balloons on the spot.

Which led our family to Harris Teeter's party section on Sunday.

The buffet of helium options had Hobie's eyes popping out of his head. To his two-year-old credit, he didn't think he needed them all—threw no temper tantrum when we repeatedly said, "Pick just one." He was focused. His neck bent back, he toddled around the balloon booth.

Hutch ran over with a large, inflated Panthers helmet, shoving it on Hobie, hoping he liked that one. The silver and black made majestic metallic reflections as late-morning sunshine streamed in the grocery's front sliding doors. "This one, Hobie? Pick this one!"

"No, Huh-chee." Hobie kept walking. (Sidenote: The way Hobie says Hutch's name is the second-best thing he utters after, "Chanch-you, Momma" to thank me.)

"NO, Hutch!" Parker came in hot. "Hobie doesn't want a helmet. He wants this one!" She pointed to a large soccer ball flying high. The black and white hexagons were super shiny. An attached red string was long and curled at the end, adding flair.

"No, Sissy," Hobie replied. He is used to them trying to "win" him. He didn't want them to make his gift of a balloon selection theirs.

Slowly, he walked, in as thoughtful of a pace as a two-year-old can make. Wes and I patiently watched. Truth be told, it was relaxing. All three kids entertained in one corralled spot for free, walking in circles, with no screens, and looking up? That's a pretty good Sunday.

There were scary Halloween witches, and some friendly-looking Caspers. Various sports equipment on circle balloons, numbers to mark birthdays, and every color in the rainbow. Some were already blown up, easy to touch. Others were in a book of added options that could be inflated. Large and small. Shiny and matte. Colorful strings. Lots of attempts at convincing by the older two. Glorious time for Wes and me to stand quietly. It felt easy, for a moment. I found myself wishing for a delicious Dunkin' coffee to wrap my hands around, as if this was a spa-like experience.

"Chatch one." Hobie pointed to—I'll just say it—a boring-looking straw man painted on a tan circle. It was small. Green around the rim with orange leaves woven in as decoration, made to represent the fall season. Not Thanksgiving-themed, as I saw pumpkins near the smiling straw man—wait, is that a straw woman?—but a country balloon obviously on display because the calendar had hit autumn.

"You want that one?" Parker sounded as confused as I felt. Here we were in the balloon heaven of Hobie's dreams, telling him to pick any one he wanted, and he chose the puniest-looking runt.

"Yesh."

Hobie nodded. He pointed up to it. The balloon had floated behind a big number four, which was next to an equally large zero, both beside a large "Happy Birthday" spelled out in neon letters. Tiny green-and-orange edging peeked out, now overshadowed by the larger, more impressive neighbors.

"Okay, Hobie," Hutch said quickly, wanting to, as always, come off like his little brother's hero. "I'll help you get that one." Hutch turned down the aisle to run toward the Harris Teeter worker.

Minutes later, we were in the car with Straw Person, its orange string tied to a yellow clip. Balloon clips are key. This, we've learned. Clips allow you to attach helium balloons to a child, a stroller, a toy basket, a preschool bag, car seat buckle, etc. Clips keep balloons nearby, even if a child loses their grasp and lets one fly.

From there, we drove. All of us—Wes, Parker, Hutch, Hobie, Straw Person, Kure, and I—headed ninety minutes away to a soccer game. Hobie was content the entire long and uncomfortable ride as his older siblings fought and Kure whined, wishing for more space. I pined more for that Dunkin' drink.

Once we arrived, it started raining. Hobie was the only one who didn't care. We were cold. Wet. Far from home. Yet, Hobie was a clapping, joyful spectator. He trotted back and forth as his sister played on a field below, walking Straw Person in the drizzle.

Check his grin in this photo. He was in a dirty diaper, in the rain, we were all hungry, and Hobie was running left to right on that sidewalk, thinking Straw Person was "chasing" him. Not a negative thought in his little head. Hobie made a miserable experience bearable. Nothing more contagious than a gleeful kid.

It's not about the biggest, the best, the shiniest, or the most visibly impressive. That's something two-year-olds inherently know—something not trained out of them yet by age and life. Two-year-olds don't keep up with others. They don't compare their worlds to what else might be beyond. They just want what they want because they like it. Because for some inexplicable reason a little thing speaks to them, and brings joy.

Toddlers like Hobie know that happiness is where you find it.

COMMENTS:

Molly. Close-up of Straw . . . Person. Your guess is as good as mine.

Joy B. I really enjoy that Hobie saw beauty where no else around him did. He checked his two-year-old heart and was certain of his own decision. Fabulous.

Taylor L. our children will cherish these stories someday.

Krista H. Maybe he thinks Straw Person looks like him?

OCTOBER

A Birthday List

Happy day to Hutch. For today's big day, he wanted a new backpack with extra zippers and pockets, a WBTV baseball hat, a blue ribbon to wear to school, and a Ouija board. There is a rhyme to his reason, even if the rest of us don't fully understand. Life is way more fun with your perspective, Hutchie, and we love you endlessly.

Will It Ever End?

Update on this unexpected saga:

Straw Person is still inflated and alive. Remarkably. Add to that, a few days ago Hobie's friend, Mr. John, got Straw Person some friends. Another Green Star (like the first one that died), and Soccer Ball. Hobie now walks through the house with all three clipped to his pants. They also ride in the car and play outside, like his own personal gang of helium that follows him around. An admitted hassle in moments to work around those long strings, but him? His face. His entire being. One glance makes everything worthwhile.

Hot Air Balloon Festival

Seventy-five thousand people on a picture-perfect fall day in one of the nation's largest hot air balloon festivals with the nation's biggest toddler fan. He lost his little two-year-old mind.

BEST
KID
BEST
KID
BEST
KID

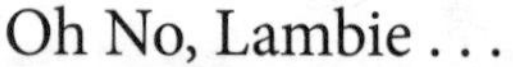

Oh No, Lambie . . .

Here we are. Again. Hutch's most beloved item in life is also, sadly, Kure's. Our whole family knows to keep Lambie protected from her. We remember reviving Lambie months ago, which is why Hutch sleeps with Lambie close to his chest and takes great care of Lambie's already-repaired self. Hutch will leave everything else lying around the house and at eight years old can't pick up his things even if I ask eight times, but he is conscientious of keeping Lambie safe.

Two nights ago, though, Hutch moved in his sleep. Wouldn't have mattered, except that this particular shift pushed Lambie to the floor. When Hutch awoke he looked over the side of his bed, saw stuffing everywhere, and a massive puppy-torn hole in Lambie's head.

I don't know how Kure knew to sneak into Hutch's room before the sun even rose, sniff out Lambie, and chew him. I just know that Kure has a sixth sense about this one stuffed animal. Hutch came downstairs screaming, holding pieces of Lambie together while running into my room.

I sent a text to Ms. Linda, our previous savior. She replied quickly that she'd recently hurt her wrist and can't sew for a bit.

Think, Molly. Think. Think. Think. Think critically.

As Hutch sobbed beside me, screaming, "He's broken forever!" it felt like an actual crisis.

A new name appeared on my brain: Susan Hancock.

Susan is our newsroom momma and everyone's favorite. She cares for all employees, orders food, helps set schedules, and is the person you want to go to for anything, at any time, whenever you might need help, no matter what help you need. She's also amazing with crafts, knitting, and sewing.

I brought multiple pieces of Lambie into work yesterday in a plastic grocery bag and walked straight to Susan's desk before hitting my own. Handed the bag over. She didn't say anything, just opened the gray plastic. We stood there looking at the white stuffing, the string from one black animal eye dangling from a blue piece of decapitated head. There was an odor to the bag opening, like wet dog, or pee. Did Kure pee on Lambie? It might have been the smell came from the fact that I hadn't washed Lambie in months. Didn't matter, honestly, as the odor wasn't the main concern. Susan looked up at my eyes that were asking for her help. She understood, and said aloud to my silence, "I'll try."

No doubt, because this is Susan, something better than nothing will be accomplished.

Hutch is aware that Lambie is currently at "Susan's Hospital" undergoing his second surgery.

There is no end to this story yet, however, I have high hopes.

COMMENTS:

Susan Hancock. Patient Lambie was presented to me with severe head trauma and some shoulder lacerations due to canine mangling. His surgeries went well and he's recovering nicely with bed rest, hydrotherapy, and time spent outdoors. Hospital discharge date is Tuesday.

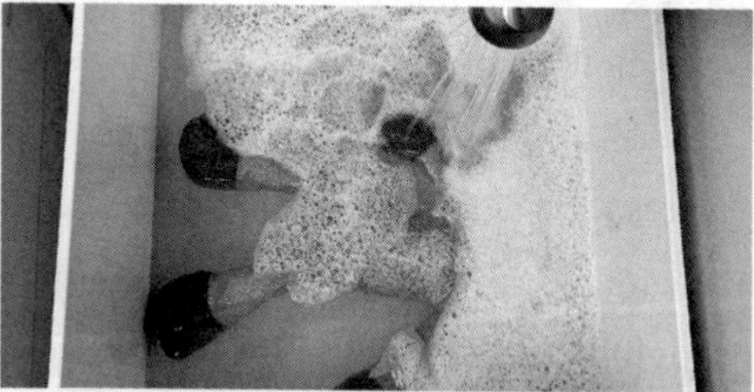

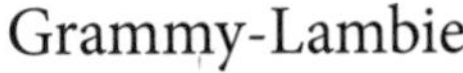

Grammy-Lambie

Tuesday. Lambie was waiting on my desk, with treats and a new hand-knit scarf Susan made with soft, beautiful yarn, *from my mom*. My mom used to knit, and when she died, I didn't know what to do with her skeins of yarn, so I gifted them to Susan. She was the only other person in this world I knew who knit.

Susie used my Mom's yarn to make Lambie a piece of Grammy to wear around his neck to cover his sutures. He got some hair from Grammy, too.

Susan is an angel.

I can't wait to show Hutch.

Showed Him

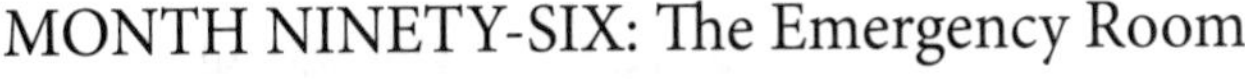

MONTH NINETY-SIX: The Emergency Room

Wes and I spent last night in the ER with Hobie. This picture is twenty-four hours later.

While at the pediatric ER, we got an inside view of our overwhelmed healthcare system. It was a tough look. There aren't enough hospital beds. People have to wait a long time for care. Healthcare workers are slammed with RSV and respiratory illnesses as they're taking over ICUs and ERs across the country. We've been reporting these things, but seeing it personally is more telling.

Doctors say one reason why it's the worst RSV season in thirty years is because our kids were cooped up for two years from COVID, and they didn't have time to build strong immune systems.

Some school systems are going virtual because so many students are calling out. Daycares are sending out warnings. Signs are up around doctors' offices begging you to have your kids wash their hands with soap and water.

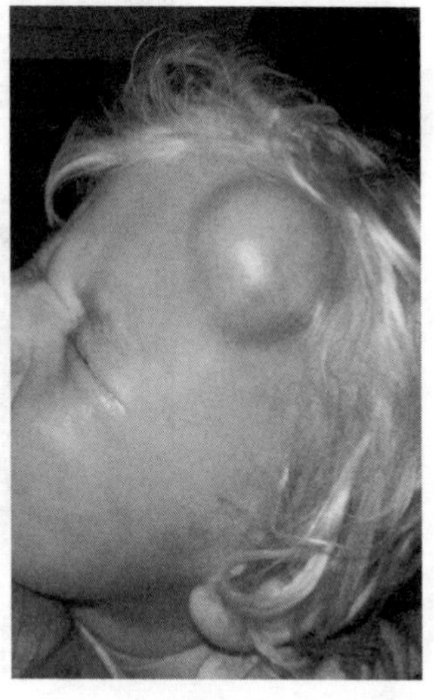

But, Hobie. Why were we there?

He fell off his new toddler bed this past Tuesday while I was at work, in the middle of the 5:00 p.m. news. The original picture his sitter, Meredith, texted was wildly scary. I didn't post it then on Facebook because I didn't want to have people scroll quickly, not actually reading how "he's okay," and sharing the image in a sensational way. I am putting it in this book so you can see the reality.

When I first saw that awful photo of a swollen hockey-puck sized lump on his left temple light up my phone, I feared head trauma. I called Meredith during a commercial break and heard Hobie's hysterical screams. Moments later the 5:00 p.m. newscast wrapped. I walked off set, into my boss's office, and showed her the photo.

She instantly—supportively—said, "Go."

I packed up, went home, and held him. Took only an instant to know he was groggy and lethargic. He'd hold his head up then lay it on my shoulder. I decided to go to the ER. You don't mess with head injuries.

If you've been to the ER before with kids, you know the high level of patience needed. But I was also trying to get there quickly and grabbed a bag with diapers and snacks and let him bring along his two comforting helium balloons. (Straw Person is now done.) We checked into the ER right after 6:00 p.m., got into triage fast for nurses to check his vitals, and then were sent back to the waiting room.

There was not a chair, not one open chair, on which to sit. The packed waiting area had infants wrapped in blankets with their moms standing up rocking them, back and forth, back and forth. There were kids screaming. Exhausted parents with heads in hands. Some children, napping on adult shoulders, looked pained and cold. One little boy was yelling because he was hungry and had apparently been there since 1:00 p.m. and his dad had no food. Another child's mom had tied a trash bag behind his neck, so it stuck out like a trough beneath his chin. *Smart move*, I remember thinking. If her son puked, it'd hit the bag and she wouldn't be running him to a restroom.

Every adult was masked, but every child was coughing. Kids with masks had noses exposed. Hobie's age and younger weren't wearing them at all.

We were there for a major head bump. Another teen in a wheelchair looked like had a sprained knee. Every single other patient was showing virus-like symptoms. I started counting. A total of fifty-nine people in that waiting room. Not fifty-nine patients—kids would have an adult or two with them—but fifty-nine people.

The nurse told us, and I quote, "We only have one doctor here."

Fifty-nine people. One doctor.

Too many sick people, not enough beds, not enough staff. A random Tuesday night. Another nurse later told me it didn't matter the day of week; every single day in the past three to four weeks had been like this, with no relief, ever.

As worried as I was for Hobie, as much as I hated that he'd hit his head hard, other children around us looked like they deserved attention first and fast. As time went on, Hobie's swelling was going down, his appetite going up, and he started to be more like himself. Other children around us were so ill they couldn't move. My heart broke for their parents. They were scared and desperate to be told anything. Some said they'd been waiting eight hours.

The receptionists as front-line greeters were doing what they could. They'd smile and receive questions, answering if able, but couldn't give either timelines or advice, presumably for legal reasons. Their non-committal answers enraged some of the frightened adults, sitting for hours with their feverish children in a state of high stress. Moms and dads would get in front of the receptionists, separated by plexiglass, and flail their arms. Some would beg. I saw a mom breakdown. The whole waiting room heard a dad screaming for attention. I understood his aggravation, though both sides of the frustration seemed fair. The receptionists couldn't create beds, but no parent expected such a long wait. They'd come to the emergency room because they needed help.

Notably, lots of security guards were also milling around, standing protectively behind the healthcare staff.

The patient, professional workers were doing the best they could, but we're talking sick kids and hours of wait.

After a solid four hours for us, Hobie had visibly improved

enough for me to feel okay about the future. He was running around the waiting room. I'd also gotten a hold of Hobie's pediatrician on the phone. She advised us to just go home. Said it would most likely be a long time before we got back into the ER, scans might not be necessary, and if it made me feel better, she'd see him in the doctor's office in the morning.

We left.

Since then I've researched more. There are currently more RSV cases than flu cases in North Carolina—in some cases, doctors say kids are getting both. They're recommending you don't stop living your lives, just be aware. Get up to date on vaccines and boosters, flu shots, wash hands with soap and water, try not to touch your face as much (hard for kids), and with Halloween approaching, be aware of the many hands that go in one candy bowl.

As for Hobie, the next morning, his pediatrician saw him. She said the big bruise might drop with gravity and end up around his eye—just in time for Halloween.

COMMENTS:

Carrie W. We're seeing post-COVID effects. So many healthcare workers left the field and industry.

Emily Mc. Thank you for sharing struggles of those in healthcare who have been in the trenches for years now. They are—we are—weary.

Follow The Yellow Brick Road

“There’s no place like home,” said the Lion who refused his mane, the Tin Man who thought he was missing a brain *and* heart, the dog who ate her Flying Monkey costume, the Scarecrow who was over his Witch-y wife’s creative ideas, and Dorothy, the only one who understood the Halloween assignment.

NOVEMBER

Taller

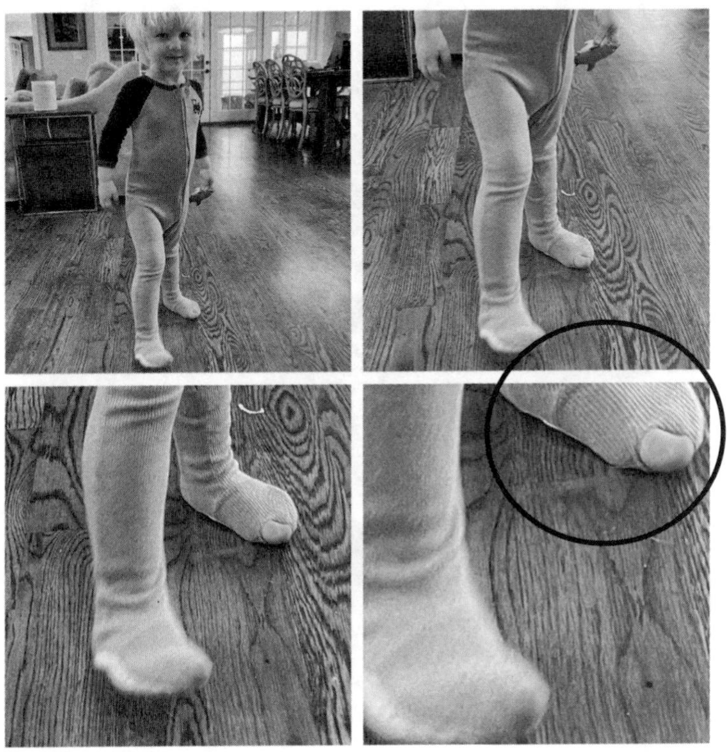

Tell me you had an overnight growth spurt without saying a word.

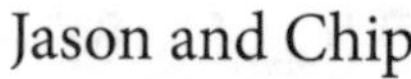

Jason and Chip

We're thirty-six hours past the worst and most personal breaking news story I've ever covered.

Faith and family are all I've been thinking about since just after noon on Tuesday when we first got word our news helicopter, Sky3, had gone down, killing meteorologist Jason Myers and pilot Chip Tayag.

I can't stop thinking about their wives: Jillian Myers and Kerry Tayag. Our newsroom is devastated, trying to pick each next right step. I'm worried for our team, but it's Kerry and Jillian in the forefront of my mind. Please send your good thoughts to them. They deserve help and comfort.

Jillian and Jason have four children. Ages thirteen to nineteen. Jason talked about his beautiful wife and four kids all the time at work. He publicly posted pictures and shared soccer sideline stories. He loved weekend family activities. As a friend, I can tell you from standing near him every day—he was in the weather center and I was behind the news desk in the studio—Jason lived the title "Family Man." All coworkers knew about his faith and family. Faith and family. Faith and family. Faith and family.

Faith and family. Jillian and Jason. Kerry and Chip.

People first. Heart wins. Words matter. It's very real, and final. Thank goodness for coanchor Jamie Boll and our partnership. In some ways, talking live for seven hours straight, commercial-free, helped us get through. Our office is filled with incredible people, and Jamie and I have worked together a long time. We leaned on each other to stay calm and helped each other to find the next right word. He'd talk, then I'd talk. I'd talk, then he'd talk. Staying professional, real, and loving was how we could honor Jason and Chip, but also help every producer, editor, reporter, manager, jour-

nalist, intern, staff member, coworker, and friend in that newsroom watching—and feeling.

Thank all of you who were watching for giving us grace and having patience as we waited to make sure notification had been given to Chip's and Jason's families before announcing their names on the news.

As WBTV figures out how best to move forward and help, we'll share what we know. Much of our newsroom is here today, the day before Thanksgiving, trying to bring you dignified newscasts tonight that honor and respect our friends.

Faith and family.

Wes and I feel lucky to have spent this past Saturday night with Jason and Jillian. We were all at a March of Dimes fundraising event representing the TV station. I'll remember those conversations and the big hugs we exchanged forever. I'd posted this group picture after the event on Sunday, but seeing Jason with his arm around Jillian now has hugely different meaning.

My God. You never know.

COMMENTS:

Pamela P. We are not promised tomorrow. Yesterday as I watched all hours straight, I felt as though I'd lost two of my brothers. You come into our home every day and become family members through the television.

Kelly F. I want to step into that newsroom and hug you all.

Alan H. I watched yesterday. Our whole family did. My wife and I knew you guys knew who was on board, and knew you were talking about your friends, but couldn't release the names.

Billie F. We could see your hearts breaking while watching, and that any minute any of you—you and Jamie or reporters—wanted to break down. But you held it together and delivered the professionalism in a time I'm not even sure professionalism was expected.

Courtney N. I'm amazed that was the sole focus of the seven hours. Never even a commercial. No other news. You took time to show respect to your colleagues because that is truly all that mattered. The Journalism School grad in me watched in admiration.

Vickie F. Thank you for sharing the wives' names.

Waters W. It's hard to watch you guys have to hold in your emotions, but then I think of Jillian and Kerry and know nothing we're seeing from your team comes close to how they're feeling.

Jennifer R. I woke up thinking of their wives this morning. Just twenty-four hours before then, they were full of assurance they'd see each other later. Later is never guaranteed.

MONTH NINETY-SEVEN: Two Weeks and One Day

Photo credit: Samuel Martin, @SPMartin on Instagram

Clinging to each other, Kerry Tayag and Jillian Myers looked into the camera lens and said it all without saying a word.

This picture was taken at Jason Myers's visitation, three days after the helicopter went down. Jillian tells me that Kerry was the first person in line. She'd come early and stood tall. Prepared, clearly, to meet—and honor—the only person in the entire world who might have had an inkling of what she felt herself.

The two women had never met before.

Good photographers capture the eyes. Your eyes give everything away, even if you're trying to make your mouth lines express something opposite. Look at these two attempting to smile, while their eyes show a rawness, the sole exit off a one-lane expressway transporting feelings up from their hearts.

Two weeks and one day ago, meteorologist Jason Myers and pilot Chip Tayag went down in a Sky3 crash that numbed our newsroom and, more importantly, shattered these two women's lives. Chip and Kerry had been married since 2019. She said, in a statement days after the wreck, he was the love of her life. Jillian had a similar statement. She said Jason was her one true love. They'd met as children, been friends their whole lives, and she'd had a crush on him growing up. They finally started dating in college. Fell in love. Got married. Built a life together. They now have four beautiful children, all teenagers.

The helicopter went down five minutes after it took off from our station hangar helipad the Tuesday before Thanksgiving. Clear day, good weather, right after noon. A full investigation by the NTSB and FAA will take at least a year. At this point, all I unequivocally know is, (A) It hurts to lose two friends and coworkers in a split second, and, (B) I've been in awe of these two women in the two weeks since.

Right after the wreck, many of you posted/texted/messaged/called/said/wrote, "You never know what will happen." You're right. We don't. But two weeks later, a new thought has crept in. This new thought shifted my mental focus from what someone can't control—"you just never know"—to what someone *can* control.

As in, your reactions

Then I thought, How would you react?

Jillian and Kerry had zero preparation. No practice for the unfathomable. They didn't train to plan services, or how to figure out sleeping alone. They didn't know when they said goodbye to Jason and Chip on that day, that was it. Yet, they're holding themselves up in the course of this horror and showing the rest of us who are hurting how to put one foot in front of the other and move forward.

"How would you react?"

I ask myself this every day.

Would I be as composed as Kerry, able to stand across from the casket of, as she called her husband, my "one true love," and hug each and every person who showed up at the visitation, many of whom she had never met and had to introduce herself to? I waited in that line and studied Kerry. I listened to the murmured conversation and watched how she held onto people's hands even after the hug had broken. As the line slowly moved ahead, I heard Kerry's conversations. She shared multiple sentences with mourners. When it was my turn, she wrapped me in her arms. I asked how she was holding up. She said, "Up and down," then graciously asked, "How is the WBTV staff holding up?"

What? She was concerned about us?

I remember thinking she didn't sound disconnected from reality, rather, she sounded *so* connected that it threw me. How could this woman be wondering about others, despite the reality?

And Jillian, oh, the exceptional Jillian. We'd happened to meet the weekend before the accident for the first time. Fate sometimes puts things in place before humans realize why. Jillian and Jason had talked about their four kids and their futures, and they and Wes and myself had enjoyed a kid-free date night for a good cause.

Looking back on that evening, the thing I'll forever remember is seeing Jason's love for his wife. They laughed across the table in their own conversation. He had his hand on her arm; they were a couple with history. Their body language spoke with eloquence.

Could I, if crisis struck, be like Jillian? Could I quickly set up a public funeral and visitation to bury a spouse after a surprise death? Could I then stand at his funeral, dignified and serene, and lead every person there and watching online through a moving, positive eulogy I'd written myself? Could I encourage my kids to write their own words about their dad, and stand beside them as a beacon?

Jillian and I had coffee yesterday morning. She told me she never even read what her oldest son wrote before he said it that day. She had full trust that whatever words he chose to eulogize his father would be right.

Could I be that open to receiving whatever came next, with that little control, but also lead by purposeful example? Could I—while living in deep grief—show the watching world how to walk through forever-pain with acceptance?

Could you?

೧೩೭೦

The grace and goodness of Kerry. The rock-like sweetness of Jillian. It is these two women who will be most impacted by the events of the Tuesday before Thanksgiving in every day going forward, and also these two women who deserve all our credit, our thoughts, our respect.

They are teachers. Watching them these couple weeks has been a masterclass on the authentic strength a woman can exude. We are seeing how to react to personal crisis with fortitude, sensitivity, and love.

Kerry and Jillian: This picture shows your soft grit and brave vulnerability. You're leading us; we're watching you by the thousands. It's okay to not be okay, while also being two bright, phenomenal lights, trying to figure it out.

COMMENTS:

Carol A. These words.

Katie S. Wow, wow, wow. These two women. This descriptive post is everything.

Hycindia L. Women leading women. Women leading us. Powerful words about two powerful, soft, broken, strong women. Thank you.

Cheryl K. Hope Jillian and Kerry take comfort in knowing how many of us want to help lift them up. Will be watching from afar.

Garret A. This is truly a poignant image.

DECEMBER

The Instinct of Children

He insists on big love whenever I head to work. It can be *pretty* hard sometimes to leave. He's just being himself. He has no idea how much kid love can help a human heal.

Truth

Newest favorite compliment: “You look just like Molly Grantham, if she didn’t brush her hair.”

Happy real-life weekend.

Stunned Excitement

Walked into preschool to a balloon arch. He couldn't even talk.

Christmas Eve

A record-breaking cold snap in the Carolinas over Christmas week. Our pipes froze last night when the heat broke downstairs. Wes and I are relieved cold water is now dripping, and the pipes never burst, but there will be no showers or baths. Add that to the older two kids fighting all day, Hobie's runny nose not going away, and how Amazon forgot to send a much-needed power cord to a Santa project tonight, and this Christmas Eve is becoming proof sometimes things you want a certain way just aren't.

My heart goes out to the many stranded around the country

with this record-breaking weather. Mother Nature majorly messed with many of us this year.

It's a nice time to dig deep and choose to find magic in the mess, something Hutch always does. In a card he left Santa beside two cookies and many carrots, he wrote, "Merry Christmas, Santa have a holly jolly Christmas. Tell Rudolph we said hi." Full belief. We're dirty and cranky, and yet, Hutch has huge eight-year-old assurance that the season will deliver.

Two chocolate chip cookies—one for Santa, and one to take to Mrs. Claus. Why so many carrots?

"Because there are eight reindeer plus Rudolph, Mom," he said. "They'll all get hungry. I want to make sure they have energy."

The sparkle of the season might be extra hidden, but if you look hard enough, it's always there.

Merry Christmas Eve.

COMMENTS:

Deb G. My Christmas Eve didn't go so well either, but I'm grateful for gas logs. We missed water and food and loved ones, but looking for the good.

Reed A. I feel you. Our pipes froze and are still frozen. No plumbers available. We're hoping for a Christmas miracle tomorrow.

Jerry G. I didn't sleep much as I was up and down running water through my pipes and running a space heater.

Gail B. The joy of Christmas from a child's perspective. Says it all.

Christmas Eve Again

I wrote that previous, positive post before remembering this Hobie project. It's now 10:45 p.m. and we're opening the box to a plastic bulldozer that he can ride.

Any guesses on how long it'll take to finish? 12:30 a.m.? 1:00 a.m.? Over? Under?

Also, I never went to pick up a bunch of helium balloons today for Santa to bring because of the house disaster. Moving ahead and reminding myself of words I wrote a mere ninety minutes ago: "There is magic in the mess."

Merry Eve a second time.

COMMENTS:

Molly.
2:24 a.m.
Proud.

Paige H. Just put my son's together as well!

Sameena O. If you happen to leave the directions out, just say, "Do you know what that means? Santa sat right here in our house and put it together while we were sleeping! Trust me. It works.

Samantha S. Two of four members of my household have COVID (yes it's still a thing!). We are quarantined separately. We were out of power for seven hours. I literally threw all the presents into one bag for each kid, unwrapped, and no stockings this year. It's also the first year in my forty-nine years there wasn't my grandmother's pound cake. Just is what it is.

Lindsey H. Doing the same construction build with a Jeep. It is so cold in the mountains where I live, I may have gotten frostbite carrying things inside from the detached garage.

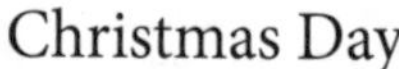

Christmas Day

Worth every late-night minute.

Mermaid in the Mountains

Arizona sunsets.

#MoreToCome.

Confidence

"Mom, I'm a professional rock climber." —Hutch.
#MoreToCome

Baby on the Back

Climbing toward clouds, carrying a two-year-old.

#MoreToCome

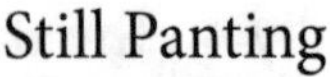

Still Panting

CLT. 1:00 a.m. We made it. We're whipped, but we're home.

If you happened to be in Dallas-Fort Worth tonight and saw an eleven-year-old girl and her father sprinting—SPRINTING—through a terminal like some Hollywood movie, they were trying to get to the night's final plane to Charlotte. As our flight into Dallas was landing late, Wes and I had made the strategic decision to send Parker and him ahead to hopefully convince a gate agent to hold the plane for all of us. I'd run behind with Hobie, Hutch, and all our carry-ons.

I moved as fast as you can while carrying a child, two bags, and Hobie's little Cars roller suitcase. Hutch was trying so hard to help, and Hobie was screaming that he wanted to walk, trying to wiggle out of my arms. We were a disaster. People were staring and parting for us in the terminal. I noticed the looks and didn't care. Nothing mattered except making that flight, thereby avoiding having to sleep on an airport floor overnight.

The boys and I finally got on the Skylink monorail to get to the other terminal. I saw Parker's many texts: "Mom, pls hurry Mom you have to get here Mom Mom Mom two min it'll close." There were five missed calls from Wes. I texted him we were on the Skylink.

Two minutes later, we got off the Skylink and I saw Wes at the bottom of the escalator. He'd run back to meet us there. I threw Hobie at him. My eyes said wordlessly what we both knew: *Just get who you can on that plane.* He and Hobie took off. I told Hutch to run as fast as he could. He got ahead of me because of bags dragging me down and I heard myself yelling, "Keep going Hutch! Gate C20! Just get to C20!"

I had this thought beating through my brain: *At least Wes, Parker, and Hobie will get home. Maybe even Hutch. I have all the diapers in my carry-on, but the baby won't be sleeping in this airport.*

I don't know why I thought about logistics and packing in that moment of crisis, but I did. It was a very clear thought. Mom minds work in peculiar ways.

Gate C20 was the farthest from the Skylink. I was so tired I almost walked, but didn't. I could see Parker far away looking for me. Wes and Hobie were arriving. The back of Hutch's green fleece was almost there. Parker's voice suddenly yelled, "MOM, THIS DUDE SAYS CLOSING IN FIFTEEN SECONDS!"

I made it. The gate agent—Parker's "dude"—scanned in my pass and I wanted to collapse. A few minutes later, with all of us seated on the plane, I still couldn't catch my breath. I started taking a video to remember how stressed and thankful I felt in that exact moment, but couldn't even talk. Hutch, beside me, took over in the commentary. I'll never delete it. All the feels and fears are heard in my deep exhales.

I'm writing this all now to decompress before falling asleep. We're all at home. What a travel day.

What a full two weeks.

Safe and grateful.

#MoreToCome on why we were traveling in the first place.

COMMENTS:

Melissa G. Why is the gate you need always at the farthest terminal?

Elizabeth K. My husband works for airlines. My sons have been flying since babies. One trip through Pittsburgh, we were trying to get a close connection. My husband picked up my three-year-old son to run and check us in while I wrangled the coats and bags. My son thought they were leaving me and was reaching over his shoulders crying and screaming for me like he was being kidnapped. I had to assure other passengers that it was okay. I do feel this pain.

Grant K. Out of breath just reading the words.

Judy H. That happened to us once, but with a cruise ship. They actually held the ship for us for five minutes. The captain was a woman and a mom herself. Captain Anne. Will never forget her.

Mary C. Ooooo . . . I have so been there. The strength to hold a toddler who needs to do it "myself," but you have to run. And hoping your other child ahead of you remembers his numbers because you are so far behind you can't scream anymore. Plus, the strategy in your mind. Mumbling prayers into the toddler's ears that you want to "just make it." For us it was a Denver airport trying to get to Charlotte.

Connie C. I went through this once years ago in Houston, only I was alone with my three-year-old and nine-year-old girls. We were loaded down with heavy carry-ons, without wheels, and were literally running from one end of the crowded terminal to the other to catch a connecting flight with a different airline. We made it with seconds to spare; I thought my chest was going to explode as I took the rest of the flight to catch my breath again. Running with a toddler and carry-ons is a challenge.

Donna D. I'm watching you now at 4:00 p.m. and you look fresh. If only everyone watching knew.

MONTH NINETY-EIGHT: #MoreToCome Explained

After my mom died in 2017, within that deep hole of sadness, a beautiful thing was birthed. My brother, Jay, suggested we take what was left in her account and put it into a special fund we'd touch once a year. The only thing that money would be spent on—ever—would be an annual joint trip. At the time, Jay and I had two kids each. He said this would allow the cousins to grow together. We could decide year to year where we'd go. Could be driving to the North Carolina mountains for Christmas Eve, spending Thanksgiving at Disney, last year's remarkable Bahamas excursion, or, this year, an after-Christmas trip to Arizona to expose our kids to the Great American West.

The fund, he figured, would last eight years. Just enough to have the oldest two—his son and Parker—get close to high school graduation.

We didn't know then the deep perfection of Jay's idea. We also didn't know that his wife, Amy, and I would both end up having another baby, making it six cousins. I say with conviction: Jay's idea was brilliant.

My mom would *love* the concept of a Grammy trip. Her two kids, two kids-in-law, and six grandchildren spending quality time with her as the backdrop? Yes. She'd love a legacy that makes memories while keeping her name fresh. We talk about her on these excursions. All her grandchildren, either very young when they knew her or not yet born, talk about her. We share funny stories and pass her personality down through laughter. My mom's spirit is with us every year, no matter where we go.

This year in Arizona, she was in the sunsets—the Crayola-orange puffed-up clouds with yellow streaks and fiery red reflecting from rocks. She was in the dry streams that let us cross a trail with six children, to continue up-up-up-up-up toward the tip of a mountain so high, it was covered on an overcast day. She was in the jokes as all ages played card games at night with three decks. She was in the New Year's Eve champagne toast we celebrated at 10:00 p.m. because we were too tired to wait till midnight. She was in the pigtail French-Dutch braids both Parker and her girl cousin wanted so they'd match as we rode horses. She was in the early-morning quiet coffees and delicious authentic Mexican food, though we all knew Grammy, a proud caterer and chef, would've critiqued every bite.

Grammy felt present to me last week in Arizona. Not alive physically, but with us.

I think she's proud of her six grandkids. I know she's proud of Jay. She probably wonders how I've gotten to the age I am without learning to cook.

As for Arizona, the state is a different type of gorgeous. I'm drawn to blues and piers and sounds of waves. Arizona is the opposite of that kind of pretty. It's mountainous and neutral with prickly cacti and curvy roads. The United States of America is impressive in how it expands. Different parts look like different countries, even though we're all one. We're diverse in our people and landscapes. Traveling to see a one-eighty from your normal is awesome.

We stayed in Tucson. I've spent quality time out West and know that you get used to the clay structures, low buildings, and high terrain. But there's an added special mood in Tucson. The Sonoran Desert is a protected space that only survives in this area of Arizona, very southern California, and parts of northern Mexico. That's it. So, to stand in that desert and see haphazard farm-like aisles of cacti is jarring; you've never seen it anywhere else. It resembles the stark surface of the moon, though not gray. After a day or two, that new visual becomes comforting. You start to feel like if you lived there, you'd miss it when away.

My kids are city kids. We walk around Uptown. They ride scooters on Carolina Panthers game days among 50,000 people trying to walk toward an NFL stadium, see skyscrapers, and complain about waiting in traffic jams.

Last week, we showed them . . .

. . . space.

They could hike and climb. I could think.

Space.

I know my hippie mom, who loved dreaming about remote cabins, listening to birds chirp, and who appreciated nature and art, would've loved seeing *space* through the eyes of her next generation.

Think I just made my New Year's resolution:

Carve out space.

ଓଃଃ

Grammy died too young, but her memory and the essence of her soul live on. Because of her, Jay and I are shaping new memories and hearing her happiness in our kids. I only hope that however heaven is laid out, she has a good seat, able to see what she created.

COMMENTS:

Patty S. A chance for family to come together and celebrate each other is the best tribute around.

Becky G. I absolutely love Jay's idea. Such great memories to be had. And you're right, Arizona has its own kind of beauty. I lost my mom in October of last year and I think this might be something I should discuss with my siblings. She loved to travel.

Joelle C. Hooray for Grammy trips! Tomorrow is one year since I lost my mom. It's hard. What your family is doing, every year, remembering her on purpose. With purpose. That's priceless.

JANUARY

Spread the Word

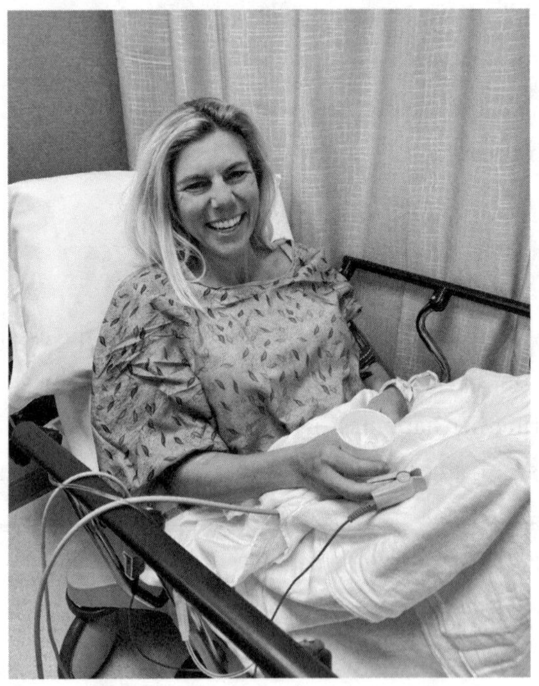

I had my first colonoscopy yesterday.

I know that sentence comes out of nowhere, but I'm trying to normalize this procedure. My dad died of colon cancer and my mom died of breast cancer. I write about getting my yearly mammograms, so why am I not giving the same awareness to colonoscopies? I know what colon cancer can do to a person and their family, yet, I had no idea what to expect in this totally common process. I'd never heard anyone describe the actual steps.

I know, I know . . . a colon. An unpretty body part most people don't want to talk about. But you know what? Colonoscopies can save lives. I only wish my dad had one before his first at age fifty-six. Maybe then his cancer wouldn't have been stage 3 by the time it was discovered.

My doctor referred me. With my family history, it was time. It took multiple calls to schedule, and I was surprised to hear you need a day off work because of anesthesia. That's why I wasn't on air yesterday. After you schedule, a big packet of information arrives in the mail. I put it to the side until a few days out. I'd recommend opening your packet earlier—there's lots of good information about prep work and what to eat/not eat the week before.

In that packet was a prescription for pills. The pills are part of the prep work, and a newer form of clearing out your system. You used to have to drink a nasty drink before the procedure. Either way—pills or liquid shake—the goal is to get your colon clean so doctors can see more.

I filled the prescription the day before my appointment; that took no time. But, the pills are hefty. Twelve pills the night before, with tons of water, and that's just one dose. Seven hours before the procedure, another twelve big pills. (Though they still seem easier than the multiple drinks I've heard others describe.)

The biggest part is that you can't eat twenty-four to thirty-six hours before the procedure. From Monday night at 7:00 p.m. to

Wednesday's 1:45 p.m. appointment, I had nothing but water and chicken broth. No coffee and creamer two mornings in a row. For me, honestly, that was the hardest part.

Someone has to drive you there, then sign paperwork that they'll stick around and drive you home. Wes took his work conference calls from the waiting room—his coworkers had no idea of his environment. I think that's funny.

The actual procedure was basic. Again, I had no idea what to expect and hope spelling it out here helps you to understand more. You're asked if you completed your prep work, are given a medical gown, lie down in a hospital bed, and then you get an IV. A CRNA came in and described how the anesthesia would take ten seconds to kick in and knock me out.

"It'll be the best nap of your life," she said. Her name was Julie. I remember thinking she looked like my sister-in-law, Amy, who also wears her brown hair in a cute ponytail.

"Once the procedure is over and we stop the anesthesia, it'll take you thirty to sixty seconds to wake up," she said. "You will be groggy, but that will fade."

Then, I was wheeled back to the room. The doctor introduced himself, asked me to confirm my name and date of birth, and three minutes later the medicine was put into the IV. After that, nothing. I felt nothing and remember nothing.

Thirty-ish minutes later, I was being shaken out of a dream, and like most dreams, don't remember what I was dreaming, I just know it was vivid. Julie was there, waking me up and I was (surprise, surprise) talking. Later I wrote down word-for-word what she recalled I'd said.

While coming out of the fog, I opened my eyes, stared right at her, called her the wrong name, and said with strength:

"Amy. Amy. Amy! Thank you soooooo much for my Christmas present. It was the best gift I ever received. Now, let's take our presents and hit the highway. We need to gooooooooo. On the road. You ready? Let's go."

Hysterical for multiple reasons:

(1) I thought Julie was Amy.
(2) Amy didn't get me a Christmas present . . .
(3) . . . our family picks Secret Santa names and she didn't pick mine.
(4) I, however, did choose hers.
(5) I got Amy a purse.
(6) I liked the purse so much, I got myself the same one.
(7) (Don't judge.)
(8) Amy and I both live hectic lives with three kids and full plates.
(9) I know Amy gets sick of the rat race, as I do.
(10) We talked about it while hiking over Christmas in Arizona.

So, in my dream state, I was imagining . . . Amy and me running off with pretty purses to "hit the highway." A fashionista version of Thelma and Louise.

Julie said she helps eleven to seventeen patients a day wake up, and most of what people say is funny. Men often look at her and say, "You're not my wife. WHERE IS MY WIFE!" Like they're accusing her of kidnapping the woman they know.

Once awake, the doctor tells you what the colonoscopy showed. I had three polyps, none cancerous. He removed all three. They also found diverticulosis, which basically means a swelling of the colon. He then handed me a packet of pictures, and told me he wants to see me again in three to five years. If you have a totally clean colon and no family history, you don't need to return for another ten. I'm happy to go in three. I'll feel better making sure to stay on top of this, knowing my dad's diagnosis.

Then he left. Another nurse helped me to discharge and—this is almost unbelievable—it was the *same nurse* who helped after I delivered Parker eleven years ago! Her name is Susan. She's in a whole new job, in a new facility, but remembered swaddling Parker in a blanket for her hospital crib. What is that likelihood? A picture of the two of us is here. Susan then gave the formal recommendations for the night:

"Don't post anything, don't buy anything online, and don't drink alcohol. You need to hydrate."

Don't post or buy online?

"Your mind is still foggy," she said. "We've had people get on

Amazon and make massive financial mistakes. So now we have to tell them not to buy things after anesthesia."

She then wheeled me to meet Wes. He and I went out for nachos. I was starving.

That's pretty much it. The prep work was yucky, but worked effectively and you feel great after the whole thing is over.

ʚϪɞ

If this feels slightly uncomfortable to read, maybe that's a good thing. We don't talk enough about this absolutely normal procedure. My dad's journey taught me to get checked and keep up with your own health. Funny enough, he only got his colonoscopy after seeing Katie Couric do one live on the *Today Show*, way back then. She impacted many people by making it a conversation. Because Katie got hers, my dad scheduled his.

My hope is that on a more micro level, writing this will encourage someone else. Colon cancer is the second most common cause of cancer death in the United States, says CNN, and there are fifteen million colonoscopies performed in our country each year. Which sounds like plenty, but delve into statistics and you'll find many more people who are scared of them. The *New England Journal of Medicine* did a big study on colon cancer in late 2022, inviting 28,000 people who hadn't had a colonoscopy in recent years to get one. A meager 42 percent, actually, would get the colonoscopy, most citing the reasons they wouldn't as fear of the procedure itself.

Colonoscopies aren't that hard. They can save your life. Spread the word, and ask your doctor when the right time is to get yours.

COMMENTS:

Linda M. I absolutely hate the prep, but if you say it's easier now, I will get mine this year. Going to schedule now . . .

Ken L. I read this word for word. You don't know how timely it is. I was supposed to have mine a year ago, and didn't. My brother, a physician, said over Christmas that I need to. My doctor last week, during my checkup, again said I need to. But I've been anxious about it and putting it off. No family history, no obvious issues, but being fifty years old, it's past time. (The new recommendation is forty-five, apparently.) Thank you for posting this, Molly. I will call tomorrow to schedule mine. And thanks for the heads up on the coffee with no cream. That will definitely be the most brutal.

Nancy V. My dad died of colon cancer in 1995. I've had breast cancer, but many years now cancer-free. Awareness to both these procedures is so important.

Julie L. Colonoscopies can save lives. One saved mine.

Lynesha D. I have to get a colonoscopy every five years. Not a pleasant subject, true, but a highly necessary one. Colon cancer is silent.

Andrea R. As a stage 3 colon cancer Survivor, diagnosed at thirty-seven years old, it makes me happy you are writing and bringing awareness to this absolutely normal procedure.

Toddlerville

HE IS NOT SLEEPING AT NIGHT AND THEN HAS THE TWO-YEAR-OLD AUDACITY TO LOOK ANGELIC WHILE FALLING ASLEEP ON THE WAY TO PRESCHOOL.

SCREAMING, AS I YAWN.

COMMENTS:

Lea M. Most relatable thing I'll see on the internet today.

Rash Y. Cracked up reading this.

FEBRUARY

MONTH NINETY-NINE: All Aboard

One thing rises to the top this month. One, and only one:

Kid-like addictions.

Kids get attached to certain things, and it's uncertain why or from where the addiction stems. This is not a new thought. But of all the obsessions my three children have had over the past eleven years, I've never experienced anything like Hobie's current need for . . . wait for it . . .

Choo-choo trains.

He previously was obsessed with sauces. Then bulldozers. Then balloons. Now, if I have to play with one more locomotive or watch one more train video on YouTube, or be awoken at 3:00 a.m. one more time by hot toddler breath on the side of my face saying, "All aboard!" I might flee into the wild.

Sounds cute, doesn't it? It was. For a bit. Kinda like the balloon thing until I found myself dragging helium green stars and large shiny latex soccer balls on strings to the grocery store, preschool, and dinner breaks. They became a responsibility. That high level of tediousness is where Hobie now sits with trains, only worse. I'm so over his obsession it almost hurts to write down the details. I have to, though. For posterity. This two-year-old's life currently revolves around locomotives, and if I don't record it, there will be a gap in the story of his toddler journey.

So, Hobie, when you get to this chapter years from now, please know, you're *killing us* (in the most innocent of ways) because your love for trains is at a more indescribable level than what you felt for balloons (and that was bad), bulldozers (that one was sort of fun), or sauces (that now seems minor). It's worse than Hutch's need for lanyards and work passes (which lasted years), and Parker's belief she was a mermaid (we're still recovering).

Surely it's not that bad, you say? Mm-hmm.

Hobie wakes up every day and says in third person, "Hobie

watch choo-choo trains." His very first words, daily, seven days a week, for many past weeks. Problematic for many reasons.

(1) I don't want to.
(2) He doesn't care about eating or being an interactive human.
(3) Soon after his eyes open, he's staring at a screen. Unhealthy.

Yet, I give in. I'm aware I'm feeding the beast and that turning on the TV every morning now will only make it harder in the future to tear him away from screens, but IT'S SO HARD. During the hightailed, hectic nature of a morning, while getting one to middle school and one to elementary school, it's enticing to have a way to keep the preschooler content on the couch.

In good news, it's not only screens: he also plays with toy trains lying around the house. We had a mini Polar Express that circled the Christmas tree during December. We didn't pack it away with other holiday decorations knowing that would shatter Hobie's heart. That train remains in the house with pieces of tracks and multiple long cars scattered across our hardwood floors. He'll walk through a room and drop to the floor when he sees one to start pushing his trains, forgetting where he'd been heading. Get up close and you can hear him lovingly whisper words, like "steam" and "caboose" and "chug-a-chug-a, chug-a-chug-a, choo-choo . . ." I bought a basket with the sole purpose to keep the trains organized, but since he wants to play with the trains so many times every hour, the basket is generally empty. The floor feels full.

Dangerous, like a minefield. You could fall over one if you don't carefully plot your steps.

The other night Hobie slept with an engine the length of his arm. *He slept with it.* His version of Brown Bear and Grammy-Lambie, I suppose. I was worried a plastic piece from the rigid toy would scratch his soft face. It didn't. He walked down early morning carrying the engine and uttered his morning greeting: "Hobie watch choo-choo trains."

As much as this makes me batty, being a parent means being in the moment, or at least trying. Recognizing that 80 percent of Hobie's words center around trains, our whole family has given in. This means we crawl on hardwoods and race choo-choos around the kitchen. He laughs with wonderment. Meet your kids where they are, right?

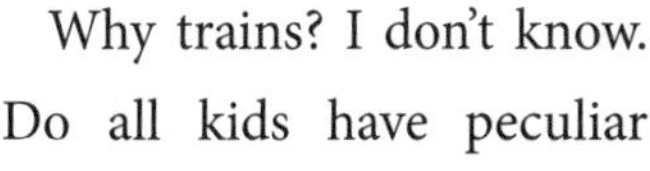

Why trains? I don't know. Do all kids have peculiar obsessions? I don't know. As I've said before, I hope my get-after-it-attitude I passed down to the three of them isn't fully to blame. Give me a mission: it will get completed. I don't miss deadlines, even if it means forgoing sleep. My book editor, actually, gave me a certain day to get this book's first draft into her hands. I stayed in the newsroom after the 11:00 p.m. show was over, through the overnight hours, still at my desk when the morning crew arrived, continuing to edit and write when that team went live at 4:30 a.m., with my butt *still* in the chair and eyes on the computer when they wrapped at 7 a.m. My editor had it by lunch. Bam. Goal achieved.

So, I don't mind pulling all-nighters or doing what needs to be done to deliver on a commitment, but are my kids now also preprogrammed to throw themselves on whatever they love? All in, whatever it might be?

The other day Hobie saw the light rail in Uptown out his car window. He screamed so abruptly that Wes almost crashed. Hobie couldn't believe his eyes. "A TRAIN A TRAIN A TRAIN!"

You know Thomas? The Tank Engine? (Hobie calls him "Thomas the Train.") There are two versions of the show on Netflix—both cartoons. Hobie knows all episodes and will ask for specific ones. He'll then know when that episode is nearly ending and will yell to anyone within earshot, "Hobie wants other train!" Like we're his remote-control servants. He then puts up his arms indicating he wants you to carry him to the TV screen and have you scroll through other available episodes until he sees what he wants.

"That one!" He'll be frantic with excitement when you highlight the desired episode. You hit play and then he'll then reach back toward the couch, meaning, drop him there and please leave him alone.

Parker's and Hutch's kid addictions faded. I hope this one for Hobie will do the same. Until then, you can find me going in circles around my kitchen island, literally spinning my wheels, trying to connect with my two-year-old.

Texts with a Preteen, Segment Two

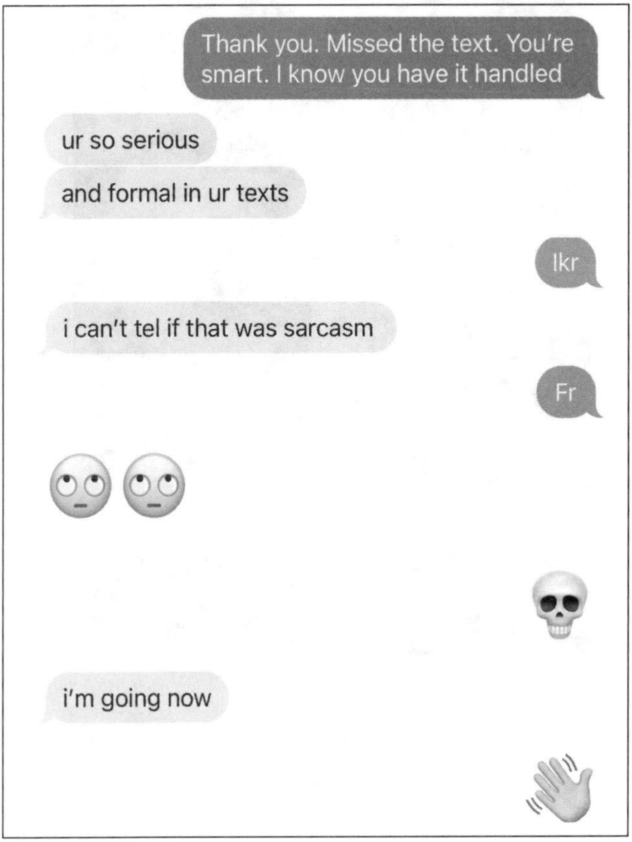

Thank you. Missed the text. You're smart. I know you have it handled

ur so serious

and formal in ur texts

Ikr

i can't tel if that was sarcasm

Fr

🙄🙄

💀

i'm going now

👋

COMMENTS:

Carolyn W. Ah, the next phase of parenting. I'm hip deep in the mire myself with three teenagers. You got her here, Mom.

Pam Q. My fourteen-year-old asked why I was writing a text like a letter.

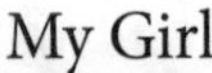

My Girl

Last night I watched Parker walk on stage, shake out her nerves, take the mic from my hands, and give a talk to a sold-out crowd of 1,400 people at Dancing with the Stars Charlotte. She wrote the speech herself and spoke from the heart about how cancer impacts a whole family, including kids. I didn't know what to expect.

As it was happening and I watched from the wings, what I saw was elegance and poise. This morning I found myself watching her again, this time from a soccer sideline as she played a tough game. I watched her this afternoon jump with excitement after her volleyball team went into a fifth set to win their match.

I'm around Parker all the time. But in the last twenty-four hours, her emotional maturity at eleven years old has blown me away.

☙❧

Here's to strong women.

May we know them. May we be them. May we raise them.

COMMENTS:

Linda H. Not a dry eye in those moments. She captivated and wowed all 1,400 last night.

Catherine M. She was so authentic and beautiful and spoke so eloquently and naturally. Your mom would be bursting.

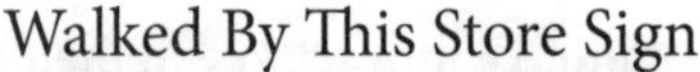

Walked By This Store Sign

"Mom, I really like what that says."

He didn't grow up with MC Hammer, and has no idea of the '90s reference, but possesses a self-assuredness you can't teach.

COMMENTS:

Darin A. Hutch is so cool.

Larken E. Please tell me you taught him the dance.

For Our Moms

An Emmy!

Last night a story with more personal meaning than any story I've done in my twenty years at WBTV won an Emmy. Remember a year and a half ago when ten-year-old Parker interviewed DeAngelo Williams's remarkable ten-year-old daughter, Rhiya Williams? We submitted it to the Emmys, which is a grueling process. It was one of four stories nominated in the category of "Interview/Discussion." The Emmys were virtual this year, and our newsroom team had a watch party.

Parker was there too, but when our category came up was in the bathroom (of course) and ran in late. Her friend was with us at the watch party and hopped on her back. They both squealed exactly as you'd imagine two eleven-year-old girls would sound.

Photojournalist John Sparks and former managing editor Michael Cable and I are all excited to win, but this is sincerely about Rhiya, Parker, and their grandmothers. I called DeAngelo last night. He said Rhiya was as pumped as Parker. They educated many in that segment on how a cancer diagnosis impacts everyone in a family, including kids.

An Emmy, with my daughter, about my mom. Work wins don't get much better than recognition because your child honored your parent so well.

MONTH ONE HUNDRED: The End

One hundred.

I started these monthly posts when Hutch was six days old. He's now eight and a half. I've been writing every single month, learning how to parent while living a full life and loving a career—for one hundred months.

Progress, not perfection. You don't start out losing weight

by running five miles. You walk ten minutes, day after day. You don't learn an instrument by picking it up and just knowing it. You learn one note, then another, then another. You don't cook a Michelin-star dish the first time you put those ingredients together. You make it repeatedly, until you're sure of the prep and process.

We were taught wrong as kids. It's not "practice makes perfect." It's "practice makes . . . progress."

One step at a time, and you might be surprised what happens.

One hundred months ago, I told myself to try writing what was in front of me, once a month. It was a self-imposed deadline. Progress was slow, but consistent. I never missed an entry. My kids now have colorful details about their childhoods, in tangible form. God forbid if something happens to me tomorrow, they could read one hundred months of words and know for eternity how I breathed them in at times rapturous, at times exhausted and feeling defeated, at times smitten, and often at times, with simple wonderment.

Eight and a half years of progress.

Eight and a half years of life lived through words.

But now, my friends, it's done.

Month One Hundred seems a perfect place to stop. I still have intentions of writing and posting about the kids as things pop up. I know me. I know I'll want somewhere to put these thoughts and funny stories. Parenting is not for the faint of heart. Recording what happens can be therapeutic and fun.

But I don't want to make myself write something *every* month.

One hundred months seems like a good run.

One hundred months. Three books. A mighty good run.

Why end now? Two reasons.

First, 100 is a tidy number. Stopping at 178 or 215 or 438 sounds weird.

Second, more importantly, I'm stopping for Parker.

Writing about a middle schooler is different than writing about a baby. These writings started when she was three and a half. She'll be twelve in two months. She's older. Her coaches and teachers and friends can read what's here. I want to help her build a path to be her. *Her.* It's time to free Parker from my words. I want to guide her—not tell everyone what they should know about her, which is not on her terms.

Soon enough, Hutch will be at that phase too. I'll want to give him the same gift of letting him live his own life. Way down the road, it'll be Hobie.

For now, though, it's about P.

I've learned that having a daughter is like holding a mirror up to yourself. You see things you like and things you don't. Parker Meade—we share a middle name (I'm Molly Meade)—is not an exact reflection. She handles middle school with more maturity than I did at eleven. She drops clever one-liners with great timing, things I'd never think to say. And her summer camp adventures are filled with confidence and new friends every year, whereas I was on the same hometown swim team my entire childhood, never thinking to branch out.

Watching Parker grow teaches me about *me*. When she yells at Hutch, she uses my angry tone. When she loves on Hobie, it's with my unconditional adoration. She makes me hear and see both my good and bad. I learn, while trying to teach.

Is that all moms and daughters, in some form or fashion? She unknowingly influences me, not just the other way around. I love her style. Her savvy. Her smarts. I see how she can be a little too controlling, but also see her not scared to challenge herself. Like all eleven-year-olds, she's figuring out cell phones, social media, and filtered comparisons. This can cause disagreements between us, but standing by her as she navigates this challenging world makes me more proud than frustrated.

She is my first gift, my only girl, and watching her is motivating, scary, and awe-inspiring.

Parker has never complained that I write about her or her brothers. Never. She has never known anything different. I told her my decision to stop, before announcing it publicly. It was a relatively quick discussion. At first, she said, "But I know you like to write, Mom."

"Oh, I'll still write," I told her.

"I thought you just said . . . "

I'll write, I explained, but probably more about the boys. Public things, like her Dancing with the Stars speech or our Emmy win, are exciting to share. But I want to be more strategically careful about *her.* She's nearly twelve, in middle school, and doesn't need people to know her business.

She gave me a hug and said two words only: "Thank you."

That, you guys, is how I know that this is the right call. Parker has never hated being the focus of my attention. I have many memories of her bouncing with anticipation to go to book signings. But her instinct to give me a hug when she heard that I want to be careful about her was important.

Think that means she sees me making her a priority. She might not remember our exact sixty-second conversation about why I'm ending here, however, I hope she recalls my longer-term intentions.

ঙ৪ৠ

The picture at the top of this chapter was yesterday after all three kids had haircuts with Miss Tiffany. As that second maternity leave with Hutch wrapped years ago, it was Miss Tiffany who encouraged me to keep writing about motherhood once I was back in the newsroom. (You can read about that in the beginning of *Small Victories.*)

Because of her pushing, I took that first step. Made progress by writing one post when back at work. Then another a month later. Then another. Then another. Practice makes . . . progress. These one hundred posts are in many ways because of her. It's only fitting the final photo, to lead off the final chapter of the final book in this series, is influenced by the woman who got the journey on track.

ଔ

Make no doubt, One Hundred Months is the best thing I ever accidentally started.

Practice makes progress. Do what you can, when you can, and watch small victories add up to big wins.

The End.

COMMENTS:

Hadley G. Giving Parker a chance to grow as anonymously as kids can these days is a perfectly perfect gesture. Someday these one hundred months of observations will mean even more to all three of them.

Lauren B. Applause, applause. You've been honest and open to those of us who needed that and didn't know we did. Big thanks from this working momma. Love your honesty and humor.

Keilah McM. This post made me cry. I don't know why. I have two girls who are in their early twenties, but I still see myself so much within your words about you and Parker. The mirror analogy is true. I hope even through my failures, my successes will be remembered and treasured.

Lauren T. I found you around Month One or so, when I was also suddenly a mom of two, juggling an infant, and an almost four-year-old. It felt validating to read the perspective of another working mom at the same stage. Thank you for sharing your stories, making us laugh, and shedding tears along the way (the ear-piercing story from *Small Victories* was probably one of my favorites).

Nina T. My first thought was, "No!" I have loved these updates on your family. But as I read on, I agree. Month One Hundred is a great number and it is time to let Parker fly. She said it best: thank you. Thank you, from us. We've all learned something.

Karen B. Molly, I think I started following you about the time of Parker and "the black dress." That story has stuck in my mind. Trust your instincts. That's all any of us can do to try our best in life. When Parker one day tries that dress on from Santa she received so many years ago, please, ask her if it's okay for you to share with us?

Molly. What an excellent idea to tie the first book in this series to the last. Here is Parker in her strapless mini black dress at the age of five during Month Twenty-Five from *Small Victories*, to today, nearly twelve years old.

Month Twenty-Five

Month One Hundred

AFTERWORD and ACKNOWLEDGMENTS

If you take nothing else from these stories in your hand, take this: *write it down.* Send letters. Jot ideas into a diary. Document through a laptop or your phone. Create a scrapbook, digitally or handmade. They both count. It all counts. Our minds get twisted and filled—what's happening now will be forgotten. Recording actions, the context you see, the texture you think—that's your life. Never would I have believed the pithy bullet points in my head one hundred months ago would matter. They do. Realities fade. Having your truth in front of you is more than an archive, it's your legacy.

Writing about the months you just read through was a phenomenal ride. Month Sixty-Six started in a pandemic and a forced requirement to slow down. Now, after Month One Hundred, that lesson seems lost. We're back to packed schedules and taking for granted our kids are in school five days a week. I'm thankful it's written down as a reminder of how life was lived.

The first book, *Small Victories,* was on a super-fast track (eleven-week production schedule, start to finish). The second book, *The Juggle Is Real,* came out as the pandemic began. There were no bookstores open, no signings, no launch parties. I've made myself be patient with this third one. It's the final in the "Off-Camera Life of an On-Camera Mom" series, and I've taken the time to make it exactly what it needs to be.

ଔ

None of my children have read any of these three books so far. Though I can't wait for them to devour their childhoods through my perspective, the time hasn't yet been right. When they do, and they get here to "The End," I hope they see their individualized beauty.

Parker: My reflection. Thank you.
Hutch: My imagination. Thank you.
Hobie: My spark. Thank you.

The three of you should never doubt how you make your parents whole.

To Wes: We are a beautiful partnership. Your patience calms me, your thoughtfulness teaches me, and your ability to humor my grand ideas and color-coded calendars shows love. Your actions utter respect louder than actual words. I married someone grander than I deserved and know I'm the luckiest girl.

Betsy Thorpe, literary consultant extraordinaire: Did you ever think we'd get to three books? Our first meeting over lunch, with you holding my hand to coach me through Publishing World 101? What a hoot. To Diana Wade and her graphic artistry who in the first book placed 155 photos on 323 pages, in the second book placed 167 photos in the 315 pages, and in this one, outdid herself by placing 262 photos on 406 pages. (That's, ahem, a ton.) To friends Nicole Taylor, who shot the book cover and somehow coaxed my kids to be nice to each other during the photo shoot (she totally captured their personalities), and Jen and Julianne, for reading advanced copies before publication. And to the final member of this dream team, Katherine Bartis: thank you for finding all editing errors I couldn't and for helping make these words read as smooth as possible.

Finally, the biggest note to all of you, who took the time to read posts, and who are now reading this book. May we support one another, learn from the past, look forward to the future, and recognize how much we don't know. Words matter. Heart wins. *Write it down.*

—Molly

www.mollygrantham.com

BONUS PAGE: A Comparison

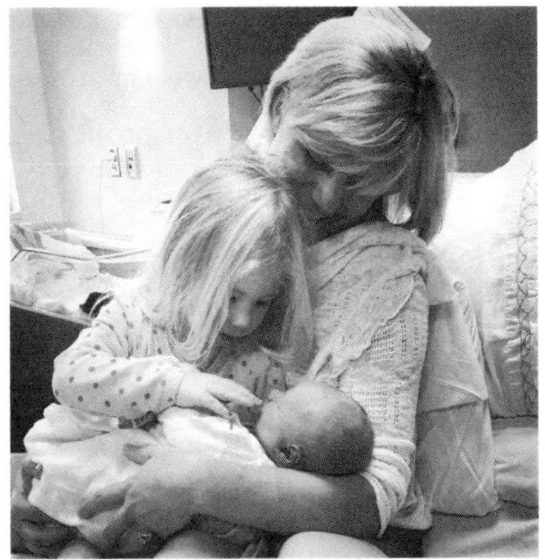

Month One

Month One Hundred

ABOUT THE AUTHOR

Molly Grantham is a four-time Emmy-award-winning journalist who anchors three live shows a day, is a popular speaker, an author of three books, founder of a non-profit pediatric network, activist for various cancer causes, and a mom. She graduated from the University of North Carolina at Chapel Hill with a degree in broadcast journalism and is launching Practice Makes... Progress on her twentieth anniversary at WBTV News. You can request her to speak to your group at www.mollygrantham.com.